Systems, Reproduction, and Growth

elevate science

MODULES

SAVVAS

LEARNING COMPANY

You're an author!

As you write in this science book, your answers and personal discoveries will be recorded for you to keep, making this book unique to you. That is why you are one of the primary authors of this book.

✎ **In the space below, print your name, school, town, and state. Then write a short autobiography that includes your interests and accomplishments.**

YOUR NAME ....

SCHOOL ....

TOWN, STATE ....

AUTOBIOGRAPHY ....

....

Your Photo

The cover photo shows a Saguaro Cactus with a flower cluster in Saguaro National Park.

Front cover: Saguaro Cactus, Jack Dykinga/naturepl.com; Back cover: Science Doodle, LHF Graphics/Shutterstock.

ISBN-13: 978-1-418-29156-3
ISBN-10: 1-418-29156-0
6 20

Program Authors

ZIPPORAH MILLER, Ed.D.
Coordinator for K-12 Science Programs, Anne Arundel County Public Schools
Dr. Zipporah Miller currently serves as the Senior Manager for Organizational Learning with the Anne Arundel County Public School System. Prior to that she served as the K-12 Coordinator for science in Anne Arundel County. She conducts national training to science stakeholders on the Next Generation Science Standards. Dr. Miller also served as the Associate Executive Director for Professional Development Programs and conferences at the National Science Teachers Association (NSTA) and served as a reviewer during the development of Next Generation Science Standards. Dr. Miller holds a doctoral degree from the University of Maryland College Park, a master's degree in school administration and supervision from Bowie State University and a bachelor's degree from Chadron State College.

MICHAEL J. PADILLA, Ph.D.
Professor Emeritus, Eugene P. Moore School of Education, Clemson University, Clemson, South Carolina
Michael J. Padilla taught science in middle and secondary schools, has more than 30 years of experience educating middle-school science teachers, and served as one of the writers of the 1996 U.S. National Science Education Standards. In recent years Mike has focused on teaching science to English Language Learners. His extensive experience as Principal Investigator on numerous National Science Foundation and U.S. Department of Education grants resulted in more than $35 million in funding to improve science education. He served as president of the National Science Teachers Association, the world's largest science teaching organization, in 2005–6.

MICHAEL E. WYSESSION, Ph.D
Professor of Earth and Planetary Sciences, Washington University, St. Louis, Missouri
Author of more than 100 science and science education publications, Dr. Wysession was awarded the prestigious National Science Foundation Presidential Faculty Fellowship and Packard Foundation Fellowship for his research in geophysics, primarily focused on using seismic tomography to determine the forces driving plate tectonics. Dr. Wysession is also a leader in geoscience literacy and education; he is the chair of the Earth Science Literacy Initiative, the author of several popular video lectures on geology in the *Great Courses* series, and a lead writer of the *Next Generation Science Standards**.

*Next Generation Science Standards is a registered trademark of Achieve. Neither Achieve nor the lead states and partners that developed the Next Generation Science Standards were involved in the production of this product, and do not endorse it. NGSS Lead States. 2013. *Next Generation Science Standards: For States, By States.* Washington, DC: The National Academies Press.

REVIEWERS

Program Consultants

Carol Baker
Science Curriculum

Dr. Carol K. Baker is superintendent for Lyons Elementary K-8 School District in Lyons, Illinois. Prior to this, she was Director of Curriculum for Science and Music in Oak Lawn, Illinois. Before this she taught Physics and Earth Science for 18 years. In the recent past, Dr. Baker also wrote assessment questions for ACT (EXPLORE and PLAN), was elected president of the Illinois Science Teachers Association from 2011–2013, and served as a member of the Museum of Science and Industry (Chicago) advisory board. She is a writer of the Next Generation Science Standards. Dr. Baker received her B.S. in Physics and a science teaching certification. She completed her master's of Educational Administration (K-12) and earned her doctorate in Educational Leadership.

Jim Cummins
ELL

Dr. Cummins's research focuses on literacy development in multilingual schools and the role technology plays in learning across the curriculum. *Elevate Science* incorporates research-based principles for integrating language with the teaching of academic content based on Dr. Cummins's work.

Elfrieda Hiebert
Literacy

Dr. Hiebert, a former primary-school teacher, is President and CEO of TextProject, a non-profit aimed at providing open-access resources for instruction of beginning and struggling readers, She is also a research associate at the University of California Santa Cruz. Her research addresses how fluency, vocabulary, and knowledge can be fostered through appropriate texts, and her contributions have been recognized through awards such as the Oscar Causey Award for Outstanding Contributions to Reading Research (Literacy Research Association, 2015), Research to Practice award (American Educational Research Association, 2013), and the William S. Gray Citation of Merit Award for Outstanding Contributions to Reading Research (International Reading Association, 2008).

Content Reviewers

Alex Blom, Ph.D.
Associate Professor
Department Of Physical Sciences
Alverno College
Milwaukee, Wisconsin

Joy Branlund, Ph.D.
Department of Physical Science
Southwestern Illinois College
Granite City, Illinois

Judy Calhoun
Associate Professor
Physical Sciences
Alverno College
Milwaukee, Wisconsin

Stefan Debbert
Associate Professor of Chemistry
Lawrence University
Appleton, Wisconsin

Diane Doser
Professor
Department of Geological Sciences
University of Texas at El Paso
El Paso, Texas

Rick Duhrkopf, Ph.D.
Department of Biology
Baylor University
Waco, Texas

Jennifer Liang
University of Minnesota Duluth
Duluth, Minnesota

Heather Mernitz, Ph.D.
Associate Professor of Physical
 Sciences
Alverno College
Milwaukee, Wisconsin

Joseph McCullough, Ph.D.
Cabrillo College
Aptos, California

Katie M. Nemeth, Ph.D.
Assistant Professor
College of Science and Engineering
University of Minnesota Duluth
Duluth, Minnesota

Maik Pertermann
Department of Geology
Western Wyoming Community College
Rock Springs, Wyoming

Scott Rochette
Department of the Earth Sciences
The College at Brockport
 State University of New York
Brockport, New York

David Schuster
Washington University in St Louis
St. Louis, Missouri

Shannon Stevenson
Department of Biology
University of Minnesota Duluth
Duluth, Minnesota

Paul Stoddard, Ph.D.
Department of Geology and
 Environmental Geosciences
Northern Illinois University
DeKalb, Illinois

Nancy Taylor
American Public University
Charles Town, West Virginia

Teacher Reviewers

Jennifer Bennett, M.A.
Memorial Middle School
Tampa, Florida

Sonia Blackstone
Lake County Schools
Howey In the Hills, Florida

Teresa Bode
Roosevelt Elementary
Tampa, Florida

Tyler C. Britt, Ed.S.
Curriculum & Instructional
 Practice Coordinator
Raytown Quality Schools
Raytown, Missouri

A. Colleen Campos
Grandview High School
Aurora, Colorado

Ronald Davis
Riverview Elementary
Riverview, Florida

Coleen Doulk
Challenger School
Spring Hill, Florida

Mary D. Dube
Burnett Middle School
Seffner, Florida

Sandra Galpin
Adams Middle School
Tampa, Florida

Margaret Henry
Lebanon Junior High School
Lebanon, Ohio

Christina Hill
Beth Shields Middle School
Ruskin, Florida

Judy Johnis
Gorden Burnett Middle School
Seffner, Florida

Karen Y. Johnson
Beth Shields Middle School
Ruskin, Florida

Jane Kemp
Lockhart Elementary School
Tampa, Florida

Denise Kuhling
Adams Middle School
Tampa, Florida

Esther Leonard, M.Ed. and L.M.T.
Gifted and talented Implementation Specialist
San Antonio Independent School District
San Antonio, Texas

Kelly Maharaj
Challenger K–8 School of Science
 and Mathematics
Spring Hill, Florida

Kevin J. Maser, Ed.D.
H. Frank Carey Jr/Sr High School
Franklin Square, New York

Angie L. Matamoros, Ph.D.
ALM Science Consultant
Weston, Florida

Corey Mayle
Brogden Middle School
Durham, North Carolina

Keith McCarthy
George Washington Middle School
Wayne, New Jersey

Yolanda O. Peña
John F. Kennedy Junior High School
West Valley City, Utah

Kathleen M. Poe
Jacksonville Beach Elementary School
Jacksonville Beach, Florida

Wendy Rauld
Monroe Middle School
Tampa, Florida

Anne Rice
Woodland Middle School
Gurnee, Illinois

Bryna Selig
Gaithersburg Middle School
Gaithersburg, Maryland

Pat (Patricia) Shane, Ph.D.
STEM & ELA Education Consultant
Chapel Hill, North Carolina

Diana Shelton
Burnett Middle School
Seffner, Florida

Nakia Sturrup
Jennings Middle School
Seffner, Florida

Melissa Triebwasser
Walden Lake Elementary
Plant City, Florida

Michele Bubley Wiehagen
Science Coach
Miles Elementary School
Tampa, Florida

Pauline Wilcox
Instructional Science Coach
Fox Chapel Middle School
Spring Hill, Florida

Safety Reviewers

Douglas Mandt, M.S.
Science Education Consultant
Edgewood, Washington

Juliana Textley, Ph.D.
Author, NSTA books on school science safety
Adjunct Professor
Lesley University
Cambridge, Massachusetts

Go to SavvasRealize.com to access your digital course.

 **VIDEO**
- Public Health Advisor

 **INTERACTIVITY**
- What All Living Things Have in Common
- Mom's Car Must Be Alive
- Classify It
- Life as a Single Cell
- Viruses by the Numbers
- Vaccines and Populations
- There's Something Going Around
- Modifying a Virus
- Different Cells, Different Jobs
- Identifying an Organism
- Organization of Organisms

VIRTUAL LAB
- Madagascar Mystery

ASSESSMENT

eTEXT

HANDS-ON LABS

Connect Is It an Animal?

Investigate
- Cheek Cells
- Living Mysteries
- A Mystery Organism No More!
- Life In a Drop of Pond Water
- Algae and Other Plants

Demonstrate
It's Alive!

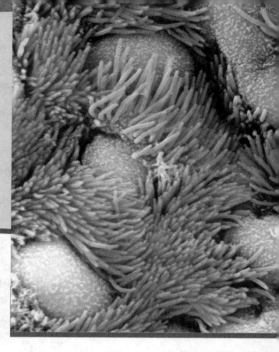

Go to SavvasRealize.com to access your digital course.

VIDEO
• Illustrator

INTERACTIVITY
• Through a Microscope • Functions of All Cells • A Strange Specimen • Structure Function Junction • Build a Cell • Specialized Cells • Cell Transport • Entering and Leaving the Cell • A Cell Divides • How Does a Broken Bone Heal? • The Cell Cycle

VIRTUAL LAB
• Living or Not?

ASSESSMENT

eTEXT

HANDS-ON LABS

иConnect What Can You See?

иInvestigate
• Observing Cells
• Comparing Cells
• Egg-speriment with a Cell
• Modeling Mitosis

иDemonstrate
Design and Build a Microscope

 Go to SavvasRealize.com to access your digital course.

▶ **VIDEO**
• Nutritionist

👆 **INTERACTIVITY**
• Human Body Systems • Interacting Systems • Balancing Act
• Communication and Homeostasis
• Joints • A Variety of Symptoms
• Bits and Pieces • Investigating Cells and Homeostasis • A Day in the Life of a Cell • Body Highways and Byways
• Testing a Training Plan • Circulatory System • Body Systems Revisited
• Humans vs. Computers • Flex Your Reflexes

📖 **VIRTUAL LAB**
• Physiology and Fitness

☑ **ASSESSMENT**

📖 **eTEXT**

HANDS-ON LABS

иConnect How is Your Body Organized?

иInvestigate
• Observing Cells and Tissues
• Parts Working Together
• Measuring Calories
• Body Systems Working Together
• Parts of the Nervous System

иDemonstrate
Reaction Research

TOPIC
4
Reproduction and Growth

The Essential Question What factors influence the growth of organisms and their ability to reproduce?

MS-LS1-4, MS-LS1-5, MS-LS3-2

Go to SavvasRealize.com to access your digital course.

▶ **VIDEO**
• Zookeeper

👆 **INTERACTIVITY**
• Inheritance of Traits
• Animal Reproduction
• Twin Studies
• Designer Flowers
• Plants and Pollinators
• They're Acting Like Animals
• Fireflies
• See How They Grow
• Breeding Bigger Bovines
• Growing Crops

📱 **VIRTUAL LAB**
• You've Got to Divide to Multiply

☑ **ASSESSMENT**

📖 **eTEXT**

📱 **APP**

HANDS-ON LABS

иConnect To Care or Not to Care
иInvestigate
• Is It All in the Genes?
• Modeling Flowers
• Behavior Cycles
• Watching Roots Grow

иDemonstrate
Clean and Green

Elevate your thinking!

Elevate Science takes science to a whole new level and lets you take ownership of your learning. Explore science in the world around you. Investigate how things work. Think critically and solve problems! *Elevate Science* helps you think like a scientist, so you're ready for a world of discoveries.

Explore Your World

Explore real-life scenarios with engaging Quests that dig into science topics around the world. You can:

- Solve real-world problems
- Apply skills and knowledge
- Communicate solutions

Quest KICKOFF

What do you think is causing Pleasant Pond to turn green?

In 2016, algal blooms turned bodies of water green and slimy in Florida, Utah, California, and 17 other states. These blooms put people and ecosystems in danger. Scientists, such as limnologists, are working to predict and prevent future algal blooms. In this problem-based Quest activity, you will investigate an algal bloom at a lake and determine its cause. In labs and digital activities, you will apply what you learn in each lesson to help you gather evidence to solve the mystery. With enough evidence, you will be able to identify what you believe is the cause of the algal bloom and present a solution in the Findings activity.

Make Connections

Elevate Science connects science to other subjects and shows you how to better understand the world through:

- Mathematics
- Reading and Writing
- Literacy

Math Toolbox
Graphing Population Changes

Ohio's Deer Population

Changes in a population over time, such as white-tailed deer in Ohio, can be displayed in a graph.

Deer Population Trends, 2000–2010

Year	Population (estimated)	Year	Population (estimated)
2000	525,000	2006	770,000
2001	560,000	2007	725,000
2002	620,000	2008	745,000
2003	670,000	2009	750,000
2004	715,000	2010	710,000
2005	720,000		

Relationships Use the data

800,000
750,000

READING CHECK   Determine Central ideas
What adaptations might the giraffe have that help it survive in its environment?

Academic Vocabulary
Relate the term *decomposer* to the verb *compose*. What does it mean to compose something?

uEngineer It! Sustainable Design **STEM**

MS-LS2-1, MS-LS2-3

Eating Oil

Do you know how tiny organisms can clean up oil spills? You engineer it! Strategies used to deal with the Deepwater Horizon oil spill, the worst in U.S. history, show us how.

The Challenge: To clean up harmful oil from marine environments

Phenomenon On April 20, 2010, part of an oil rig in

INTERACT

Design your o clean up an oil

litt

Build Skills for the Future

- Master the Engineering Design Process
- Apply critical thinking and analytical skills
- Learn about STEM careers

Focus on Inquiry

Case studies put you in the shoes of a scientist to solve real-world mysteries using real data. You will be able to:

- Analyze Data
- Test a hypothesis
- Solve the Case

Case Study

MS-LS2-1

THE CASE OF THE DISAPPEARING

Cerulean Warbler

The cerulean warbler is a small, migratory songbird named for its blue color. Cerulean warblers breed in eastern North America during the spring and summer. The warblers spend the winter months in the Andes Mountains of Colombia, Venezuela, Ecuador, and Peru in northern part of South America.

Enter the Lab

Hands-on experiments and virtual labs help you test ideas and show what you know in performance-based assessments. Scaffolded labs include:

- STEM Labs
- Design Your Own
- Open-ended Labs

Alike and Different: Living Things

Click the pictures.
Compare how living things and their parents are alike and different.
Write your answer below.

Type your answer here.

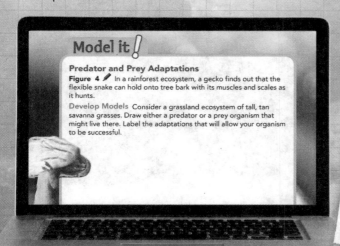

Model it

Predator and Prey Adaptations

Figure 4 In a rainforest ecosystem, a gecko finds out that the flexible snake can hold onto tree bark with its muscles and scales as it hunts.

Develop Models Consider a grassland ecosystem of tall, tan savanna grasses. Draw either a predator or a prey organism that might live there. Label the adaptations that will allow your organism to be successful.

HANDS-ON LAB

Investigate Observe how once-living matter is broken down into smaller components in the process of decomposition.

TOPIC
1

Living Things in the Biosphere

NGSS PERFORMANCE EXPECTATIONS

MS-LS1-1 Conduct an investigation to provide evidence that living things are made of cells; either one cell or many different numbers and types of cells.
MS-LS1-2 Develop and use a model to describe the function of a cell as a whole and ways parts of cells contribute to the function
MS-LS1-3 Use argument supported by evidence for how the body is a system of interacting subsystems composed of groups of cells.
MS-LS4-2 Apply scientific ideas to construct an explanation for the anatomical similarities and differences among modern organisms and between modern and fossil organisms to infer evolutionary relationships.

HANDS-ON LAB

иConnect Expand your knowledge of what might be an animal.

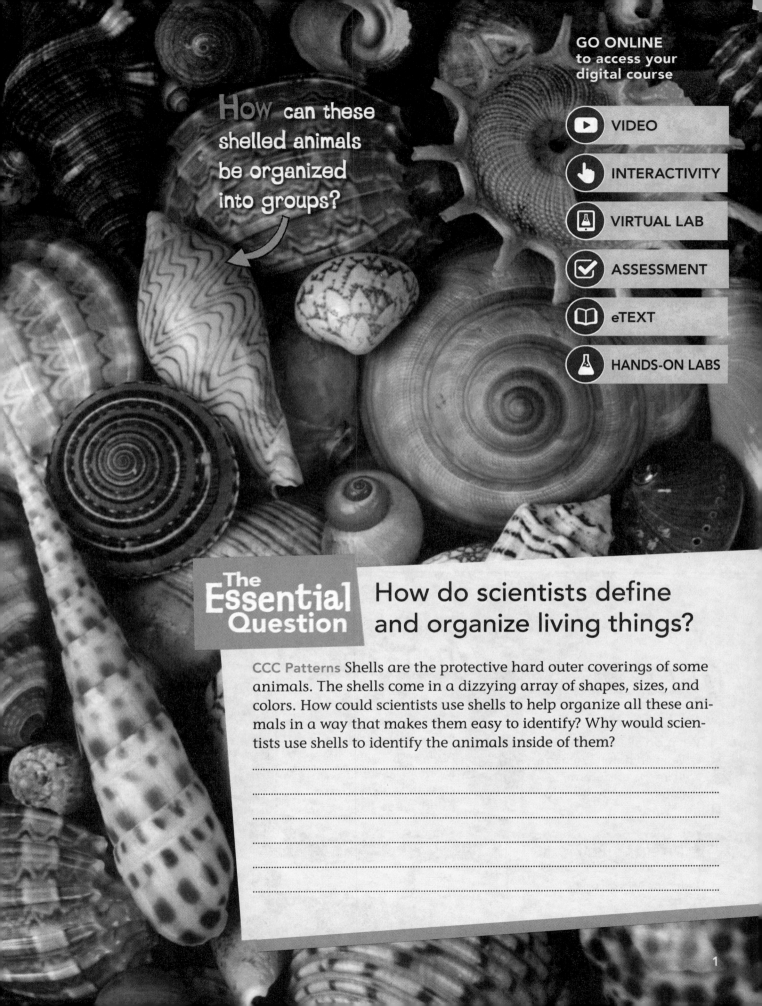

How can these shelled animals be organized into groups?

GO ONLINE to access your digital course

▶ VIDEO

👆 INTERACTIVITY

⚗ VIRTUAL LAB

☑ ASSESSMENT

📖 eTEXT

⚗ HANDS-ON LABS

The Essential Question

How do scientists define and organize living things?

CCC Patterns Shells are the protective hard outer coverings of some animals. The shells come in a dizzying array of shapes, sizes, and colors. How could scientists use shells to help organize all these animals in a way that makes them easy to identify? Why would scientists use shells to identify the animals inside of them?

....

....

....

....

....

....

Quest KICKOFF

How can you design a field guide to organize living things?

Phenomenon A 2011 scientific study estimates that there are around 8.7 million, plus or minus 1.3 million, species on our planet. Guess how many species have actually been identified! About two million. To identify these new organisms, taxonomists look at characteristics. Taxonomy is the branch of science that classifies organisms. In this problem-based Quest activity, you will design a field guide to help people identify the different organisms they may see at a nature center. By applying what you learn in each lesson, digital activity, or hands-on lab, you will gather key Quest information. With this information, you will develop your field guide in the Findings activity.

👆 **INTERACTIVITY**

Sort Out Those Organisms

MS-LS4-2 Apply scientific ideas to construct an explanation for the anatomical similarities and differences among modern organisms and between modern and fossil organisms to infer evolutionary relationships.

📺 **NBC LEARN** ▶ VIDEO

After watching the Quest Kickoff video about discovering and categorizing organisms, choose two organisms that you observe in your daily life. Complete the Venn diagram by describing what makes them similar and different.

Quest CHECK-IN

IN LESSON 1

What do all living things have in common? Analyze specimens to determine whether they are living or nonliving.

👆 **INTERACTIVITY**

Under the Microscope

Quest CHECK-IN

IN LESSON 2

What characteristics do biologists consider when grouping organisms? Model a scientific classification system using seeds.

🧪 **HANDS-ON LAB**

Classifying Seeds

Quest CHECK-IN

IN LESSON 3

What distinguishes unicellular and multicellular organisms? Classify organisms based on their characteristics as unicellular or multicellular.

👆 **INTERACTIVITY**

Discovering Rainforest Organisms

This plant can be identified by making detailed observations about its characteristics and comparing those observations to descriptions in a field guide.

Quest CHECK-IN

IN LESSON 4

How are plants and animals different from other organisms and from each other? Discover more rainforest organisms.

👆 **INTERACTIVITY**

Multicellular Rainforest Organisms

Quest FINDINGS

Complete the Quest!

Identify the criteria and constraints for your field guide. Then create a field guide that will help people identify different organisms in a local nature center.

👆 **INTERACTIVITY**

Create Your Field Guide

Is It an Animal?

How can you **make observations** and collect evidence to classify animals?

Background

Phenomenon Sometimes it is difficult to decide if a living thing is an animal. All organisms have characteristics that allow us to classify them as animals or other living things. How can you design a procedure to classify different organisms as animals or not?

Design a Procedure

☐ **1.** Make a list of 3-5 different animals.

....

....

☐ **2.** What are some things that make these animals different from one another?

....

....

....

☐ **3.** 🐁 🌱 Use your materials to design a procedure for how you can classify organisms as animals or not.

....

....

....

....

☐ **4.** Show your plan to your teacher before you begin. Record your observations and data.

Materials

(per group)
• cricket
• earthworm
• fern
• minnow
• pill bug
• potted plant
• sponges

Safety

Be sure to follow all safety procedures provided by your teacher. The Safety Appendix of your textbook provides more details about the safety icons.

Observations

HANDS-ON LAB

Connect Go online for a downloadable worksheet of this lab.

Analyze and Interpret

1. **SEP Analyze** Which organisms are animals and which are not? Use your observations to support your reasoning.

   ....

   ....

   ....

   ....

2. **SEP Use Evidence** Look at the observations you recorded about each organism. What evidence did you use to classify the animals? What characteristics do all animals share?

   ....

   ....

   ....

3. **SEP Construct Explanations** Are all living things considered animals? Are all animals considered living things? Explain your answer.

   ....

   ....

   ....

   ....

① Living Things

Guiding Questions

- What evidence is there that all living things are made of cells?
- Where do living things come from?
- What do living things need to stay alive, grow, and reproduce?

Connection

Literacy Gather Information

MS-LS1-1

HANDS-ON LAB

uInvestigate Identify structures found in the cells of living things.

Vocabulary

organism
cell
unicellular
multicellular
stimulus
response
spontaneous
  generation
homeostasis

Academic Vocabulary

characteristics

Connect It!

✏ **Circle the things in the image that appear to be living.**

SEP Conduct an Investigation Suppose you scraped off some of the pale green stuff from the tree bark. How would you know whether it was alive or not? What observations would you note? What tests could you do to see whether it's alive?

....

....

....

Characteristics of Living Things

An **organism** is any living thing. It could be a horse, a tree, a mushroom, strep bacteria, or the lichens (LIE kins) in **Figure 1**. Some organisms are familiar and obviously alive. No one wonders whether a dog is an organism. Other organisms are a little harder to distinguish from nonliving things. Lichens, for example, can be very hard and gray. They don't seem to grow much from year to year. How can we separate living from nonliving things? The answer is that all organisms share several important **characteristics**:

- All organisms are made of cells.
- All organisms contain similar chemicals and use energy.
- All organisms respond to their surroundings.
- All organisms grow, develop, and reproduce.

HANDS-ON LAB

Explore what makes a living thing alive.

Academic Vocabulary

A *characteristic* is a feature that helps to identify something. How would you describe the characteristics of a good movie or book?

....

....

....

....

....

Still Life with Lichens
Figure 1 Lichens blend in with the trees.

Characteristics of Living Things

Figure 2 All living things share certain characteristics.

SEP Analyze What is the one characteristic that all living things and only living things have in common?

....

....

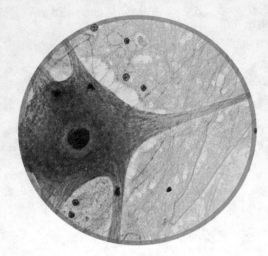

Cellular Organization
All living things are made of smaller living units called cells. **Cells** are the basic unit of structure and function in living things. In a single-celled or **unicellular** organism, one cell carries out the functions necessary to stay alive. Organisms consisting of many cells are **multicellular**. You are a multicellular organism with trillions of cells specialized to do certain tasks. The nerve cell shown here sends electrical signals throughout your body. It may signal you to let go of something hot or to take a step. In a multicellular organism, all cells work together to keep the organism alive.

The Chemicals of Life
All substances, including living cells, are made of chemicals. The most common chemical in cells is water, which is essential for life. Other chemicals, called carbohydrates (kahr boh HY drayts) provide the cell with energy. Proteins and lipids are chemicals used in building cells, much as wood and bricks are used to build schools. Finally, nucleic (noo KLEE ik) acids provide chemical instructions that tell cells how to carry out the functions of life. You've probably heard of DNA, deoxyribonucleic acid, but did you know what it looks like? The nucleic acid DNA directs the actions of every cell in your body.

Growth and Development
All living things grow and develop. Growth means becoming larger, and development is change that leads to maturity. As they develop and grow, organisms use energy. All multicellular organisms make new cells to become bigger or replace cells that have died. The mushrooms in the photo are both the same kind of organism. The larger mushroom is simply a few hours older and more developed.

Response to Surroundings Have you ever touched the palm of a baby's hand? If so, you may have observed the baby's fingers curl to grip your fingertip. The baby's grip is a natural reflex. Like a baby's curling fingers, all organisms react to changes in their surroundings. Any change or signal in the environment that can make an organism react in some way is called a **stimulus** (plural *stimuli*). Stimuli include changes in light, sound, flavors, or odors. An organism reacts to a stimulus with a **response**—an action or a change in behavior. Responding to stimuli helps the baby and all other organisms to survive and function.

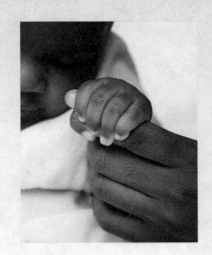

Reproduction Organisms reproduce to create offspring that are similar to the parent or parents. Some organisms reproduce asexually, creating an identical offspring with only one parent. One example is the young hydra (HY druh) budding off the parent hydra in the image. Mammals, birds, and most plants reproduce sexually. In sexual reproduction, two parents combine their DNA to create an offspring with a mix of both parents' characteristics.

Energy Use All organisms need energy to power their cells. Within an organism's cells, chemical reactions break down materials to get energy. Some organisms, called producers, can get energy from sunlight in a process known as photosynthesis, while other producers use different chemicals in their environment to make energy. Other organisms, called consumers, get energy by eating other living things. The shrew pictured here must eat more than its own weight in food every day. A shrew can starve to death if it goes five hours without eating!

HANDS-ON LAB

и**Investigate** Identify structures found in the cells of living things.

Life Produces More Life

Every spring, wildflowers seem to pop up out of the ground from nowhere. Do the plants sprout directly from rocks and soil? No, we know that the new plants are reproduced from older plants. Four hundred years ago, however, people believed that life could appear from nonliving material. For example, when people saw flies swarming around spoiled meat, they concluded that the meat produced the flies. The mistaken idea that living things arise from nonliving sources is called **spontaneous generation**. It took hundreds of years and many experiments to convince people that spontaneous generation does not occur.

Redi's Experiment In the 1600s, an Italian doctor named Francesco Redi helped to prove spontaneous generation wrong. Redi investigated the source of the maggots that develop into adult flies on rotting meat. Redi performed a controlled experiment so he was certain about the cause of the results. In a controlled experiment, a scientist carries out two or more tests that are identical in every way except one. As shown in **Figure 3**, Redi set up two jars in the same location with meat in them. Then Redi changed just one variable in his experiment and watched to see what would happen.

Redi's Experiment

Figure 3 Redi showed that meat did not cause the spontaneous generation of flies.

Relate Text to Visuals ✏️ Read the steps below. Then sketch steps 2 and 3.

> **Step 1** Redi placed meat in two identical jars. He covered one jar with a cloth that let in air, the control in the experiment.
>
> **Step 2** After a few days, Redi saw maggots (young flies) on the decaying meat in the open jar.
>
> **Step 3** Redi reasoned that flies had laid eggs on the meat in the open jar. The eggs hatched into maggots.

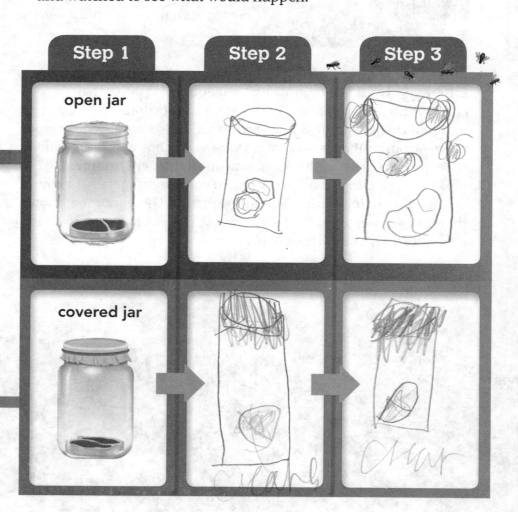

Step 1	Step 2	Step 3
open jar		
covered jar		

Pasteur's Experiment Even after Redi's experiment, many people continued to believe in spontaneous generation. Almost 200 years after Redi's experiment, French chemist Louis Pasteur (pah STUHR) decided to put spontaneous generation to the test. In his experiment, Pasteur used a control group. A control group is exposed to the same factors as the experimental group, except that it is not exposed to the variable being tested. **Figure 4** shows the experiment that convinced the scientific community that spontaneous generation was just a myth.

☑**READING CHECK** **Gather Information** How did both the Redi and Pasteur experiments prove there was no such thing as spontaneous generation?

....

....

....

Pasteur's Experiment
Figure 4 Pasteur carefully controlled his experiment.
1. **Relate Text to Visuals** 🖊 Draw and label the flasks in steps 2 and 3. Label the control and experimental flasks.

2. **Draw Conclusions** What did the bacterial growth in Step 3 confirm for Pasteur?

....

....

....

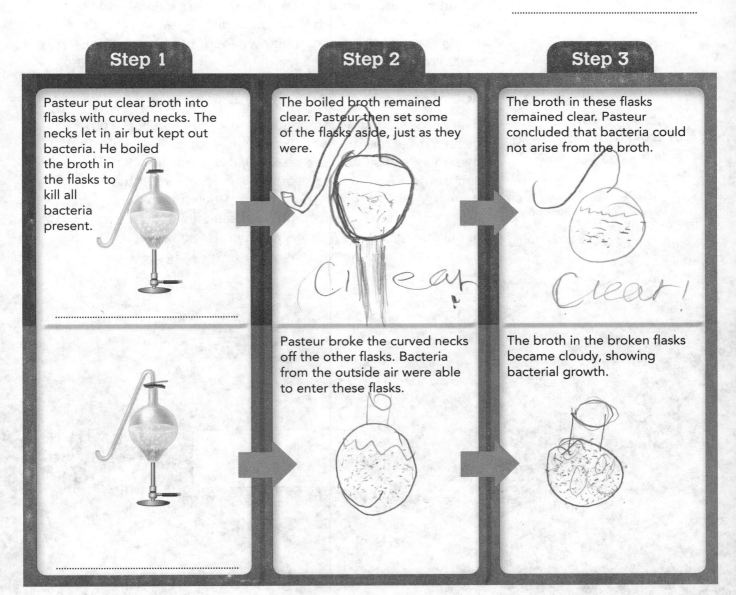

Step 1

Pasteur put clear broth into flasks with curved necks. The necks let in air but kept out bacteria. He boiled the broth in the flasks to kill all bacteria present.

....

Step 2

The boiled broth remained clear. Pasteur then set some of the flasks aside, just as they were.

Clear!

Pasteur broke the curved necks off the other flasks. Bacteria from the outside air were able to enter these flasks.

Step 3

The broth in these flasks remained clear. Pasteur concluded that bacteria could not arise from the broth.

Clear!

The broth in the broken flasks became cloudy, showing bacterial growth.

....

Autotrophs and Heterotrophs

Figure 5 Every organism has to eat!

CCC Energy and Matter ✏ Write whether each organism is an autotroph or a heterotroph in the space provided.

Needs of Living Things

Though it may seem surprising, pine trees, worms, and all other organisms have the same basic needs as you do. All living things must satisfy their basic needs for water, food, living space, and homeostasis.

Water All living things depend on water for their survival. In fact, some organisms can live only for a few days without water. All cells need water to carry out their daily functions. Many substances dissolve easily in water. Once food or other chemicals are dissolved, they are easily transported around the body of an organism. About half of human blood is made of water. Our blood carries dissolved food, waste, and other chemicals to and from cells. Also, many chemical reactions that take place in cells require water.

Food All living things consume food for energy. Some organisms, such as plants, capture the sun's energy and use it to make food through the process of photosynthesis. Producers are organisms that make their own food. Producers are also called autotrophs (AW toh trohfs). *Auto-* means "self" and *-troph* means "feeder." Autotrophs use the sun's energy to convert water and a gas into food.

Every organism that can't make its own food must eat other organisms. Consumers are organisms that cannot make their own food. Consumers are also called heterotrophs (HET uh roh trohfs). *Hetero-* means "other," so combined with *-troph* it means "one that feeds on others." A heterotroph may eat autotrophs, other heterotrophs, or break down dead organisms to get energy. **Figure 5** shows an interaction between autotrophs and heterotrophs.

Crocodile

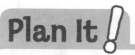

Plan It!

Can a Person Be an Autotroph?

Shelby and Michaela are learning about organisms. Shelby says she is sometimes an autotroph because she makes her own food after school, a bowl of cut fruit.

SEP Explain Phenomena How can Michaela prove to Shelby that she is not an autotroph? What could she do to help Shelby investigate how an autotroph makes its own food?

....

....

....

Space All organisms need a place to live—a place to get food and water and find shelter. Whether an organism lives in the savanna, as shown in **Figure 5**, or the desert, its surroundings must provide what it needs to survive. Because there is a limited amount of space on Earth, some organisms compete for space. Trees in a forest, for example, compete with other trees for sunlight. Below ground, their roots compete for water and minerals. If an organism loses its living space, it must move to a new place or it may die.

☑ **READING CHECK** **Cite Textual Evidence** Why do living things need water, food, and space to live?

....

....

....

Tick

Zebra

Grass

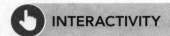
Homeostasis

When you go outside on a freezing cold day, does your body temperature fall below freezing as well? Of course not! Your body is able to keep the temperature of your insides steady even when outside conditions change. Shivering, moving to a warmer place, and putting on more clothes all help you to stay warm. The maintenance of stable internal conditions is called **homeostasis** (hoh mee oh STAY sis). All organisms maintain homeostasis to stay alive.

Organisms have many different methods for maintaining homeostasis. The methods depend on the challenges faced by the organism. Consider the marine iguana, pictured in **Figure 6**. Marine iguanas feed underwater in the ocean and swallow a lot of salty water. To maintain homeostasis, the iguanas need a way to get rid of the extra salt. In a human, extra salt would be removed in sweat, tears, or urine. The iguana has a different way of maintaining homeostasis. Iguanas produce very salty liquid that comes out near their noses. Frequent sneezing clears the salty liquid away. Homeostasis is maintained!

✓ **READING CHECK** **Determine Central Ideas** The paws of the arctic fox are covered in thick fur. How does this help the fox maintain homeostasis?

....

....

....

Salty Sneezes

Figure 6 As they eat underwater plants, marine iguanas maintain homeostasis by sneezing out salty liquid.

CCC Energy and Matter Which basic need is an iguana meeting by feeding on underwater plants?

....

....

1. **CCC Stability and Change** Why is it necessary for organisms to maintain stable internal conditions?

   ....

   ....

2. **SEP Use Models** ✏ Draw a diagram showing all the things that an organism needs to survive. Label the drawing to show how the organism can meet its needs right where it lives.

3. **SEP Plan an Investigation** A student is designing a controlled experiment to test whether the amount of water that a plant receives affects its growth. Which factors should the student hold constant and which variable should the student change?

   ....

   ....

   ....

   ....

4. **SEP Construct Explanations** What sort of evidence can you use to show that all living things grow and develop?

   ....

   ....

   ....

   ....

   ....

   ....

   ....

   ....

   ....

   ....

   ....

Quest CHECK-IN

In this lesson, you learned about the characteristics of living things and where living things come from. You also learned about what living things need to grow, stay alive, and reproduce.

SEP Evaluate Your Plan What are your plans for your field guide? How will you use the characteristics of living things to identify and categorize different organisms?

....

....

....

....

👆 **INTERACTIVITY**

Under the Microscope

Go online to observe different objects and determine whether they are living or nonliving.

The TOUGH and *Tiny* TARDIGRADE

Imagine being shrunk to the size of the period at the end of this sentence and getting plopped down in a bed of moss. You just might run into a tardigrade as big as you. Sort of cute, right? No wonder they're nicknamed the water bear.

rehydration

dehydration

All living things need water, a safe temperature range, and the right pressure to sustain functioning cells. But one microscopic organism called a tardigrade defies all those rules. Tardigrades survive the most extreme conditions on Earth.

How do they do it? Tardigrades dehydrate themselves. They shed 95 percent of the water in their bodies. Life comes to a nearly complete halt in the dried-out tardigrade. Studies suggest that tardigrades produce proteins and sugars that help to protect their cells while they are dehydrated. Add water and the tardigrade rehydrates and bounces back to life. Scientists study tardigrades to learn more about the activities inside cells that enable animals to develop and survive.

Extreme Temperatures

Tardigrades have been found in conditions ranging from polar waters to bubbling hot springs. In one lab experiment, they even survived at an unimaginable −272°C (−458°F). And they withstood temperatures well over boiling, too.

Intense Pressure

If you stood in the very deepest part of the ocean, the pressure would crush you flat. But tardigrades? They can withstand *six times* that pressure. In the vacuum of space where there's almost no pressure, your insides would start to expand until your body exploded like a balloon. But tardigrades toured outer space for ten days and came back to Earth unharmed.

Radiation

In high doses, radiation damages cells and destroys DNA. Humans can withstand only very small doses (measured in Grays, or Gy), but tardigrades can survive 5,000 Gy or more. With their ability to protect their cells from these extremes, you'd think tardigrades would live in the wildest places on Earth. But they prefer to live in the water, or in damp places, such as among wet leaves and in moist soil.

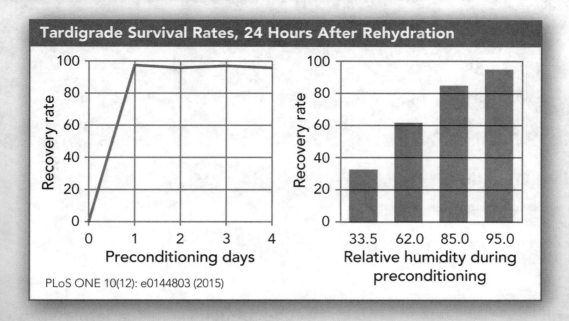

Tardigrade Survival Rates, 24 Hours After Rehydration

PLoS ONE 10(12): e0144803 (2015)

Tardigrades are exposed to different amounts of humidity (or moisture) before dehydrating. This is called preconditioning. The graphs show results from an experiment that tested whether preconditioning was necessary. The bar graph above shows the results of changing the amount of humidity in the air during preconditioning. The recovery rate is the percent of tardigrades who survive the transition from dehydration to rehydration.

1. **Analyze Properties** When you think of the common characteristics that all living things share, which one stands out the most in this experiment?

....

2. **Evaluate Data** What does the bar graph above suggest about the effects of relative humidity during preconditioning?

....
....

3. **Predict** What do you think the data would look like if the relative humidity were 45 percent?

....
....
....

4. **Synthesize Information** Why might humidity be helpful to a tardigrade?

....
....
....

② Classification Systems

Guiding Questions

- How are living things classified into groups?
- How does the theory of evolution support the classification of organisms?

Connections

Literacy Assess Sources

Math Write an Expression

MS-LS4-2

HANDS-ON LAB

ᴜInvestigate Create a taxonomic key to classify different tree leaves.

Vocabulary

species
classification
genus
binomial
  nomenclature
taxonomy
domain
evolution
convergent
  evolution

Academic Vocabulary

determine

Connect It !

✏ **Draw arrows and label parts of the organism that help you to identify it.**

SEP Make Observations   What kind of living thing do you think this is?

....

....

....

Classifying Organisms

It is estimated that there are approximately 8.7 million species of organisms on the planet, with thousands more discovered each day. A **species** is a group of similar organisms that can mate with each other and produce offspring that can also mate and reproduce. Biologists place similar organisms into groups based on characteristics they have in common. **Classification** is the process of grouping things based on their similarities. To classify the organism in **Figure 1**, you'd first need to know about its characteristics. Then you could figure out which group it belonged to.

Linnaean Naming System
In the 1730s, biologist Carolus Linnaeus arranged organisms in groups based on their observable features. Then he gave each organism a two-part scientific name. The first word in the name is the organism's **genus**, a group of similar, closely-related organisms. The second word is the species and might describe where the organism lives or its appearance. This system in which each organism is given a unique, two-part scientific name that indicates its genus and species is known as **binomial nomenclature**. Today, scientists still use this naming system that classifies organisms according to their shared characteristics.

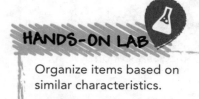

HANDS-ON LAB

Organize items based on similar characteristics.

Write About It Pick a favorite animal or plant. What is it that you find most interesting? In your science notebook, describe its characteristics.

Animal, Vegetable, or Mineral?
Figure 1 Some organisms are much harder to classify than others!

Literacy Connection

Assess Sources Books become outdated and the Internet is full of incorrect information. If you need an accurate answer to a scientific question, where would you look? Whom could you ask for help?

....

....

....

....

....

....

Taxonomy The scientific study of how organisms are classified is called **taxonomy** (tak SAHN uh mee). Scientists use taxonomy to identify the name of an unknown organism or to name a newly discovered organism. For example, if you look closely at the characteristics of the organism in **Figure 1**, you might classify it as a sea slug. It would then be simple to look up sea slugs and find out that they are animals related to slugs and snails. All sea slugs have sensitive tentacles that they use to smell, taste, and feel their way around. They eat other animals by scraping away their flesh. Sea slugs can even gain the ability to sting by eating stinging animals!

Domains In classification of organisms, the broadest level of organization is the **domain**. There are three domains: Eukarya, Archaea, and Bacteria. Eukarya (yoo KA ree uh) includes the familiar kingdoms of plants, animals, and fungi, and a less familiar kingdom, Protista, which has much simpler organisms. Members of Domain Eukarya are called eukaryotes. Eukaryotes have nuclei containing DNA. Domain Archaea (ahr KEE uh) contains a group of one-celled organisms with no nuclei in their cells. Members of Domain Bacteria, like Archaea, have only one cell and no nucleus, but bacteria have different structures and chemical processes from those of Archaea. **Figure 2** shows the levels of classification for Domain Eukarya.

☑ READING CHECK **Determine Central Ideas** What do scientists use to determine how organisms are classified in each level? Explain your answer.

....

....

....

Model It !

So Many Levels of Classification!

There are ways to memorize a long list of terms so that you can remember them months or even years later. A mnemonic (nee MON ic) can help you memorize a list of terms in order. To create one type of mnemonic, you compose a sentence from words that start with the first letter of each term in the list. One popular mnemonic for levels of classification is: "<u>D</u>ear <u>K</u>ing <u>P</u>hilip <u>C</u>ome <u>O</u>ver <u>F</u>or <u>G</u>ood <u>S</u>paghetti." In the space, devise your own mnemonic to help you remember the levels of classification.

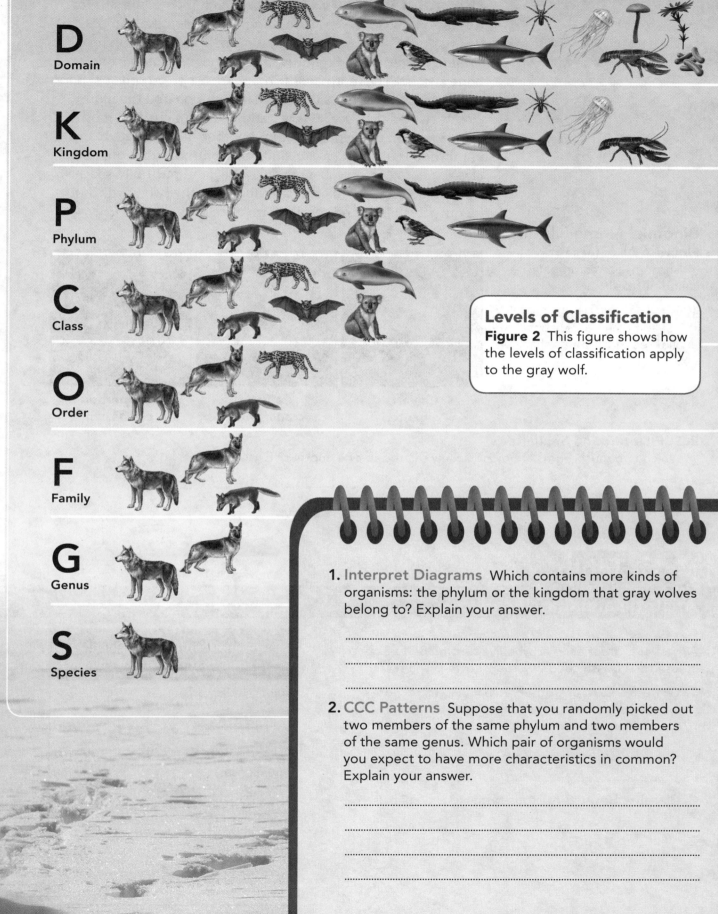

D
Domain

K
Kingdom

P
Phylum

C
Class

O
Order

F
Family

G
Genus

S
Species

Levels of Classification
Figure 2 This figure shows how the levels of classification apply to the gray wolf.

1. **Interpret Diagrams** Which contains more kinds of organisms: the phylum or the kingdom that gray wolves belong to? Explain your answer.

....

....

....

2. **CCC Patterns** Suppose that you randomly picked out two members of the same phylum and two members of the same genus. Which pair of organisms would you expect to have more characteristics in common? Explain your answer.

....

....

....

....

Binomial Nomenclature As explained at the start of this lesson, the first word in an organism's scientific name is its genus. The genus (plural *genera*) is a classification grouping of similar, closely related organisms. Each genus contains one or more species. The more classification levels two organisms share, the more characteristics they have in common and the more closely related they are. **Figure 3** shows a giant puffball mushroom found in the genus *Calvatia*. Another closely related kind of puffball is also in *Calvatia*. Still other puffballs that are not as closely related are in other genera. The giant puffball's species name, *gigantea*, describes its size. Together, the two words that identify the genus and species form the scientific name.

Binomial Nomenclature

Figure 3 All of these mushrooms are commonly called puffballs.

1. **SEP Make Observations** List some characteristics that all three mushrooms share.

....

....

....

| *Calvatia gigantea* | *Calvatia craniiformis* | *Lycoperdon echinatum* |

2. **SEP Determine Similarities** Which two mushrooms are most closely related to one another? Explain.

....

....

Math Toolbox

Aristotle and Classification

Aristotle, a Greek scholar who lived from 384 to 322 BCE, created the classification system shown in the table.

1. **Write an Expression** Use variables to write an expression to find the percentage of animals that swim. Then, complete the table.

....

....

2. **Classify** How did Aristotle organize the animals?

....

....

Animals with blood that...	Percentage of animals
fly	22%
walk, run, or hop	46%
swim	

Scientific Names

A complete scientific name is written in italics. The first letter in the first word is capitalized. You will notice that most scientific names use Latin. Linnaeus used Latin in his naming system because it was the common language used by all scientists. **Figure 4** shows how using different common names for the same organism can get confusing. Scientists also use taxonomic keys, as shown in **Figure 5**, to help name and identify organisms.

☑ READING CHECK **Determine Meaning** How are scientific names written?

....

....

Confusing Common Names

Figure 4 Is this a firefly, a lightning bug, a glowworm, or a golden sparkler? Different names are used in different parts of the country. Luckily, this insect has only one scientific name, *Photinus pyralis*.

Predict What characteristic of the insect do you think scientists used to give it the species name *pyralis*?

....

....

Using a Taxonomic Key

Figure 5 While on a hike, you find an organism with eight legs, two body regions, claw-like pincers, and no tail. Use the key to identify the organism.

1. **Interpret Diagrams** How many different organisms can be identified using this key?

   ....

2. **CCC Patterns** Use the taxonomic key to identify the organism you observed on your hike.

   ....

Taxonomic Key			
Step		**Characteristics**	**Organism**
1	1a.	Has 8 legs	Go to Step 2.
	1b.	Has more than 8 legs	Go to Step 3.
2	2a.	Has one oval-shaped body region	Go to Step 4.
	2b.	Has two body regions	Go to Step 5.
3	3a.	Has one pair of legs on each body segment	Centipede
	3b.	Has two pairs of legs on each body segment	Millipede
4	4a.	Is less than 1 millimeter long	Mite
	4b.	Is more than 1 millimeter long	Tick
5	5a.	Has clawlike pincers	Go to Step 6.
	5b.	Has no clawlike pincers	Spider
6	6a.	Has a long tail with a stinger	Scorpion
	6b.	Has no tail or stinger	Pseudoscorpion

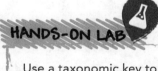

HANDS-ON LAB

Use a taxonomic key to identify an unknown pest.

Investigate Create a taxonomic key to classify different tree leaves.

Evolution and Classification

When Linnaeus was alive, people thought that species never changed. This point of view changed when Charles Darwin developed a new idea in the 1830s. Darwin was an Englishman. He sailed around the world for five years observing nature and collecting samples of fossils and animals. During the voyage, he was fascinated by the relationships between modern species and ancient types, as shown in **Figure 6**. Darwin was one of the first scientists to understand **evolution**, or the process of change over time. He concluded that all modern species developed from earlier kinds of life through natural selection. Natural selection is the idea that some individuals are better adapted to their environment than others. The better-adapted individuals are more likely to survive and reproduce than other members of the same species.

Common Ancestry Evolution by natural selection is the organizing principle of life science. Evidence from thousands of scientific investigations supports the idea of evolution. As understanding of evolution increased, biologists changed how they classify species. Scientists now understand that certain organisms may be similar because they share a common ancestor and an evolutionary history. The more similar the two groups are, in fact, the more recent their common ancestor.

5.2 million years ago (mya)

Pakicetus, land-dwelling, four-footed mammal

4.8 mya

Ambulocetus, "walking whale," mammal lived both on land and in water

4.1 mya

Dorudon, "spear tooth," water-dwelling mammal

Evolution of the Dolphin

Figure 6 Darwin compared ancient and modern species to develop his theory of evolution by natural selection. Skeletons of dolphin ancestors show how the species evolved.

Form a Hypothesis Why do you think the ancient ancestor of the dolphin became a water-dwelling animal?

....

....

2.2 mya

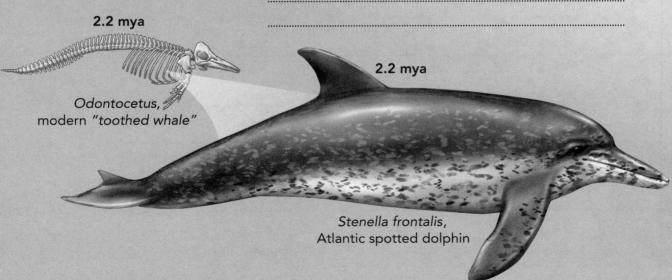

Odontocetus, modern "toothed whale"

2.2 mya

Stenella frontalis, Atlantic spotted dolphin

Convergent Evolution

Figure 7 These three organisms evolved a similar characteristic over time.

1. **Identify** 🖊 Circle the characteristic that the three organisms share.

2. **Form a Hypothesis** Why did the same characteristic evolve?

....

....

....

....

Evolutionary Relationships Scientists **determine** the evolutionary history of a species by comparing the structures of organisms. Scientists also compare the genetic information contained in the DNA of organisms' cells. Sometimes, unrelated organisms that live in similar environments evolve similar characteristics, as shown in **Figure 7**. Sharing common characteristics, however, does not necessarily mean that organisms are closely related. The process by which unrelated organisms evolve similar characteristics is called **convergent evolution**. When scientists discovered convergent evolution, they had to change the placement of organisms within the classification system. Because scientific research leads to discovery and new knowledge, scientists sometimes reclassify organisms to account for new evidence. In this sense, the system of classification also evolves.

Academic Vocabulary

To determine is to find out an answer by doing research. When have you determined the answer to an important question?

....

....

....

....

☑ **READING CHECK** **Assess Sources** Suggest one reliable source of information about Charles Darwin. What makes this source reliable?

....

....

....

1. Draw Conclusions What can you conclude about two organisms that can mate and produce fertile offspring?

....

2. SEP Interpret Data Use the chart. Which two species are most closely related? How do you know? Which species is the least related to the other three? Explain.

Some Types of Trees				
Common Name	Kingdom	Family	Genus	Species
Bird cherry	Plants	Rosaceae	*Prunus*	*avium*
Flowering cherry	Plants	Rosaceae	*Prunus*	*serrula*
Smooth-leaved elm	Plants	Ulmaceae	*Ultima*	*minor*
Whitebeam	Plants	Rosaceae	*Sorbus*	*aria*

....

....

....

....

....

....

3. SEP Construct Explanations How are evolution and classification related?

....

....

....

4. SEP Construct Explanations How did Darwin's discoveries change scientists' understanding of species?

....

....

....

....

....

....

5. SEP Evaluate Claims A friend claims her pet ferret is descended from the wild polecat. You want to learn more about this ferret ancestor. An online search shows several different kinds of polecats. How could you figure out which one is the ferret ancestor?

....

....

....

....

Quest CHECK-IN

In this lesson, you learned how scientists classify living things based on shared characteristics.

CCC Systems and System Models What are some limitations of using a classification system to categorize living things?

....

....

....

....

....

HANDS-ON LAB

Classifying Seeds

Go online for a downloadable worksheet of this lab. Model a scientific classification system using seeds. Then brainstorm ideas for how you might use classification in your field guide.

MS-LS4-2

Classification:
What's a Panda?

What's in a name? In the Linnaean classification system, an animal's name tells what species it is. And with millions of species on Earth, this naming system comes in handy.

The naming system is based on observable physical characteristics—an animal's coloration, number of legs, the shape of its wings, and so on. But with today's technology, scientists can now classify animals from the inside out, by using their DNA.

DNA has helped scientists to figure out pandas, which have posed quite a puzzle. *Giant* pandas share a lot of physical traits with bears—their shape, size, shaggy fur, and lumbering movement. But smaller *red* pandas have more in common with raccoons. So what exactly is a "panda"?

Recent DNA studies show that giant pandas and red pandas are not closely related after all. Giant pandas share more DNA with bears and have been classified in the bear family (*Ursidae*). Red pandas, however, didn't make the cut. They're not bears, and, currently, they're not raccoons either. For now, they are classified in their own family, *Ailuridae*. But with further DNA evidence, this could change. Until then, the red panda is an animal unto itself.

MY DISCOVERY

Is a red panda a raccoon? The evidence points in different directions, and scientists are still debating. Read up on these animals and see what you think.

The red panda has a bushy, ringed tail, much like a raccoon's.

Are giant pandas really bears? DNA evidence reveals the answer.

Viruses, Bacteria, Protists, and Fungi

Guiding Questions

- What are all living things made of?
- What are the characteristics of viruses, bacteria, protists, and fungi?
- How do viruses, bacteria, protists, and fungi interact with nature and people?

Connections

Literacy Cite Textual Evidence

Math Analyze Relationships

MS-LS1-1

HANDS-ON LAB

uInvestigate Discover unicellular and multicellular organisms in pond water.

Vocabulary

virus
host
vaccine
bacteria
protist
parasite

Academic Vocabulary

resistant

Connect It!

✏️ **Write a checkmark on one individual of each kind of living thing you see.**

SEP Make Obsesrvations Describe the different types of organisms you see.

....

....

SEP Explain Phenomena Why might it be unwise to drink water straight from a pond?

....

....

Microorganisms

When people think of organisms, they picture plants or animals. Yet many of the organisms we come in contact with every day are so small that you need a microscope to see them. These microorganisms are vital for the survival of all plants and animals. **Figure 1** shows some amazing microbes living in a single drop of pond water.

Protists are classified in Domain Eukarya and are simpler than the plants, animals, and fungi they are grouped with. However, organisms in Domains Archaea and Bacteria are less complex than protists. Archaea and bacteria are unicellular microorganisms that do not have a nucleus. These microorganisms are classified in different domains because of their different characteristics.

Many archaea live in extreme conditions and make food from chemicals. You might find archaea in hot springs, very salty water, or deep underground. Archaea is a great example of how science is always changing. The domain Archaea was only proposed by taxonomists in 1977!

Bacteria have different structures and chemical processes than archaea do. Some bacteria are autotrophs, meaning they can make their own food. Other bacteria are heterotrophs who must find their food. Still other types of bacteria are decomposers that absorb nutrients from decaying organisms. Bacteria are found in soil, water, and air. In fact, bacteria are found everywhere, even inside you.

☑ **READING CHECK** **Determine Central Ideas** If you had a powerful microscope, how could you determine whether a cell was from a eukaryote?

....

....

....

Life in a Drop of Water
Figure 1 A single drop of pond water is home to many kinds of life.

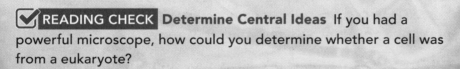

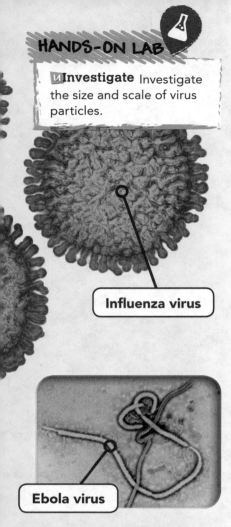

Influenza virus

Ebola virus

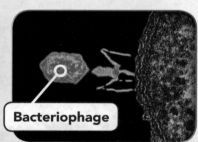

Bacteriophage

Viral Variety

Figure 2 Viruses come in many shapes. These images have been magnified and colorized to show details.

SEP Determine Similarities ✏ Circle the virus that most closely resembles a cell. Explain your choice.

Viruses

You may have noticed that viruses were not included in the domains of living things. That's because viruses are not alive. A **virus** is a tiny, nonliving particle that enters and then reproduces inside a living cell. They lack most of the characteristics of living things. Some viruses may look like cells, but they are not cells. Viruses cannot reproduce on their own. Instead, they cause the cells they enter to reproduce more viruses. Viruses do not use food for energy or to grow. They also do not respond to their surroundings or produce wastes.

Shapes and Names Viruses can be round or shaped like bricks, threads, or bullets. Some viruses even have complex, robot-like shapes, as shown in **Figure 2**. Viruses are so small that they are measured in units called nanometers (nm), or one billionth of a meter. The common cold virus is 75 nm in diameter. The diameter of a red blood cell—7,500 nm—is much larger. Scientists name some viruses after the disease they cause or after the area where they were discovered.

Reproduction A virus is very small and simple. All viruses contain genetic material with a protein coating. The genetic material contains chemical instructions for making more copies of the virus. To reproduce, a virus attaches itself to a host cell, as shown in **Figure 3**. A **host** is an organism that provides a source of energy or a suitable environment for a virus to live. The virus either enters the cell or injects its genetic material into the host cell. Inside the host cell, the virus's genetic material takes over and forces the cell to make more copies of the virus! Finally, the host cell bursts open, releasing many new viruses which then infect other healthy cells, repeating the process.

Disease Many copies of a virus attacking your cells at once may cause a disease. Some viral diseases are mild, such as the common cold. Other viral diseases can produce serious illnesses. Viruses spread quickly and attack the cells of nearly every kind of organism. Fortunately, scientists have developed vaccines to prevent many dangerous viral diseases. A **vaccine** is a substance used in vaccination that consists of pathogens, such as viruses, that have been weakened or killed but can still trigger the body to produce chemicals that destroy the pathogens. **Figure 4** shows the vaccination process.

✓ READING CHECK **Distinguish Facts** What makes viruses so dangerous and vaccines so important?

....

....

Virus Invasion!

Figure 3 A cell invaded by a virus becomes a kind of zombie. All the cell's energy goes into making more and more new viruses.

SEP Apply Scientific Reasoning Which evolved first: viruses or living organisms? Explain.

....

....

....

VIRUS

HOST CELL

Step 1 Virus injects genetic material into host cell.

Step 2 Cell makes copies of virus.

Step 3 Cell bursts, releasing many new copies of virus.

The virus that causes a disease is isolated. The virus is then damaged by heat, and a vaccine is prepared from it.

After being injected with a vaccine, the body prepares defenses against the virus.

The body can now resist infection by the disease-causing virus.

Vaccine Protection

Figure 4 Vaccinations can prevent measles and other viral diseases.

SEP Construct Explanations Why is it important to use a weakened virus in a vaccine?

....

....

....

Math Toolbox

A Viral Epidemic

When a virus sickens many people at the same time within a limited geographic area, the outbreak is called an epidemic. During the 2014–2015 Ebola epidemic in West Africa, people began to get sick faster and faster beginning in May. There were about 375 new Ebola cases at the beginning of June. By July first, there were about 750 new cases.

1. **SEP Identify Variables** On the graph, circle the variable that depends on the other.

2. **SEP Interpret Data** Explain the relationship between the number of cases reported and time.

....

3. **Write an Expression** 🖊 Find the number of new cases expected by September. Use an expression to plot the number of new cases for both September and October on the graph. Then finish drawing the line.

....

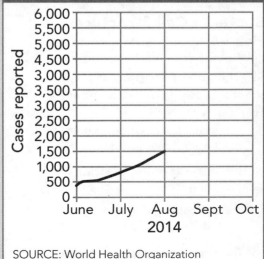

Ebola Cases in West Africa, 2014

Cases reported: 6,000 / 5,500 / 5,000 / 4,500 / 3,000 / 3,500 / 3,000 / 2,500 / 2,000 / 1,500 / 1,000 / 500 / 0

June July Aug Sept Oct
2014

SOURCE: World Health Organization

Bacteria Shapes

Figure 5 The shape of a bacteria helps a scientist to identify it.

CCC Structure and Function Label the shape of each bacteria.

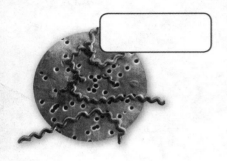

□□□□□□

□□□□□□

Bacteria

If life were a movie, bacteria would be both villains and heroes. Bacteria would also make up most of the supporting cast. Bacteria make up the great majority of organisms on Earth. Bacteria are very small; millions can fit into the period at the end of this sentence. The smallest bacteria are about the size of the largest viruses. Most bacteria are one of three basic shapes: ball, rod, or spiral. You can see some of these shapes in **Figure 5**. The shape of the cell helps scientists identify the type of bacteria.

Infectious Bacteria You have probably heard of *E. coli*, *Streptococcus* ("strep throat"), and *Staphylococcus* ("staph"). They are types of infectious, or disease–causing, bacteria. Someone can become infected when the bacteria enter the person's body. The bacteria then grow and multiply quite quickly. Because these bacteria give off toxins (dangerous chemicals that damage surrounding cells and tissues), they can cause serious infections. Luckily, fewer than one percent of bacteria are actually infectious.

Bacterial Cell Structures Bacteria are single-celled organisms, also known as prokaryotes, that lack a nucleus. Each cell is a separate living organism that performs all the functions needed for life. **Figure 6** shows the structure of a typical bacterial cell. Bacteria have cell walls that protect them from attacks and keep them from drying out. Inside the cell wall is a cell membrane. The cell membrane controls what substances pass into and out of the cell. Some bacteria have structures attached to the cell wall that help them move around. Flagella whip around like propellers to drive some bacteria toward their food.

Model It!

Bacterial Cell Structures

Figure 6 Structures in a bacterial cell help them function and survive.

SEP Develop Models ✏ Use the descriptions below to label the structures.

cytoplasm everything inside the cell membrane

genetic material string-like chemical instructions for cell

pili tiny hairs that help cell move and reproduce

ribosomes round structures where proteins are made

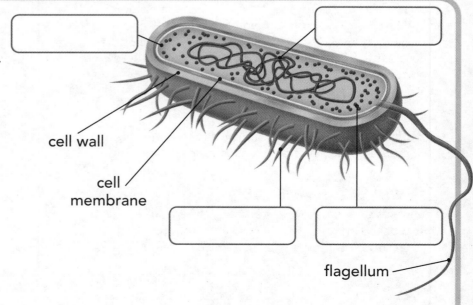

cell wall

cell membrane

flagellum

Obtaining Food

Some bacteria make their own food from sunlight, like plants do. Other bacteria create food from chemicals. Chemicals from underwater volcanoes feed the bacteria in **Figure 7**. A third group of bacteria take in food through their cell walls. Food for these bacteria could be milk, sugar, meat, or dead cells. Your digestive system is a good home for bacteria! Some bacteria use the energy from food to make poisonous chemicals called toxins. Toxins cause the pain and sickness you feel when you get food poisoning.

Survival

Bacteria cannot move fast. They cannot escape intense heat or hunt for food. In harsh conditions, some bacteria survive by sheltering in place. A thick-walled shell forms around genetic material and cytoplasm, forming a tough endospore. The endospore can grow back into a full cell when conditions improve.

Bacterial Reproduction

Bacteria also keep ahead of predators by reproducing rapidly. Even if predators eat some individual bacteria, there are always more. Bacterial reproduction is shown in **Figure 8**. Most bacteria reproduce asexually by growing and then dividing into two identical cells. Asexual reproduction in bacteria is called binary fission.

Bacteria can also pass genetic material to a neighboring bacteria through conjugation. Conjugation occurs when two bacteria cells come together and exchange genetic material. Conjugation does not produce more bacteria, but it does allow genetic information to spread. For example, one bacterial cell could be **resistant** to antibiotics. The antibiotic-resistant cell could pass the resistance on to other bacteria by conjugation. Soon, the whole bacteria population can become resistant and the antibiotic will stop working.

INTERACTIVITY

Observe and compare different unicellular organisms.

Undersea Mystery
Figure 7 These "rocks" are layers of bacteria that have grown up around the mouth of the seafloor volcano.

Academic Vocabulary

Resistant means able to work against or hold off an opposing force. When have you been resistant?

....

....

Bacterial Reproduction

Figure 8 🖊 Label the diagram with these terms: asexual reproduction, binary fission, conjugation, and transfer of genetic material. Then, match the number in the diagram to the step it describes below.

_____ Cells separate; one now has some genetic information from the other cell.

_____ Cell splits into two identical cells.

_____ Cell grows larger before dividing.

_____ One cell passes some of its genetic information to another cell.

Cite Textual Evidence
Would you classify bacteria as harmful or helpful? Explain.

....
....
....
....

The Many Roles of Bacteria

Figure 9 🖊 Bacteria do other things besides make people sick. They have many important roles in nature and human life. There are many ways we interact with bacteria. Circle or highlight one or more examples of harmful bacteria.

☑ **READING CHECK** **Cite Textural Evidence** According to what you have read, how do bacteria protect their genetic material and cytoplasm during harsh conditions?

....
....
....

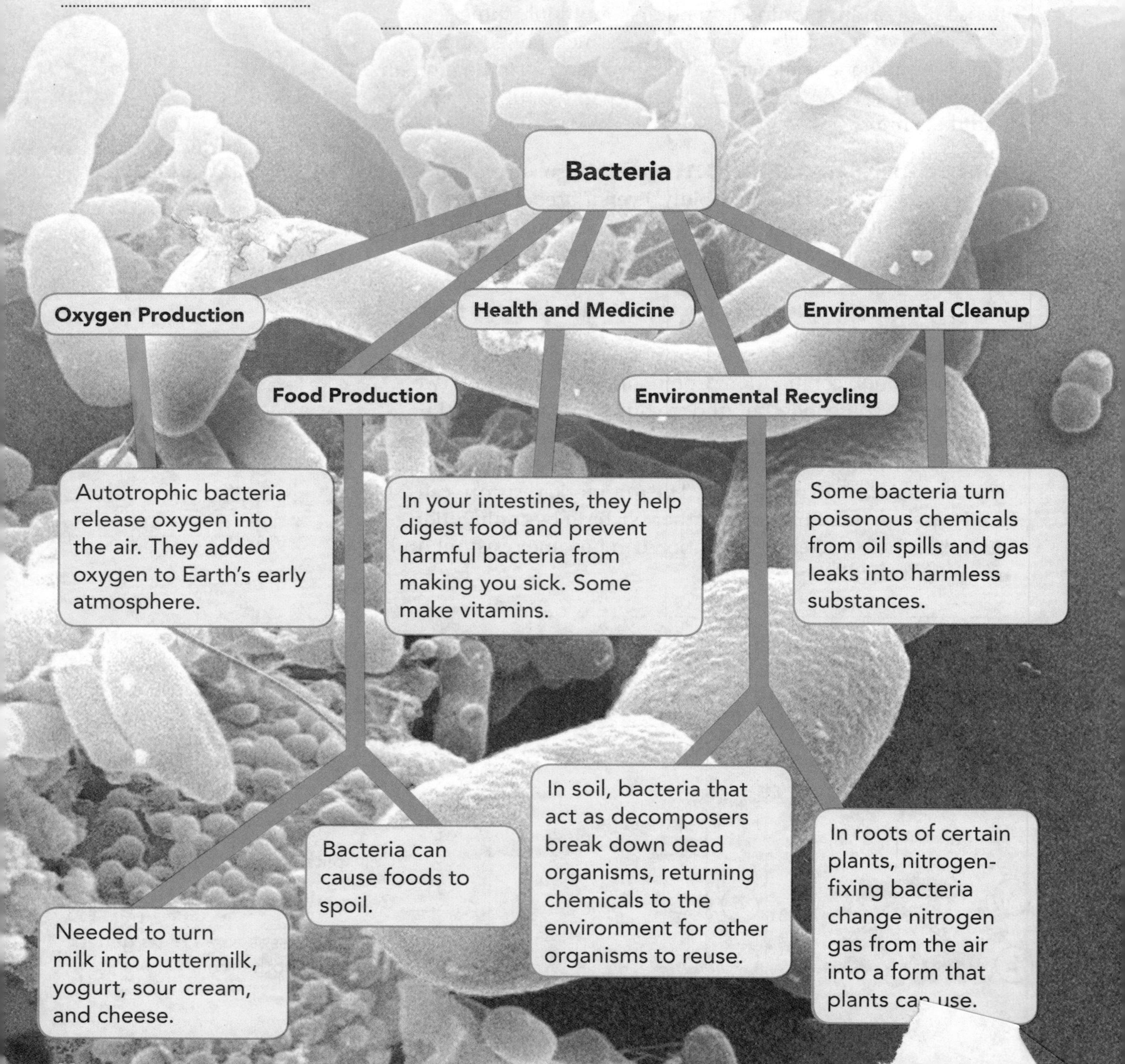

Bacteria

Oxygen Production

Health and Medicine

Environmental Cleanup

Food Production

Environmental Recycling

Autotrophic bacteria release oxygen into the air. They added oxygen to Earth's early atmosphere.

In your intestines, they help digest food and prevent harmful bacteria from making you sick. Some make vitamins.

Some bacteria turn poisonous chemicals from oil spills and gas leaks into harmless substances.

In soil, bacteria that act as decomposers break down dead organisms, returning chemicals to the environment for other organisms to reuse.

Bacteria can cause foods to spoil.

In roots of certain plants, nitrogen-fixing bacteria change nitrogen gas from the air into a form that plants can use.

Needed to turn milk into buttermilk, yogurt, sour cream, and cheese.

Protists

Protists are eukaryotic organisms that cannot be classified as animals, plants, or fungi. **Figure 10** shows that protists have a wide range of characteristics. All protists live in moist environments and are common where humans interact. Most protists are harmless, but some can cause illness or disease. Most harmful protists are **parasites**, organisms that benefit from living with, on, or in a host. Drinking water contaminated with these protists can cause fever, diarrhea, and abdominal pain. For example, a person can become ill after drinking water containing the protist *Giardia*. The protist attaches itself to the small intestine, where it takes in nutrients and prevents those nutrients from entering the human. The person gets ill from the disease giardiasis. Another parasitic protist travels with a mosquito. When a mosquito that is carrying the protist *Plasmodium* bites a human, the protist infects the red blood cells, causing malaria.

☑ **READING CHECK** **Cite Textual Evidence** Tasha and Marco examine a cell through a microscope. Tasha suggests that the cell is a protist. Marco thinks it might be a bacterium. What evidence would prove Tasha right?

....

....

HANDS-ON LAB

☑**Investigate** Discover unicellular and multicellular organisms in pond water.

Diversity of Protists

Figure 10 Protists are classified in Domain Eukarya and Kingdom Protista. The three separate types are shown in the table below.

Identify Use information in the chart to identify the three photos of protists below. Write the name of each type of protist in the space provided.

	Animal-like Protists	Plant-like Protists	Fungi-like Protists
Food	Heterotrophs	Autotrophs; some also heterotrophs	Heterotrophs
Features	Unicellular	Unicellular or multicellular	Unicellular, but often live in colonies
Movement	Free-swimming	Free-swimming or attached	Move during some part of life cycle
Reproduction	Asexual and sexual	Sexual and asexual	Asexual
Examples	Amoebas: surround and trap food particles Giardia: common parasite, has eight flagella	Red algae: seaweeds people eat, known as nori Dinoflagellates: glow in the dark	Slime molds: brightly colored, grow in garden beds Water molds: attack plants, such as crops

Fungi

What's the largest organism ever to exist on Earth? Good guesses would be a dinosaur, a blue whale, or a giant tree. These are wrong. The biggest living thing is a honey fungus colony growing under a forest in Oregon. The colony is larger than a thousand football fields! Like all other fungi, the honey fungus has eukaryotic cells with cell walls. Fungi are heterotrophs that feed by absorbing food through their cell walls. Most of the honey fungus is unseen underground. The cells of fungi are arranged into hyphae, or threadlike tubes. Hyphae, like those shown in **Figure 11**, give fungi structure and allow them to spread over large areas. Hyphae also grow into food sources and release chemicals. Food is broken down by the chemicals and then absorbed by the hyphae. Some fungi act as decomposers and consume dead organisms, while others are parasites that attack living hosts.

Fungal Reproduction
Fungi occasionally send up reproductive structures called fruiting bodies. Some fruiting bodies are the familiar mushrooms that you eat or see growing in damp environments. Fruiting bodies produce spores that are carried by wind or water to new locations. Each spore that lands in the right conditions can then start a new fungal colony. Fungi can also reproduce sexually when hyphae from two colonies grow close together and trade genetic information.

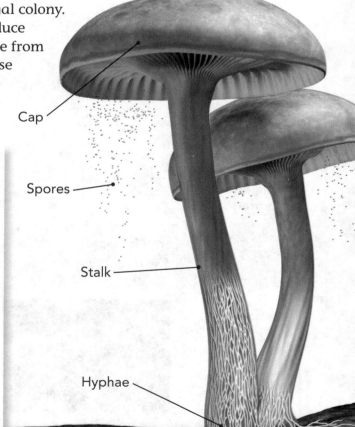

Cap

Spores

Stalk

Hyphae

Structure of a Honey Mushroom
Figure 11 The part of a mushroom you can see above ground is tiny compared to the network of hyphae underground.

Hypothesize What is a possible relationship between the fungus and the tree root?

....

....

☑ READING CHECK **Determine Central Ideas** What is the purpose of fungal spores?

....

....

Roles of Fungi Fungi come in many forms and have varying lifestyles. We depend on fungi for many services. **Figure 12** explores some of the ways that fungi are helpful and harmful. At the same time, fungi can destroy our property and food and make us sick. You've probably heard of *athlete's foot* and *ringworm*. These are both common rashes—mild skin infections caused by fungi in the environment. They are easily treated. Some fungi, however, can cause serious diseases. In fact, more people die each year from fungal infections than from malaria and certain common cancers. There are no vaccines to prevent fungal infections.

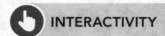
INTERACTIVITY

Use research to develop medicine needed for someone that is ill.

Fungi Files

Fungi: Friend or Foe?

Figure 12 ✏ Circle or highlight evidence of harm in the image descriptions.

1. CCC Energy and Matter Why would a fungus growing on a rock need a partner to provide it food?

....

....

2. SEP Construct Explanations Why would fungi be better than seeds at absorbing water?

....

....

Mycorrhiza

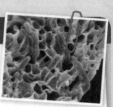

Grows around plant seeds and roots.

Brings water to plant and eats plant sugars.

Helps plants grow.

Penicillium Mold

Grows on food products.

Spoils food.

Produces chemicals used in antibiotics.

Some produce poisons or cause allergic reactions.

Shiitake Mushroom

Grows on and consumes dead logs.

Provides nutritious food.

Breaks down dead wood and makes nutrients available for living things.

Lichen

Forms partnership with autotrophic algae or bacteria.

Provides water, shelter, and minerals, while partner provides food.

Produces chemicals used in dyes, perfumes, and deodorant.

Provides food for animals in harsh environments.

Yeast

Eats carbohydrates, turning them into alcohols and carbon dioxide.

Helps to bake bread and make beverages.

Causes diaper rash and yeast infections.

Destroys stored foods.

MS-LS1-1

1. Apply Concepts What is unique about parasites?

....

....

....

2. Identify What are three ways that fungi interact with other kinds of living things?

....

....

....

3. SEP Construct Arguments Could you have two or more viral infections at the same time? Explain, using evidence to support your argument.

....

....

....

....

....

4. SEP Use Scientific Reasoning Which of these taxonomic groups are most closely related: Fungi, Archaea, Bacteria, Protista? Explain.

....

....

....

....

5. SEP Develop Models ✏ Draw a Venn Diagram to compare and contrast two types of infectious agents.

Quest CHECK-IN

In this lesson, you learned about the characteristics of viruses, bacteria, protists, and fungi. You also discovered how some of these living and nonliving things interact with nature and people.

SEP Integrate Information When developing a classification system, do you think identifying similarities or identifying differences is more helpful? Explain.

....

....

....

....

☝ INTERACTIVITY

Discovering Rainforest Organisms

Go online to classify organisms as unicellular or multicellular.

A Disease Becomes a Cure

INTERACTIVITY

Explore how viruses are engineered to solve problems.

Viruses make you sick when they work their way into healthy cells. They can do serious damage as a result. But some scientists are taking advantage of a virus's ability to invade cells to make people better.

The Challenge: To use viruses to deliver targeted therapy to cells.

Phenomenon Cancer therapies battle cancer cells, but they often damage healthy cells in the process. This can lead to serious side effects, from severe nausea to hair loss. Scientists are looking for better methods to target diseased cells while leaving healthy ones alone.

To tackle this problem, scientist James Swartz looked to nature for inspiration. Viruses, he realized, are great at targeting specific cells. He and his team re-engineered a virus by removing the disease-causing properties, leaving a hollow shell that might carry medicine inside. Next, they altered the spiky surface of the virus and attached tiny "tags" to it. The tags send the virus to sick cells to deliver medicine.

Swartz and his team still have to do a lot of research and testing to see whether this improved delivery system works. If it does, they'll have engineered a virus that works in reverse—infecting you with medicine rather than disease.

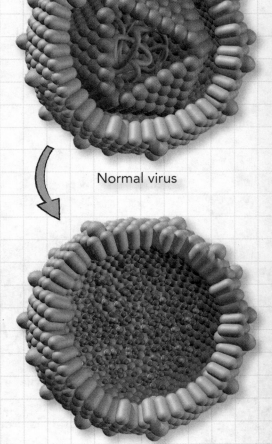

Normal virus

Re-engineered virus

The redesigned protein coat in the middle section of this virus removed the disease-causing properties, leaving the protein able to carry medicine. The spiky virus surface contains tags to direct the virus to the correct cells.

 **DESIGN CHALLENGE** Can you engineer a virus to perform a specific function? Go to the Engineering Design Notebook to find out!

 4 Plants and Animals

Guiding Questions

- What makes animals and plants different in form and function?
- Which special structures inside plant and animal cells determine an organism's characteristics?
- How do similar cells work together to help plants and animals function?
- Which traits are unique to animals?

Connection

Literacy Gather Information

MS-LS1-1, MS-LS1-2, MS-LS1-3

HANDS-ON LAB

uInvestigate Discover where land plants come from.

Vocabulary

tissue
vascular plants
nonvascular
  plants
vertebrates
invertebrates
organ
mammals

Academic Vocabulary

symmetry

Connect It!

🖉 **Circle a plant and place a square around an animal.**

SEP Determine Differences What characteristics of each organism helped you identify it as either a plant or an animal?

....
....
....
....

Form and Function

The plants and animals you see in **Figure 1**, along with protists and fungi, are all classified in Domain Eukarya. As eukaryotes, they share some characteristics. They are all made of one or more cells, and each cell contains a nucleus with DNA. However, they also have characteristics that set them apart, such as how they get energy and move around. These differences are what separate plants into Kingdom Plantae and animals into Kingdom Animalia.

All living things need water and food for energy. Plants are autotrophs, or producers. They use photosynthesis to make their own food. Plant cells have specialized structures that make food. Animals are heterotrophs, or consumers. They get food by eating other organisms. Animals have specialized body structures that break down food they consume.

Mobility, the ability to move around, also separates plants and animals. To get food, animals need to move around. Structures such as legs, fins, and wings allow movement from one place to another. Because most plants are anchored to the ground, they cannot move around.

☑ **READING CHECK** **Summarize Text** Why are plants and animals placed in different kingdoms?

....

....

👆 **INTERACTIVITY**

Explore the different types of cells that make up multi-cellular organisms.

Plants and Animals
Figure 1 Plants and animals are classified in the same domain, but their differences place them in two separate kingdoms.

Characteristics of Plants

All land plants are multicellular. In addition, nearly all plants are autotrophs. DNA analysis has led some scientists to classify green algae as part of the Kingdom Plantae. Almost all algae are single-celled organisms and live in the water. All plants undergo photosynthesis to make food. Plants take in carbon dioxide, water, and sunlight to produce food (and oxygen as a by-product). Specialized structures, called stomata, are located on each leaf (**Figure 2**). Each stoma (plural: stomata) is a small opening on the underside of a leaf through which oxygen, water, and carbon dioxide can move. It also prevents water loss.

Plant cells have specialized structures that serve specific functions. Look at the plant cell in **Figure 2**. Surrounding the plant cell is a strong rigid cell wall, which is used for structural support and protection. The largest structure inside the cell is the vacuole. It stores water, wastes, and food. The chloroplasts, which look like green jellybeans, are the cell structures where food is made. Chloroplasts contain a green pigment called chlorophyll that absorbs sunlight, the energy that drives photosynthesis.

HANDS-ON LAB

Investigate Discover where land plants come from.

Plant Cell Features

Figure 2 🖊 Plants need specialized structures to carry out their life functions. Label the stoma, cell wall, chloroplast, and vacuole. Then list the function of each part. Finally, circle where the chlorophyll is located.

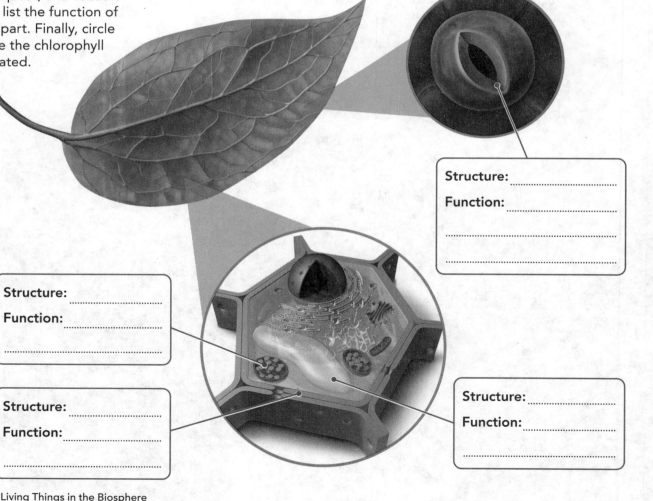

Structure: ....

Function: ....

....

....

Structure: ....

Function: ....

....

Structure: ....

Function: ....

....

Structure: ....

Function: ....

....

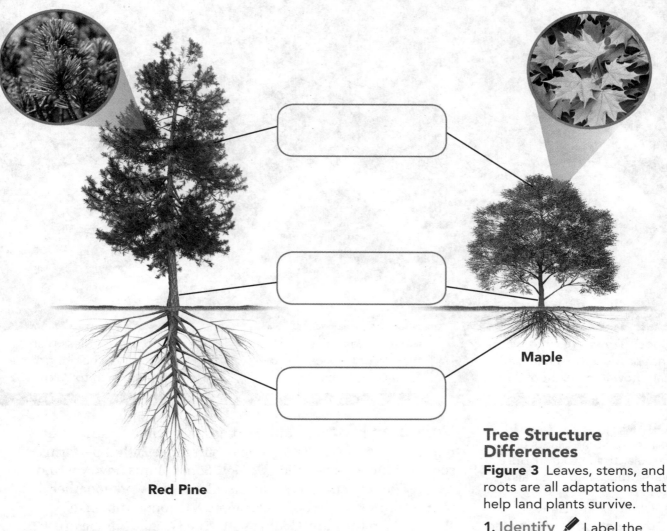

Red Pine

Maple

Plant Structure

Think about the aquatic plants you identified in **Figure 1**. To make food, they need water and sunlight. But land plants need special structures to get the water they need to make food. There are three main parts to a land plant: leaves, stem or branch, and roots. A leaf has two functions: to capture light energy and gas exchange. The stem provides support and stores food for the plant. The stem is where leaves, flowers, cones, and buds grow. Stems also connect roots to leaves, so that leaves can get the water they need to carry out photosynthesis. The roots of trees have three major functions. First, roots absorb water and nutrients from the ground. Second, roots anchor the plant to the ground. Third, roots store food and nutrients. See if you can identify the different tree structures in **Figure 3**.

☑ READING CHECK **Cite Textual Evidence** What is the function of the stem on a plant?

....

....

Tree Structure Differences

Figure 3 Leaves, stems, and roots are all adaptations that help land plants survive.

1. **Identify** 🖉 Label the roots, stem, and leaves in the diagram.

2. **CCC Structure and Function** Explain any differences in the trees' structures.

....

....

....

....

....

....

Beech Trees are seed plants that produce beechnuts and can grow to a height of 35 m.

Moss are seedless plants that do not typically grow taller than 10 cm.

Ferns are seedless plants that range in height from less than 1 cm to 25 m.

Plants

Figure 4 Some plants have vascular tissue to transport water, food, and minerals.

1. **Claim** 🖊 Circle two different types of vascular plants in the picture.

2. **Evidence** What evidence supports your claim?

....

....

....

3. **Reasoning** Explain how the evidence supports your claim.

....

....

....

....

....

....

....

....

Vascular Plants

Tall, short, large, or small, plants are made up of many cells. A group of similar cells that perform a specific function are called **tissues**. Some plants have vascular tissue. The cells that make up vascular tissue work together to transport water, food, and minerals through tube-like structures in the plant. Plants with true vascular tissue are **vascular plants**.

Characteristics of Vascular Plants

Vascular plants have vascular tissue, true roots, and a cuticle on their leaves. Vascular tissue carries important materials like water and nutrients to all the parts of a plant. Because of the way cells are grouped together, vascular tissue also strengthens the body of the plant. This support gives plants stability and allows plants to have height. The roots of vascular plants anchor the plant to the ground, but they also draw up water and nutrients from the soil. Vascular plants have a waxy waterproof layer called a cuticle that covers the leaves and stems. Since leaves have stomata for gas exchange, the cuticle inhibits water loss.

Vascular Tissue

There are two types of vascular tissue that transport materials throughout vascular plants. Food moves through the vascular tissue called phloem (FLOH um). Once food is made in the leaves, it must travel through phloem to reach other parts of the plant that need food. Water and minerals, on the other hand, travel through the xylem (ZY lum). Roots absorb water and minerals from the soil and the xylem moves them up into the stem and leaves.

Nonvascular Plants The characteristics of nonvascular plants are different from those of vascular plants. The moss in **Figure 4** is a **nonvascular plant**, a low-growing plant that lacks vascular tissue for transporting materials. Most nonvascular plants live in moist areas and feel wet, because they obtain water and minerals from their surroundings. They are only a few cell layers thick, so water and minerals do not travel far or quickly. Nonvascular plants do not have true roots that take up water and nutrients from the soil. The function of their roots is to anchor them to the ground. Also, their cell walls are thin, which prevents them from gaining height.

☑ READING CHECK **Determine Central Ideas** Name three characteristics of vascular plants that make them different from nonvascular plants.

....

....

Plan It!

Plants need water, carbon dioxide, and sunlight to grow. You want to determine the impact of sunlight on plant growth. Consider how you could prove that sunlight is an important factor in plant growth.

SEP Plan an Investigation 🖉 Design a procedure to investigate how sunlight affects the growth of a plant. Include a sketch of your investigation.

Procedure:

....

....

....

....

....

Sketch:

Academic Vocabulary

In math class, how would you explain an object that had symmetry?

....

....

....

Characteristics of Animals

All organisms are classified according to how they are related to other organisms by comparing DNA, body structure and development. All animals are classified based on whether or not they have a backbone. **Vertebrates** are animals with a backbone. Animals without a backbone are classified as **invertebrates**.

Structure of Animals
All animals are multicellular and most have several different types of tissue. Complex animals have organs and organ systems. An **organ** is a body structure composed of different kinds of tissues that work together. An organ performs a more complex task than each tissue could alone. For example, the eye is a specialized sense organ. It has about ten different tissues working together to enable sight. A group of different organs that work together to perform a task is called an organ system. The organization of cells, tissues, organs, and organ systems describes an animal's body structure.

Most organisms have a balance of body parts called **symmetry**. **Figure 5** shows that animals have different types of symmetry or no symmetry. Animals with no symmetry are asymmetrical and have simple body structures with specialized cells but no tissues.

Types of Symmetry

Figure 5 ✎ Symmetry occurs when the organism can be divided into two or more similar parts. Draw the lines of symmetry on the animals that have radial and bilateral symmetry.

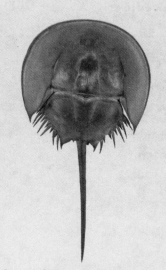

Asymmetrical Animals without symmetry, such as this sea sponge, are asymmetrical.

Radial Symmetry Animals with radial symmetry, such as this jelly-fish, live in water and have complex body plans with tissues and usually have organ systems. An animal has radial symmetry if many imaginary lines drawn through a central point divide the body into two mirror images.

Bilateral Symmetry Most animals, such as this horse-shoe crab, have bilateral symmetry. Only one line can be drawn to divide the body into halves that are mirror images.

Invertebrates Most animals are invertebrates. Scientists separate invertebrates into six main groups. **Figure 6** shows the different characteristics defining each group. While invertebrates do not have backbones, many have structures that support their bodies in a similar way. For example, arthropods have an exoskeleton, a tough waterproof outer covering that protects, supports, and helps prevent evaporation of water from the body. In contrast, echinoderms have an endoskeleton, a structural support system that is found within the animal.

☑ **READING CHECK** **Determine Meaning**
What is the difference between an exoskeleton and an endoskeleton?

....

....

....

☞ **INTERACTIVITY**

Determine how to use characteristics of an organism to identify it.

Echinoderms have a system of tubes to move and obtain food and oxygen.

Arthropods have jointed appendages and shed their exoskeleton as they grow.

Mollusks have one or two hard shells to protect internal organs.

Worms are simple animals but have a brain and digestive system.

Cnidarians have stinging cells and take food into a central body cavity.

Sponges are made of specialized cells, adults are attached, and they take food into their bodies to get energy.

Invertebrates

Figure 6 This diagram shows how scientists believe invertebrates evolved, starting with sponges and ending with echinoderms. Consider other characteristics that separate invertebrates into different groups.

CCC Relate Structure and Function Starting at sponges and moving to echinoderms, what happens to the body structures of the invertebrates?

....

....

....

....

Vertebrates

Most of the animals you see at an aquarium or zoo are members of the phylum Chordata and are called chordates. All chordates belong to Domain Eukaryota and Kingdom Anamalia and have a nerve cord. Most chordates, like you, have a backbone to protect the nerve cord. Some chordates, like sea squirts (**Figure 7**), do not have a backbone.

Common Structures All chordates have three structures in common: a notochord, a nerve cord, and pouches in the throat area. A notochord is a flexible rod that supports the chordate's back. The nerve cord runs down the back. It connects the brain to nerves. For most chordates, the throat pouches disappear before birth. In fish, they become gill slits.

Body Temperature Vertebrates must maintain their body temperature (**Figure 7**). Animals, such as amphibians and reptiles, that produce little internal body heat are ectotherms. Their body temperature changes with the environment. To stay warm, they go to a sunny spot and bask in sunlight. In contrast, endotherms control their internal heat and regulate their own temperature. Birds and mammals are endotherms. They have structures such as sweat glands, fur or feathers.

Vertebrate Groups **Figure 8** shows the five major groups of vertebrates: fish, amphibians, reptiles, birds, and mammals. Members of each group share unique characteristics. For example, a **mammal** is a vertebrate whose body temperature is regulated by its internal heat, and has skin covered with hair or fur and glands that produce milk to feed its young.

Animals Control Their Body Temperature

Figure 7 Animals control their body temperature one of two ways.

1. **SEP Apply Scientific Reasoning** Hypothesize whether each animal is an endotherm or ectotherm.

2. **SEP Construct Explanations** Would it be more difficult for a hare to live in a tropical rainforest or a frog to live in the Arctic? Explain.

....

....

....

sea squirts

Monotremes are the only egg-laying mammals. Examples include: duck-billed platypus and spiny anteaters.

Marsupials carry their young in a pouch. Examples include: kangaroo, koalas, possums, and opossums.

Placentals have live births. While developing in the mother, the embryo receives nourishment from an organ that surrounds the embryo called a placenta. Examples include: rodents, whales, cattle, dogs, and humans.

Mammals have mammary glands to feed their young milk. They are further grouped into three types: monotremes, marsupials, and placentals.

Birds have wings, lightweight bones, and a 4-chambered heart.

Reptiles have scales, thick skin, and lay their eggs on land.

Amphibians have permeable skin; live their early life in water and adult life on land.

Fish live in water, have scales, and use gills to collect dissolved oxygen.

Vertebrates

Figure 8 This diagram shows how scientists believe vertebrates evolved, starting with fish and ending with mammals. Consider other differences among these five groups of vertebrates.

1. **CCC Patterns** What is one characteristic that amphibians, reptiles, birds, and mammals share?

....

2. **SEP Determine Differences** How are amphibians different from fish?

....

Movement Adaptations

Figure 9 Animals display a wide range of adaptations for movement. ✏️ Rate each movement adaptation from 1 (fastest) to 5 (slowest) in the circles. Explain your highest rank.

....

....

....

Wings Birds and insects have wings that allow them to fly, hover, dive, and soar.

Fins Fish and whales have fins, and their bodies are streamlined to help them move through water.

Tube Feet Echinoderms have several tiny tube feet under their body. Water moves from their vascular system to the tube feet. This water movement expands each foot, causing it to move.

Muscular Foot Mollusks have a foot that is made of several thin muscles. This foot is used for digging or creeping along the surface.

Jet Propulsion Octopuses take water into a muscular sac and quickly expel it out a narrow opening to move. They also elongate and contract their arms to move.

👆 **INTERACTIVITY**

Explain the organization of different organisms.

☑ **READING CHECK**
Draw Evidence What adaptations does the octopus have that would help it open a jar?

....

....

....

....

Traits Unique to Animals

All animals have unique traits. Characteristics that organisms inherit to help them survive in their environment are called adaptations. These adaptations may be used to separate animals into minor groups.

Adaptations for Movement Animals have a variety of adaptations for movement. Humans walk on two legs, while other animals use four. Animals are best adapted to the environment in which they live. As you see in **Figure 9**, adaptations vary greatly within the animal kingdom.

Adaptations for Conserving Water Obtaining fresh water from the salty ocean or dry desert is difficult for animals. Some animals, however, have adaptations that help them hold on to as much water as they can. A reptile's kidneys can remove solid material from its waste and then reabsorb the liquid material. Because they recycle the fluid part of their waste, reptiles do not need to take in as much water. Whales, seals, and dolphins also have specialized kidneys to conserve water. Their fresh water comes from the food they eat. Their waste first passes through a filter that removes the salt. It then passes through another tube that absorbs more water.

☑ LESSON 4 Check

MS-LS1-1, MS-LS1-2, MS-LS1-3

1. SEP Determine Similarities What are two characteristics that both plants and animals have in common?

....

....

2. CCC Stability and Change How do some animals protect themselves against water loss?

....

....

....

3. Apply Concepts What is the function of a backbone in vertebrates?

....

....

4. CCC Relate Structure and Function What are the three functions of roots?

....

....

....

....

....

....

5. SEP Apply Scientific Reasoning The tallest plants on Earth are redwood trees. They can grow to heights over 100 m. How are redwood trees able to transport water and nutrients from their roots to their leaves?

....

....

....

....

....

....

....

6. SEP Construct Explanations Why are organisms that have organs classified as more complex than organisms without organs?

....

....

....

....

....

....

....

Quest CHECK-IN

In this lesson, you learned that plants and animals are classified into different groups based on their cell structures, presence of different tissue types, traits, and adaptations.

SEP Determine Differences When you create your field guide, what physical characteristics would you use to separate plants and animals?

....

....

....

....

👆 INTERACTIVITY

Multicellular Rainforest Organisms

Go online to to take a field trip to a rain forest. There, you will make observations and use them to classify various organisms.

1 Living Things

MS-LS1-1

1. What are the basic building blocks of all living things?
A. food
B. energy
C. cells
D. water

2. Which is an example of homeostasis?
A. reproduction
B. controlling an experiment
C. growth and development
D. maintaining a steady temperature

3. The kind of reproduction that requires two parents is called ....

4. CCC Analyze Systems An oasis is a place in a sandy desert where water rises to the surface. Trees and plants often grow by the water and animals make their homes there. What would happen to the organisms living in an oasis if the water dried up?

....

....

....

5. SEP Plan Your Investigation Design a controlled experiment to demonstrate that birds do not spontaneously generate on birdfeeders.

....

....

....

....

....

....

2 Classification Systems

MS-LS4-2

6. The mosquito *Aedes aegypti* is a carrier of the Zika virus. *Aedes* is the name of the mosquito's
A. order.
B. family.
C. genus.
D. species.

7. Which could happen through convergent evolution?
A. Two unrelated species could evolve into one species.
B. Two unrelated species could evolve similar features.
C. Two unrelated species could evolve very different features.
D. Two unrelated species could finish evolving.

8. Two organisms that share several classification levels will be .... and have .... in common.

9. SEP Develop Models ✏ Develop a taxonomic key that a person could use to identify the following animals: hawk, alligator, duck, snake.

hawk   alligator   duck   snake

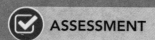

3 Viruses, Bacteria, Protists, and Fungi

MS-LS1-1

10. Which of the following groups is heterotrophic?
- **A.** Domain Archaea
- **B.** Domain Bacteria
- **C.** Kingdom Fungi
- **D.** Kingdom Protista

11. Which of the following statements is true about viruses?
- **A.** Viruses contain very small cells.
- **B.** Viruses do not eat food.
- **C.** Viruses can reproduce themselves quickly.
- **D.** Viruses have hyphae that help them take up water.

12. Two ways that bacteria help people are

.... and

....

13. SEP Defend Your Claim Why is *diverse* a good word to use to describe protists?

....

....

....

....

....

14. CCC Cause and Effect Describe three problems that could occur if all the fungi on Earth disappeared.

....

....

....

....

4 Plants and Animals

MS-LS1-1, MS-LS1-2, MS-LS1-3

15. CCC Cause and Effect Explain why vascular plants can gain height, but nonvascular plants only grow close to the ground.

....

....

....

....

....

....

....

....

....

....

16. SEP Distinguish Relationships Explain how vertebrates and invertebrates are similar and different.

....

....

....

....

....

....

....

....

MS-LS1-1, MS-LS1-2, MS-LS1-3

Evidence-Based Assessment

Naya is using a microscope to investigate the similarities and differences between two organisms. One is an animal called a rotifer and the other is a protist called a paramecium. She records her observations about both organisms in a table.

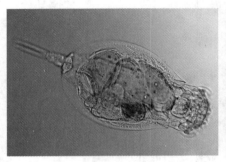

rotifer

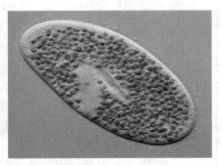

paramecium

Observations	Organism A	Organism B
Organization is more complex	X	
Injury to one cell does not affect ability of the organism to stay alive	X	
Organism's lifespan is relatively short		X
Contains substances such as water, proteins, and lipids	X	X
Creates offspring through sexual reproduction	X	X
Gets energy by using hair-like structures to move food into its mouth		X
Requires energy in order to survive	X	X
Can only be observed with microscope	X	X
Responds to surroundings		
No cell differentiation		
One cell carries out necessary functions for life		

1. **SEP Analyze Data** Based on the data in the table, which statement is true?
   A. Organism A is multicellular.
   B. Organism B is multicellular.
   C. Both organisms are unicellular.
   D. Both organisms are multicellular.

2. **SEP Interpret Data** Naya adds another row for the following observation: Can only be produced from other living cells. For which organism is this statement true?
   A. Organism A
   B. Organism B
   C. Both organisms
   D. Neither organism

3. **SEP Use Scientific Reasoning** Which organism is Organism A? Which is Organism B? Explain how you classified the organisms as you did.

   ....
   ....
   ....
   ....
   ....

4. **SEP Make Observations** Refer to the images and existing observations to complete the table for the last three observations. Write an X in the appropriate column(s).

5. **SEP Construct Explanations** Suppose that Naya decides to observe a sample of quartz, a mineral found in Earth's crust. If Naya were to add quartz to the table, which observations could she check off for it? Explain.

   ....
   ....
   ....
   ....
   ....

6. **SEP Construct Arguments** Explain why both the paramecium and rotifer are considered living things. Which organism is more complex, and which has better chances of survival?

   ....
   ....
   ....
   ....
   ....
   ....
   ....
   ....

Quest FINDINGS

Complete the Quest!

Phenomenon In a group, identify the criteria and constraints for your field guide. Then, create your guide for the nature center.

SEP Identify Limitations What are some of the drawbacks or difficulties in using classification systems in your field guide? How else could you organize living things?

....
....
....
....
....
....

👆 **INTERACTIVITY**

Create Your Field Guide

MS-LS1-1

It's Alive!

How can you **gather evidence** to **distinguish living** things from **nonliving** things?

Background

Phenomenon Before scientists could peer into microscopes, they had very different ideas about what living things were made of. It was a challenge to classify organisms when they couldn't even distinguish between living and nonliving things.

It may seem pretty obvious to you today that a flower is a living thing and a rock is a nonliving thing. But how could you explain this difference to a class of third-grade students in a way they would understand? In this investigation, you will observe samples of living and nonliving things. You will use the data you collect to develop an explanation of how living things can be distinguished from nonliving things.

Materials

(per group)

- hand lens
- samples of living and nonliving things
- prepared slides or microscope pictures of living and nonliving things
- microscope

Safety

Be sure to follow all safety guidelines provided by your teacher. The Safety Appendix of your textbook provides more details about the safety icons.

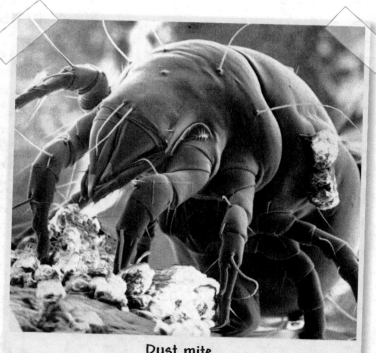

Dust mite

Procedure

1. Work with a partner. At your workstation, you should have a hand lens, a microscope, and paper and pencils for drawing.

2. Discuss with your partner what you should be looking for to help you determine whether your samples are living or nonliving. Then, from the class supplies, choose one sample and the microscope slide or microscope photograph that goes with it. Take them to your station to examine.

3. On a separate paper, make detailed observations of your sample, label it, note whether it is living or nonliving, and describe any structures you observe.

4. Return your sample and select a new one. Continue until you have examined five different samples. You should include three different organisms and two nonliving things, and include at least one fungus and one autotroph.

5. Based on your observations, complete the data table that follows. There may be some spaces that you are not sure how to fill out. If you have time, take another look at the sample(s) in question to gather more evidence.

HANDS-ON LAB

Demonstrate Go online for a downloadable worksheet of this lab.

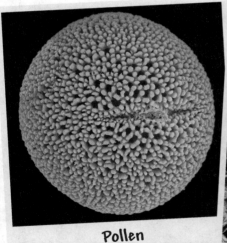

Pollen

Honey

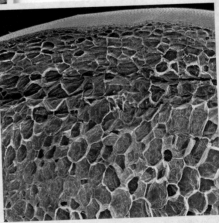

Cross-section of tomato

uDemonstrate Lab

Observations

Which Samples Are Living or Nonliving?			
Sample Name	Living or Nonliving?	Observations	Sketches

Analyze and Interpret Data

1. **CCC Evaluate Scale** Why is the microscope necessary for determining whether a sample is living or nonliving?

....
....
....
....

2. **CCC Structure and Function** Compare the appearance of the living samples to the appearance of the nonliving samples. How do you explain the differences in structures?

....
....
....
....
....

3. **SEP Characterize Data** Based on what you observed, what are some ways that the living things in this lab could be grouped or organized?

....
....
....
....

4. **SEP Construct Explanations** How would you explain to a class of third-graders the difference between living things and nonliving things? What are some examples you would give to support your thinking?

....
....
....
....
....

The Cell System

HANDS-ON LAB

uConnect Explore how an object's appearance changes when different tools are used.

NGSS PERFORMANCE EXPECTATIONS

MS-LS1-1 Conduct an investigation to provide evidence that living things are made of cells; either one cell or many different numbers and types of cells.

MS-LS1-2 Develop and use a model to describe the function of a cell as a whole and ways parts of cells contribute to the function.

MS-LS1-3 Use argument supported by evidence for how the body is a system of interacting subsystems composed of groups of cells.

MS-ETS1-1 Define the criteria and constraints of a design problem with sufficient precision to ensure a successful solution, taking into account relevant scientific principles and potential impacts on people and the natural environment that may limit possible solutions.

MS-ETS1-2 Evaluate competing design solutions using a systematic process to determine how well they meet the criteria and constraints of the problem.

MS-ETS1-3 Analyze data from tests to determine similarities and differences among several design solutions to identify the best characteristics of each that can be combined into a new solution to better meet the criteria for success.

MS-ETS1-4 Develop a model to generate data for iterative testing and modification of a proposed object, tool, or process such that an optimal design can be achieved.

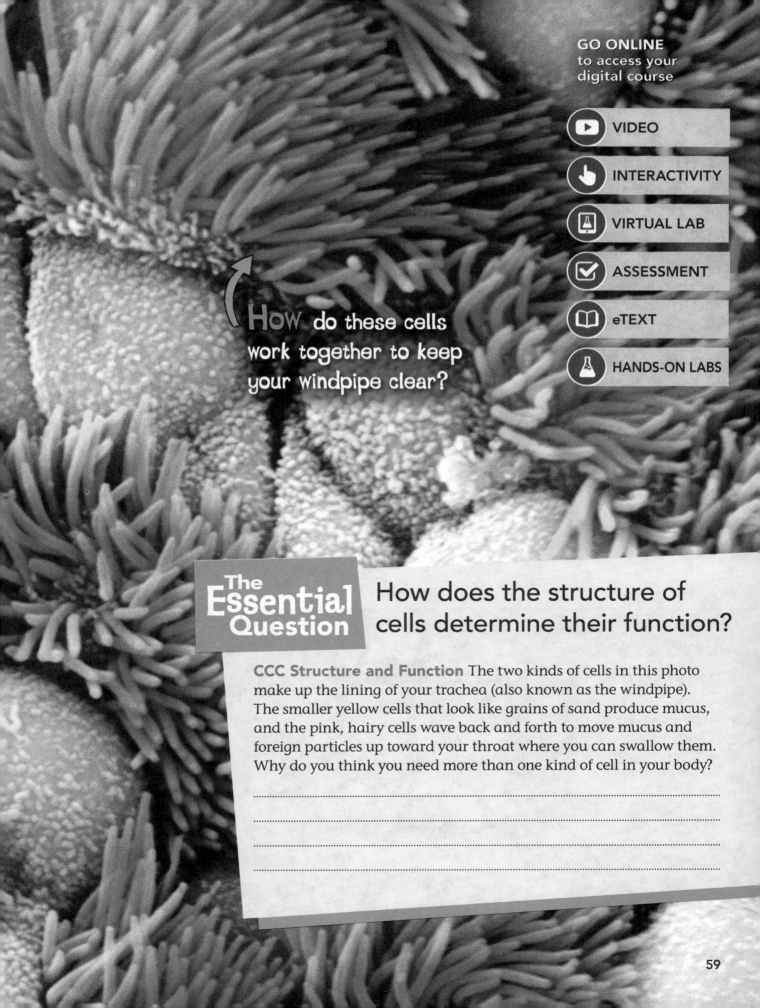

HOW do these cells work together to keep your windpipe clear?

to access your
digital course

▶ VIDEO

👆 INTERACTIVITY

🧪 VIRTUAL LAB

☑ ASSESSMENT

📖 eTEXT

⚗ HANDS-ON LABS

The Essential Question

How does the structure of cells determine their function?

CCC Structure and Function The two kinds of cells in this photo make up the lining of your trachea (also known as the windpipe). The smaller yellow cells that look like grains of sand produce mucus, and the pink, hairy cells wave back and forth to move mucus and foreign particles up toward your throat where you can swallow them. Why do you think you need more than one kind of cell in your body?

....

....

....

....

59

Quest KICKOFF

How can you design a model exhibit for a science museum?

Phenomenon Cells are often called "the building blocks of life." But that makes us think of wooden or plastic blocks that simply sit next to each other or stack neatly. In fact, cells have moving parts. And they interact with each other. To help people understand impossible-to-see processes such as these, museum staff—both scientists and engineers—try to engage and educate visitors with easy-to-see and hands-on models. In this problem-based Quest activity, you will plan and design a science exhibit on cells. By applying what you learn in each lesson, digital activity, and hands-on lab, you will gather information that will assist you in creating your exhibit. Then, in the Findings activity, you assemble, organize, and present your exhibit.

MS-LS1-1, MS-LS1-2, MS-LS1-3

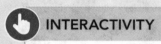

👆 **INTERACTIVITY**

Cells on Display

NBC LEARN ▶ VIDEO

After watching the Quest Kickoff video on how museum models are planned and built, think about the qualities of a good science museum display. Record your thoughts in the graphic organizer.

Qualities of a Science Museum Display	
Good Qualities	**Bad Qualities**

IN LESSON 1
What will your exhibit teach the public about cell theory? Consider the challenges of explaining and modeling things that are hard to observe.

Quest CHECK-INS

IN LESSON 2
What do cells look like? How can you represent different cell parts? Design and build a model cell.

🧪 **HANDS-ON LAB**

Make a Cell Model

Quest CHECK-IN

IN LESSON 3
What cell parts are involved in cellular transport? Create an animation that shows how materials enter and leave the cell.

 INTERACTIVITY

Put Your Cells in Motion

The Body Fantastic exhibit at the Odyssium, a science museum in Edmonton, Alberta, Canada.

Quest CHECK-INS

IN LESSON 4

Why is cell division important? Think about how to incorporate information about cell division into your exhibit.

INTERACTIVITY

The Importance of Cells

Quest FINDINGS

Complete the Quest!

Determine the best way to present your museum exhibit. Then share your exhibit with museum guests. Evaluate and compare the different exhibits.

INTERACTIVITY

Reflect on Your Museum Exhibit

What Can You See?

How can you **make observations** using different tools to describe an object?

Background

Phenomenon The observations scientists are able to make often depend on the types of tools available. In this activity, you will make and compare observations of an object using different tools.

Design a Procedure

☐ **1.** ✂ Cut a photograph out of a page in a newspaper or magazine. With only your eyes, closely examine the photo. Record your observations in the table.

☐ **2.** **SEP Plan a Procedure** Write a procedure to make additional observations of the photo. Use the hand lens, microscope and flashlight in your plan. Show your plan to your teacher before you begin.

....
....
....
....
....
....
....
....

☐ **3.** Record your observations in the table.

Materials

(per group)
- newspaper or magazine
- scissors
- hand lens
- microscope
- flashlight or other light

Safety

Be sure to follow all safety procedures provided by your teacher. The Safety Appendix of your textbook provides more details about the safety icons.

Observations

Type of Tool Used	Observations

HANDS-ON LAB

Connect Go online for a downloadable worksheet of this lab.

Analyze and Conclude

1. **SEP Make Observations** What observations did you make using only your eyes?

....

....

....

2. **SEP Make Observations** What did you see in the photo with the hand lens that you could not see with only your eyes?

....

....

....

3. **CCC Evaluate Scale** What additional details could you see with the microscope? Explain why your observations change depending on the type of tool you used.

....

....

....

Structure and Function of Cells

Guiding Questions

- What evidence is there that cells make up all living things?
- How do cells determine the structure of living things?

Connections

Literacy Determine Central Ideas

Math Represent Quantitative Relationships

MS-LS1-1, MS-LS1-2

HANDS-ON LAB

ʉInvestigate Observe objects using a microscope.

Vocabulary

cell
microscope
cell theory

Academic Vocabulary

distinguish

Connect It!

✏️ **Circle the different structures you observe in the photograph.**

CCC Cause and Effect With microscopes, we can see the cells inside us and around us. What reactions do you think people had when they first learned that they were surrounded by tiny living organisms?

....

....

....

Cells

What do a whale, a rose, bacteria, a ladybug, and you have in common? You are all living things, or organisms. All are made of **cells**, the basic unit of structure and function in living things. Cells form the parts of an organism and carry out its functions. The smallest organisms, such as the bacteria in **Figure 1,** are made of one cell, while the largest organisms may have trillions of cells.

Cell Structure The structure of an object refers to what it is made of and how its parts are put together. For example, the structure of a car depends on how materials such as plastic, metal, and rubber are arranged. The structure of a living thing is determined by the amazing variety of ways its cells are put together.

Cell Function A single cell has the same needs as an entire organism. For a cell to stay alive, it must perform biological functions. Those functions include obtaining energy, bringing in nutrients and water, and getting rid of wastes. Most organisms have bodies with many different cells that work together to help the organism to stay alive, grow, and reproduce. For example, blood cells in your circulatory system carry oxygen around your body. This blood provides you with fresh oxygen and removes the waste product carbon dioxide. Cells in your heart pump blood to every part of you. Your body's cells work together to keep you alive.

☑ READING CHECK **Determine Central Ideas** How is a single cell similar to a gray wolf?

....

....

....

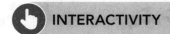

INTERACTIVITY

Explore the function of different cell types in unicellular and multicellular organisms.

Studying Cell Function
Figure 1 If you were to take a swab from someone's tongue, you might see this under this microscope. Microscope visualizations such as these help scientists study complex cell structures. Scientists can then develop and use better models to understand how cell function depends on the relationships among its parts.

63

VIDEO

Learn more about the scientists who helped to develop the cell theory.

Cell Theory

It wasn't until the 1600s that scientists realized living organisms are made of cells. The invention of the **microscope**, an instrument that makes small objects look larger, made this discovery possible. The technology of the microscope led to new knowledge of how life is organized. As this technology improved over time, scientists were able to gather new information about cells and how they function. Scientists put all these discoveries together to develop a theory about cells.

Observing Cells In the mid-1600s, English scientist Robert Hooke built his own microscopes to learn about nature. He made drawings of what he saw when he looked at the bark of cork oak trees (**Figure 2**). Hooke thought that the empty spaces he observed in the tree bark looked like tiny rooms, so he named them "cells." Tree bark, however, contains only dead cells.

Early Cell Observations

Figure 2 Hooke drew what he saw through his microscope in great detail. Draw a circle around one of Hooke's "cells."

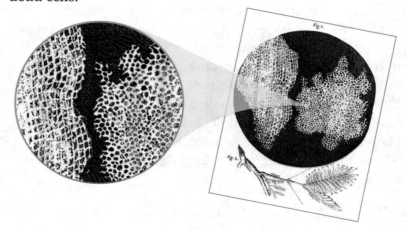

In 1674, Dutch businessman Anton van Leeuwenhoek (LAY von hook) was the first person to observe living cells through a microscope. He saw many tiny organisms swimming and hopping around in a drop of pond water. He named them "animalcules," or little animals.

By 1838, Matthias Schleiden, a scientist working with plants, noticed that all plants are made of cells. A year later, Theodor Schwann came to the conclusion that animals are made of animal cells. The timeline in **Figure 3** shows how the improvement of the microscope furthered the study of cells.

Before Schleiden and Schwann's suggestion that organisms are made up of cells, not much was known about the structure of organisms. These two scientists are credited with the development of the cell theory. Each scientist proposed a hypothesis (plural: hypotheses), a possible answer to a scientific question. Their hypotheses, supported through the observations and experiments of other scientists, led to a theory about cells and all living things.

Literacy Connection

Determine Central Ideas How did early modern scientists learn about cells without performing experiments?

....

....

....

....

....

Microscopes & Cell Theory

Anton van Leeuwenhoek observes living microorganisms under the microscope.

Robert Hooke studies bark and fossils with microscopes and coins the term "cells".

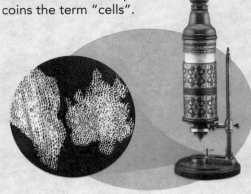

1650

1663

1674

1675

1825

Matthias Schleiden concludes that all plants are made of cells.

Theodor Schwann reaches the conclusion that all animals are made of cells.

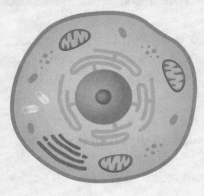

1838

1839

1850

1855

Rudolf Virchow proposes that cells are only made from other cells.

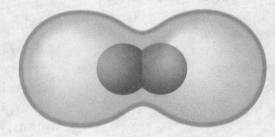

Scientists developed several types of electron microscopes that are 5,000 times more powerful than light microscopes.

1875

1925

1930s

1950

Magnifying the Power of Discovery

Figure 3 This timeline shows how technology and science advance together.

Infer Why didn't Robert Hooke recognize that cells are alive?

....

....

....

Giant Cells

Figure 4 Bubble algae, or sea pearls, look like rubber balls. The bubble shown in this life-sized photo is a single cell! Some scientists consider eggs to be single cells as well. An ostrich egg is 15 cm long and a human egg is about the size of the period at the end of this sentence.

HANDS-ON LAB

Investigate Observe objects using a microscope.

Principles of Cell Theory One of the most important ideas in biology, **cell theory** is a widely accepted explanation of the relationship between cells and living things. According to this theory:

- All living things are made of cells.
- Cells are the basic units of structure and function in living things.
- All new cells are produced from existing cells.

Even though living things differ greatly from one another, they are all made of one or more cells. Cells are the basic unit of life. Most cells are tiny. But some, like those shown in **Figure 4**, can be surprisingly large. The cell theory holds true for all living things, no matter how big or how small they are. Organisms can be made of one cell or of many cells. We can study how one-celled organisms remove wastes to sustain life. Then we can use this information to understand how multi-celled organisms carry out the same task. And, because all new cells are produced from existing cells, scientists can study cells to learn about growth and reproduction.

READING CHECK Cite Textual Evidence According to cell theory, how are bubble algae, or sea pearls, made?

....

....

Microscopes The cell theory could not have been developed without microscopes. The microscopes we use today have the same function as those used 200 years ago—to view tiny specimens. These specimens are now known as "microscopic." The advanced technology in the modern microscope, however, provides far greater detail and much clearer visualization. Light microscopes focus light through lenses to produce a magnified image. Electron microscopes are more complex. To create an image, electron microscopes use beams of electrons that scan the surface of the specimen. Look at the two different images of the same cells in **Figure 5**. Both types of microscopes do the same job in different ways, and both rely on two important properties—magnification and resolution.

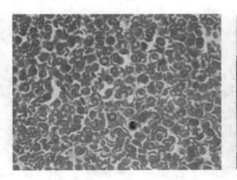 

Different Views

Figure 5 Red blood cells look very different when viewed using a light microscope (left) and an electron microscope (right).

SEP Design Solutions How could scientists today use current technologies to further support the cell theory?

....
....
....
....
....
....

Plan It

Plastic or Wood?

Two students in a science classroom are debating about whether the tables are made of wood or plastic. As the teacher passes by, she suggests, "Use cell theory to find the truth!"

SEP Plan Investigations Propose a scientific investigation to determine whether the tables are wooden or plastic. Include your hypothesis, what steps the students should take, and any materials they might need to carry out the procedure.

....
....
....
....
....
....
....
....

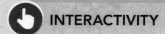
INTERACTIVITY

Explore how to use a microscope to observe specimens under different magnifications.

Magnification The compound light microscope you see in **Figure 6** magnifies an image using two lenses at once. One lens is fixed in the eyepiece. A second lens, called the objective, is located on the revolving nosepiece. A compound microscope usually has more than one objective lens. Each objective lens has a different magnifying power. By turning the nosepiece, you select the lens with the magnifying power you need. A glass rectangle called a slide holds a thin sample to be viewed. A light shines up and passes through the slide and the sample. The light then passes through the lens in the nosepiece and the eyepiece lens. Each lens magnifies the sample. Finally, the light reaches your eye and you get to see the sample in detail!

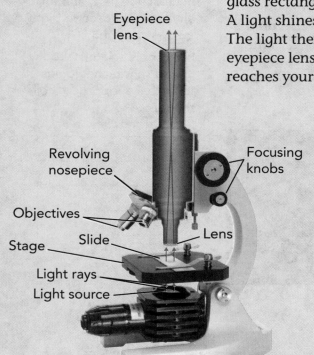

Eyepiece lens

Revolving nosepiece

Focusing knobs

Objectives

Stage

Slide

Lens

Light rays

Light source

Compound Light Microscope

Figure 6 This microscope has a 10× lens in the eyepiece. The revolving nosepiece holds three different objective lenses: 4×, 10×, and 40×.

CCC Scale, Proportion, and Quantity Which magnification would you select to look at a penny? Which would you select to look at a sample of pond water?

....

Academic Vocabulary

The verb *distinguish* has more than one meaning: "to manage to recognize something you can barely see" or "to point out a difference." What distinguishes technology from science?

....

....

....

Resolution A microscope image is useful when it helps you to see the details of an object clearly. The higher the resolution of an image, the better you can **distinguish** two separate structures that are close together, for example. Better resolution shows more details. In general, for light microscopes, resolution improves as magnification increases. Electron microscopes provide images with great resolution and high magnification. As you can see in **Figure 7**, greater resolution and higher magnification makes it relatively easy to study tiny objects.

☑ READING CHECK **Summarize Text** How does the resolution of a microscope help you to observe different structures of the cell?

....

....

....

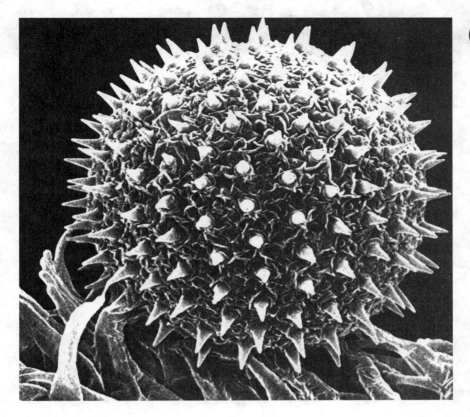

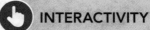

INTERACTIVITY

Investigate a sample to determine if it is living.

Extreme Close-Up

Figure 7 These plant pollen grains are magnified thousands of times.

SEP Make Observations Look closely at the image. Describe some of the details you can distinguish at this very high resolution.

....

....

....

....

Math Toolbox

Getting the Right Magnification

The total magnification of the image from a microscope equals the magnifications of the two lenses multiplied together. If the objective lens magnifies the object 10 times, and the eyepiece lens also magnifies the object 10 times, the total magnification of the microscope is 10 x 10, or 100 times (expressed as "100×"). The image you see will be 100 times larger than the actual sample.

1. **SEP Use Mathematics** Calculate the total magnification of a microscope with eyepiece lens 10× and objective lens 4×.

....

2. **CCC Scale, Proportion, and Quantity** If you use that microscope to view a human hair that is 0.1 mm across, how large will the hair appear in the image?

....

3. **CCC Scale, Proportion, and Quantity** ✏ Your lab partner examined some items under the compound microscope at 40x and began entering her data in this table. Based on the equations in questions 1 and 2, fill in the missing data.

Item	Actual size	Size at 40x
A	0.3 mm	
B		4.8 mm
C		2 mm

1. **Identify** What are three functions of all cells?

....

....

....

2. **Describe** What are the three key points of cell theory?

....

....

....

....

3. **CCC Patterns** Scientists discover new kinds of life in the deep ocean every year. What does the cell theory tell them must be true about every new organism?

....

....

....

4. **SEP Engage in Argument from Evidence** Use evidence to explain how advancements in technology influenced cell theory.

....

....

....

5. **CCC Relate Structure and Function** Compare and contrast the structure and function of a unicellular organism to that of a multicellular organism.

....

....

....

....

....

6. **SEP Use Models** ✏ In the first circle, draw a small, simple picture of something that is big enough to see without magnification. In the second circle, draw it again under 5x magnification. If it is too big to fit in the circle, draw only the part of the object that fits inside.

7. **SEP Apply Scientific Reasoning** Hooke and Van Leeuwenhoek made their discoveries around the same time. More than 150 years later, Schleiden, Schwann, and Virchow all made breakthroughs within a few years of each other. What are some possible reasons for the sudden development of the cell theory after such a long break?

....

....

....

....

....

Viewing cells through a

"Thermal Lens"

This T-cell attacks cancer cells.

Cells have complex functions. Researchers have been trying to figure out how to target cells as a way to deliver drugs and medicines. The mid-infrared photothermal microscope is a new technology that lets scientists peer directly into living cells.

Until now, research into how cells use chemicals has been limited. Infrared imaging techniques could only use samples of dried tissue. Because the water in live cells kept the infrared signals from passing all the way through, scientists could not get detailed images. But engineering advances have led to a new imaging technology that works by shining a laser onto the surface of the tissue. This creates a phenomenon called a "thermal lens" effect, much like a mirage seen over a hot road. The result is a detailed three-dimensional image of the cell.

The photothermal microscope will be essential for discovering different ways cancer treatment drugs reach and affect cancer cells. And scientists can learn more about the chemistry of living systems and find better ways to treat many diseases.

Biomedical engineers are constantly developing new technologies that help save lives. The mid-infrared photothermal microscope lets researchers see how various drug treatments affect cancer cells (left).

MY DISCOVERY

Investigate other conditions and diseases that could be better understood or treated using the new photothermal microscope.

② Cell Structures

Guiding Questions

- What are some special structures within a cell?
- How do the different parts of a cell help it function?
- How are animal cells different from plant cells?

Connection

Literacy Integrate with Visuals

MS-LS1-2, MS-LS1-3

HANDS-ON LAB

µInvestigate Investigate the differences between plant and animal cells.

Vocabulary

organelle
cell wall
cell membrane
cytoplasm
nucleus
mitochondria
chloroplast
vacuole

Academic Vocabulary

structure
function

Connect It !

✎ **Circle three different structures inside this plant cell.**

CCC Structure and Function This plant cell has been sliced in half and you are looking into one of the halves. How would you describe the structure of the cell?

....

....

....

Parts of a Cell

Humans, mushrooms, and plants are all made of many parts. If you've ever taken apart a flower, a leaf, or a nut, you've seen that it also contains smaller parts. You could keep dividing the plant up into parts until you got all the way down to the individual cells. As you learned in your study of the cell theory, cells are the smallest functional units of living organisms. But within each cell there are working structures that help the cell function like an entire organism. Each **organelle** is a tiny cell structure that carries out a specific function within the cell. You can see that the cell in **Figure 1** may have many of the same organelles, but different organelles have a different **structure**. This is because each of the different organelles has a different **function**. Also, some organelles are found only in plant cells, some only in animal cells, and some are found in both plant and animal cells. Bacteria are unicellular organisms that do not contain as many different types of cell parts as plant or animals cells. Together, all the parts of a cell keeps the cell contributing to the function of whole organism.

HANDS-ON LAB

Investigate the size of a single-celled organism.

Academic Vocabulary

Have you heard the terms *structure* and *function* used before? Using what you already know, identify two structures in your classroom and state their function.

....

....

....

Working as a Team

Figure 1 Many structures, or organelles, in this plant cell work together to help the cell survive. The cells, in turn, work together to help the plant survive and grow.

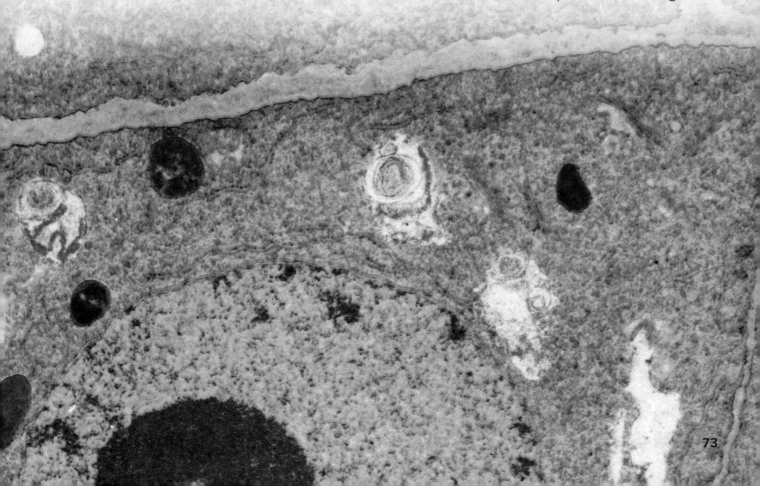

Plant and Animal Cell Differences

Figure 2 These illustrations show typical structures found in plant and animal cells. The functions of some organelles are also included.

1. **SEP Develop Models** 🖊 Fill in the functions of the cell wall and the cell membrane in the boxes provided.

2. **CCC Structure and Function** 🖊 Draw a circle around the structure *inside* the plant cell that is not inside the animal cell.

3. **Use an Analogy** How would you describe the shape of the plant cell compared to the shape of the animal cell?

....
....
....
....
....
....
....
....
....
....

Plant Cell

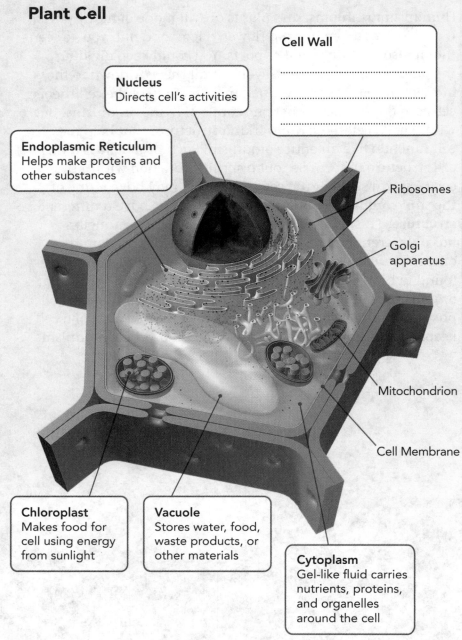

Nucleus
Directs cell's activities

Cell Wall
....
....
....

Endoplasmic Reticulum
Helps make proteins and other substances

Ribosomes

Golgi apparatus

Mitochondrion

Cell Membrane

Chloroplast
Makes food for cell using energy from sunlight

Vacuole
Stores water, food, waste products, or other materials

Cytoplasm
Gel-like fluid carries nutrients, proteins, and organelles around the cell

Cell Wall The rigid supporting layer that surrounds the cells of plants and some other organisms is the **cell wall**. While plants, protists, fungi, and some bacteria have cell walls, the cells of animals do not have cell walls. One function of the cell wall is to help protect and support the cell. The cell walls of plant cells are made mostly of a strong material called cellulose. The cell walls of fungi are made of chitin, the same material that forms the hard, outer skeleton of insects. Observe in **Figure 2** that there are small holes, or pores, in the plant cell wall. Pores allow materials such as water and oxygen to pass through the cell wall.

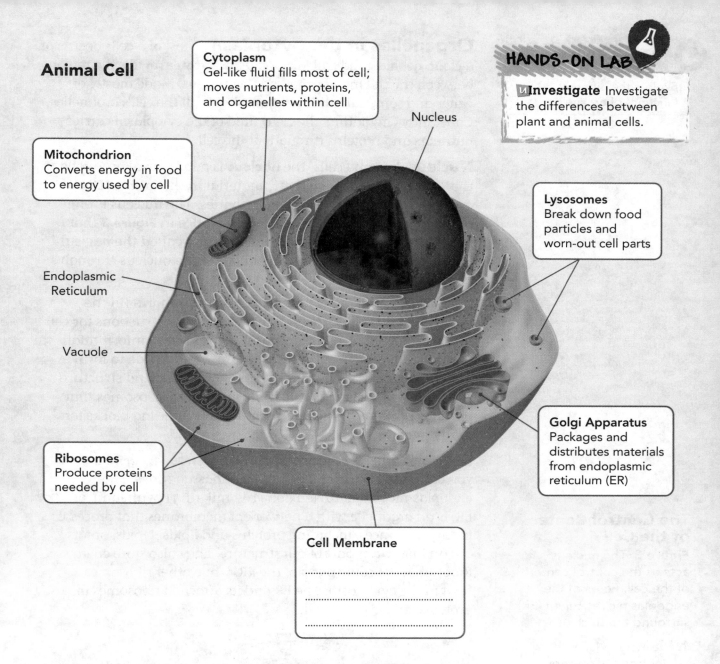

Animal Cell

Cytoplasm
Gel-like fluid fills most of cell; moves nutrients, proteins, and organelles within cell

Nucleus

Mitochondrion
Converts energy in food to energy used by cell

Lysosomes
Break down food particles and worn-out cell parts

Endoplasmic Reticulum

Vacuole

Golgi Apparatus
Packages and distributes materials from endoplasmic reticulum (ER)

Ribosomes
Produce proteins needed by cell

Cell Membrane

....

....

....

Cell Membrane The **cell membrane** is a thin, flexible barrier that surrounds a cell and controls which substances pass into and out of a cell. All cells have a cell membrane. In plant cells, the cell membrane is a fluid-like layer between the cell and the cell wall. As you can see in **Figure 2**, animal cells do not have a cell wall, so the cell membrane is the outermost layer. For all cells without a cell wall, the cell membrane forms the border between the cell and its environment. Think about how a dust mask allows you to breathe, but keeps harmful particles outside your body. One of the functions of the cell membrane is similar to that of a dust mask—it prevents harmful materials from entering the cell. Everything a cell needs, such as food particles, water, and oxygen, enters through the cell membrane. Waste products leave the same way.

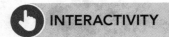
Organelles in the Cytoplasm

Most of a cell consists of a clear, gel-like fluid called cytoplasm. **Cytoplasm** fills the region between the cell membrane and the nucleus. Made mostly of water and some salt, the cytoplasm holds all the cell's organelles. Constantly circulating, the clear fluid of the cytoplasm carries nutrients and proteins throughout the cell.

Nucleus In some cells, the **nucleus** is a large oval organelle that contains the cell's genetic material in the form of DNA and controls many of the cell's activities. The nucleus is one of the largest of the cell's organelles. Notice in **Figure 3** that the nucleus is surrounded by a membrane called the nuclear envelope. Materials pass into and out of the nucleus through pores in the nuclear envelope.

Thin strands of genetic material called chromatin fill the nucleus. This genetic material contains the instructions for cell function. For example, chromatin helps to store information that will later make sure leaf cells grow and divide to form more leaf cells. Also in the nucleus is a dark, round structure called the nucleolus. The nucleolus produces ribosomes that produce proteins. Proteins are important building blocks for many parts of the body.

Endoplasmic Reticulum and Ribosomes In **Figure 3**, you can see a structure like a maze of passageways. The endoplasmic reticulum (en doh PLAZ mik rih TIK yuh lum), or ER, is an organelle with a network of membranes that processes many substances, including proteins and lipids. Lipids, or fats, are an important part of cell structure. They also store energy. Ribosomes dot some parts of the ER, while other ribosomes float in the cytoplasm. The ER and its attached ribosomes make proteins for use in the cell.

The Control Center of the Cell

Figure 3 The nucleus acts as the control center of the cell. Folds of the endoplasmic reticulum (ER) surround the nucleus.

1. Identify 🖉 On the electron microscopy photo, label the nucleus, nuclear envelope, and ER.

2. SEP Construct Explanations Why is the nucleus called the cell's "control center"?

....

....

....

....

....

....

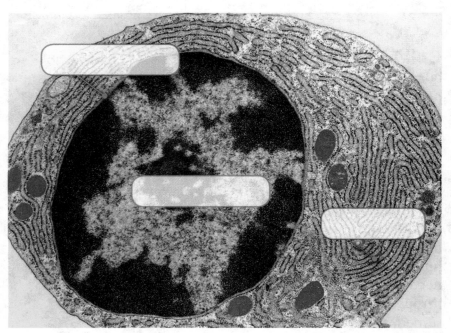

Golgi Apparatus As proteins leave the ER, they move to the Golgi apparatus, a structure that looks like flattened sacs and tubes. Considered the cell's warehouse, the Golgi apparatus receives proteins and other newly formed materials from the ER, packages them, and distributes them to other parts of the cell or to the outside of the cell.

Mitochondria Floating in the cytoplasm are rod-shaped structures. Look again at **Figure 2**. **Mitochondria** (myt oh KAHN dree uh; singular: mitochondrion) convert energy stored in food to energy the cell can use to live and function. They are the "powerhouses" of the cell.

Chloroplasts The **chloroplast** is an organelle in the cells of plants and some other organisms that captures energy from sunlight and changes it to an energy form that cells can use in making food. The function of the chloroplast is to make food, in the form of sugar, for the cell. Cells on the leaves of plants typically contain many green chloroplasts. Animal cells do not have chloroplasts because animals eat food instead of making their own food from sunlight.

☑ READING CHECK **Determine Conclusions** Suppose there is a drought and a plant cannot get enough water. What happens to the cytoplasm and the organelles in the plant cells?

....

....

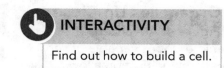

INTERACTIVITY

Find out how to build a cell.

📓 **Student Discourse** In a small group, brainstorm real-world models for a mitochondrion and a chloroplast. Consider their function, how these parts of the cell help keep the whole cell alive. What structures do you know in everyday life that function like them? Record your ideas in your science notebook.

Model It !

The Substance of Life
Earth is often called the water planet because water covers 75 percent of its surface. Cytoplasm, a gel-like fluid, is about 80 percent water. Cytoplasm has three important functions: it gives the cell form, it houses the other organelles in the cell, and it stores chemicals that the cell needs.

SEP Develop Models What could you use to model cytoplasm? What would you use to represent each organelle? List the items you would use.

....

....

....

....

Organelles Up Close

Figure 4 Advanced microscopes capable of very high magnification allow scientists to see organelles in very fine detail. The actual images are not colored. All of these images have been colorized to help you see details.

1. **Claim** ✏ For each organelle, fill in the small circle with A if it is found only in animal cells, P if it is found only in plant cells, or B if it is found in both kinds of cells.

2. **Evidence** Fill in the blank under each image with the name of the organelle. Make changes to your claim as needed.

3. **Reasoning** Explain how your evidence supports your claim.

....

....

....

....

....

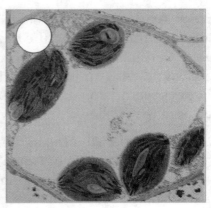

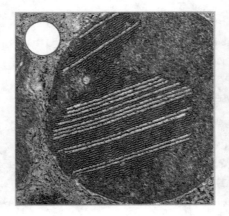

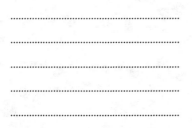

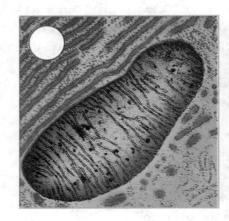

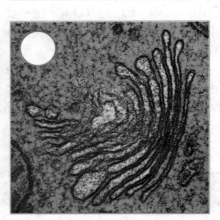

▶ **VIDEO**

Take a tour of the major structures of a cell.

Lysosomes You can think of lysosomes as a cell's recycling centers. Refer to the animal cell in **Figure 2**. Notice the small, round organelles? These are called lysosomes (LY suh sohmz). Lysosomes contain substances that break down large food particles into smaller ones. Lysosomes also break down old cell parts and release the materials so they can be used again.

Vacuoles Plant cells often have one or more large, water-filled sacs floating in the cytoplasm along with the other organelles shown in **Figure 4**. In some animals cells these sacs are much smaller. This structure is a **vacuole** (VAK yoo ohl), a sac-like organelle that stores water, food, or other materials needed by the cell. In addition, vacuoles store waste products until the wastes are removed. In some plants, vacuoles also perform the function of digestion that lysosomes perform in animal cells.

✓ **READING CHECK** **Integrate with Visuals** Use **Figure 2** to describe the main differences between lysosomes and vacuoles.

....

....

....

Cells Working Together

A unicellular organism must perform every function for the survival, growth, and reproduction of the organism. A bacterium is one example of a unicellular organism that performs all the functions that sustain life. When the only cell that makes up the bacterium dies, the organism dies. In a multicellular organism, there are many different types of cells with different functions. But whether a cell is an entire organism or one of billions, all its parts contribute to its function.

Specialized Cells Multicellular organisms are more complex than unicellular organisms. Because they are more complex, they are composed of different types of cells that perform different functions. One type of cell does one kind of job, while other types of cells do other jobs. For example, red blood cells are specialized to deliver oxygen to cells throughout your body. However, they would not travel through your body without the specialized cells of the heart, which send them to other cells needing oxygen. Just as specialized cells differ in function, they also differ in structure. **Figure 5** shows specialized cells from plants and animals. Each type of cell has a distinct shape. For example, a nerve cell has thin, thread-like extensions that reach toward other cells. These structures help nerve cells transmit information from one part of your body to another. The nerve cell's shape would not help a red blood cell fulfill its function.

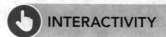

INTERACTIVITY

Investigate the functions of different specialized cells.

Literacy Connection

Integrate with Visuals Which image in **Figure 5** shows you evidence that the cells are relaying information to each other? What does it remind you of?

....

....

....

....

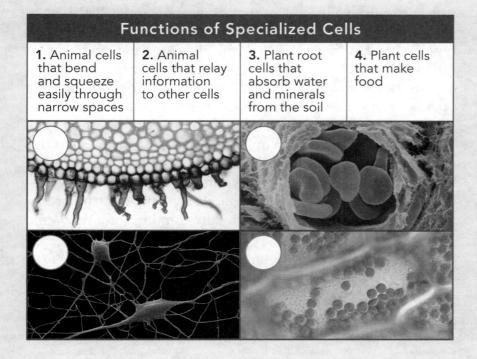

Functions of Specialized Cells

1. Animal cells that bend and squeeze easily through narrow spaces

2. Animal cells that relay information to other cells

3. Plant root cells that absorb water and minerals from the soil

4. Plant cells that make food

The Right Cell for the Job

Figure 5 Different cells carry out different functions.

1. CCC Structure and Function ✏ Match each function to a cell. Write the number of the function in the corresponding image.

2. SEP Consider Limitations Recall the animal cell in **Figure 2**. Why is that model not a true representation of different types of animal cells?

....

....

....

Levels of Organization

Figure 6 ✏ Organisms like this soccer player are organized in levels of increasing complexity. Label the levels of organization starting with the simplest and ending with the most complex. Then circle the organ system.

📓 **Reflect** Consider a time when you worked on a team. In your science notebook, describe how members of your team had special skills that helped you all work together as a group to overcome a challenge.

Cells Make Up an Organism A group of similar cells that work together to perform a specific function is called a tissue. For example, your stomach is made mostly of muscle cells that form muscle tissue. The muscle tissue helps your stomach churn your food for digestion. Your stomach also has glands that produce stomach acid. The glands are another type of tissue. As a whole, the stomach is an organ, made of different kinds of tissues that function together. A group of organs that work together to perform a major function make up an organ system. Your stomach is part of your digestive system, which breaks down your food into useful substances. The body is a system made up of many subsystems, such as the digestive system, and all are made of cells. These subsystems interact to run the whole body system. **Figure 6** shows how the body, a multicellular organism, builds up complex structures from atom to molecule to cell to tissue to organ to organ system.

☑ **READING CHECK** **Determine Central Ideas** Could a single part of a multicellular organism survive on its own? Explain.

....

....

....

☑ LESSON 2 Check

MS-LS1-2, MS-LS1-3

1. Interpret Photos What is the yellow structure, and what role does it play in a cell?

....

....

....

2. CCC Structure and Function Why do cells have so many different organelles and structures?

....

....

....

....

3. SEP Determine Differences What are the main differences between cell walls and cell membranes?

....

....

....

....

....

4. CCC Structure and Function What are three differences between plant cells and animal cells?

....

....

....

....

5. SEP Construct Explanations Are there more tissues or more organs in your body? Explain your reasoning.

....

....

....

Quest CHECK-IN

In this lesson, you learned about the different structures of plant and animal cells and how they function.

SEP Develop Models How can a model help visitors to the exhibit better understand cell structures and their functions?

....

....

....

....

....

HANDS-ON LAB

Make a Cell Model

Go online for a downloadable worksheet of this lab. Design and build a model of a plant cell.

Obtaining and Removing Materials

Guiding Question

• What is the primary role of the cell membrane in cell function?

Connections

Literacy Integrate with Visuals

Math Analyze Proportional Relationships

MS-LS1-2

ωInvestigate Model the way that water moves into and out of a cell.

Vocabulary

selectively
    permeable
diffusion
osmosis
endocytosis
exocytosis

Academic Vocabulary

maintain

Connect It!

✏ **Circle the area on the photo where you think the skunk spray odor will be strongest.**

CCC Energy and Matter How do you think it's possible for you to detect skunk spray from inside your house or from inside a moving car?

....

....

....

Moving Materials Into and Out of Cells

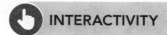
INTERACTIVITY

Discuss how objects move in and out of an area.

One afternoon, you are out walking near your home. You spy something moving around on the ground. Look at **Figure 1**. Is it a black and white cat? As you move closer to get a better look, the animal fluffs up and raises its tail. It's a skunk! You hurriedly turn around and go in the other direction. You know that if you get sprayed by a skunk, people will be able to smell the stink from far away. Odor molecules will travel through the air to be inhaled by everyone around you.

Cells rely on the movement of surrounding gases, liquids, and particles to supply them with nutrients and materials. In order to live and function, cells must let certain materials enter and leave. Oxygen and water and particles of food must be able to move into a cell, while waste materials must move out. The same mechanism that lets materials in and out of a cell also lets those skunk spray molecules—the chemical makeup of odor— seep into the specialized cells in your nose that perceive smell.

Stinky Defense
Figure 1 When a skunk starts to feel threatened, you better watch out! Being sprayed is a miserable experience, and the smell travels fast through the air through the process of diffusion. Diffusion also carries useful molecules to the cells of every living organism.

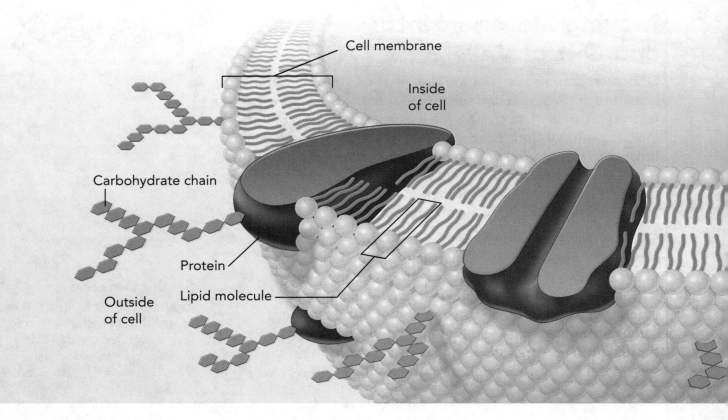

Cell membrane

Inside of cell

Carbohydrate chain

Protein

Lipid molecule

Outside of cell

A Selective Barrier

Figure 2 Carbohydrates, proteins, and lipids are important molecules that make up the structure of the cell membrane. They help move materials into and out of the cell through the cell membrane.

SEP Use Models In what way is the cell membrane like a security guard?

....

....

....

....

....

....

Function of the Cell Membrane

Every cell is surrounded by a cell membrane that lets substances in and out. This movement allows the cell to maintain homeostasis (a stable internal environment) and get all the chemicals needed to support life. The cell membrane is not rigid, but flexible. In **Figure 2**, you can see that different types of molecules play important roles in helping materials move across the cell membrane.

A permeable membrane allows liquids and gases to pass through it. Some materials move freely across the cell membrane. Others move less freely or not at all. The cell membrane is **selectively permeable**, which means some substances can cross the membrane, while others cannot. Substances that move into and out of a cell do so by means of one of two processes: passive transport or active transport.

Passive Transport

Moving materials across the cell membrane sometimes requires no energy. At other times, the cell has to use its own energy. Consider this analogy: If you pour a bucket of water down a slide, the water flows down easily with no effort on your part. Your role is passive. Now, suppose you have to push that same water back up the slide. You would have to use your own energy to move the water. The movement of dissolved materials across a cell membrane without using the cell's energy is called passive transport.

Diffusion Molecules are always moving. As they move, they bump into one another. Crowded, or concentrated, molecules collide more often. Collisions cause molecules to push away from one another. Over time, as molecules continue colliding and moving apart, they spread evenly throughout the space and become less concentrated. **Diffusion** (dih FYOO zhun) is the process by which molecules move from an area of higher concentration to an area of lower concentration. Consider a cell in the lining of your lungs. The cell is in contact with the air that you breathe. The air outside the cell has a higher concentration of oxygen. What happens? Oxygen moves easily into the cell. The diffusion of oxygen into the cell does not require the cell to use any of its energy. Diffusion is a form of passive transport. **Figure 3** shows how insects use spiracles instead of lungs to diffuse oxygen into their cells.

☑ READING CHECK **Write Informative Texts** Why is it important for a cell membrane to be selectively permeable?

....

....

....

....

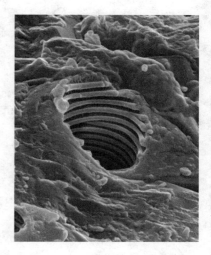

No Lungs Necessary

Figure 3 Spiracles are holes in the exoskeleton, or outer shell, of insects that allow oxygen to enter and diffuse into the cells of the insect. Spiracles connect to air passages that lead into all parts of the insect.

CCC Structure and Function ✏ Circle the area where air can enter the insect's body.

Math Toolbox

Giant Ancient Insect

The largest insects ever discovered were giant dragonflies that lived 300 million years ago. These dragonflies had a wingspan of 67 cm! Today the largest dragonfly has a wingspan of about 20 cm. The giant dragonflies existed at a time when the oxygen level in the atmosphere was about 35 percent, compared to 21 percent today. Use this information to answer the following questions.

1. **SEP Use Mathematics** Express the size of the giant dragonfly as a percentage of the size of the modern dragonfly. Show your work.

   ....

2. **CCC Scale, Proportion, and Quantity** Refer to the spiracle in **Figure 3**. What do you think the relationship is between the spiracles, insect size, and air oxygen levels?

   ....

   ....

Model It !

Raisins No More

Figure 4 In the US, most raisins grow in California—as grapes! Raisins are dried grapes—most of the water is removed. The cells of raisins are dead. If you soak raisins in water, the cells will take up water by the process of diffusion.

SEP Develop Models ✏️ Use the grape cell shown below as a reference. In the empty circles, first draw a raisin cell and then draw what the cell looks like after soaking the raisin in water overnight.

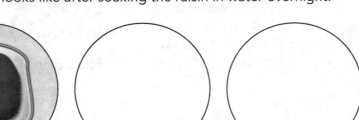

Literacy Connection

Integrate with Visuals ✏️
The Great Salt Lake in Utah is so salty that large clumps of salt crystallize out of the water. Imagine yourself soaking in the lake. Draw a diagram below to show the flow of water by osmosis between the lake water and the cells of your body.

Osmosis Like oxygen, water passes easily into and out of a cell across the cell membrane. **Osmosis** is the diffusion of water molecules across a selectively permeable membrane. Many cellular processes depend on osmosis to bring them the water they need to function. Without enough water, most cells will die. Because it requires no energy from the cell, osmosis is a form of passive transport.

Osmosis can have important effects on cells and entire organisms. The soaked raisins in **Figure 4** are lighter in color and appear plumper due to a flow of water into their cells. Under certain conditions, osmosis can cause water to move out of the cells more quickly than it moves in. When that happens, the cytoplasm shrinks and the cell membrane pulls away from the cell wall. If conditions do not change, the cells can die.

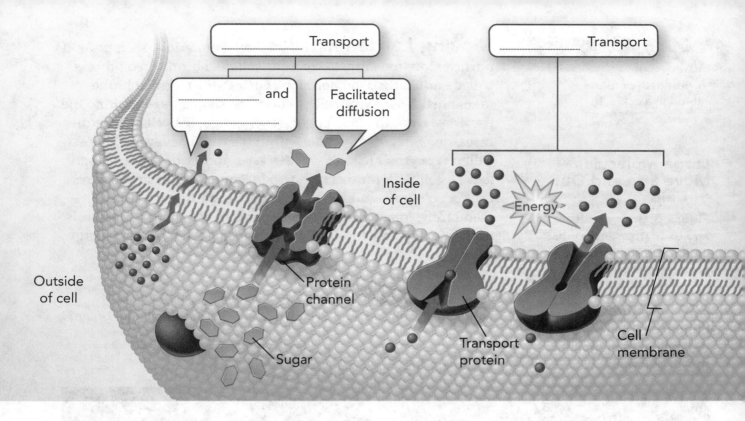

_____ Transport

_____ and

Facilitated diffusion

_____ Transport

Outside of cell

Inside of cell

Energy

Protein channel

Sugar

Transport protein

Cell membrane

Facilitated Diffusion Oxygen, carbon dioxide, and water freely diffuse across the cell membrane. Some molecules, such as sugar, cannot easily cross the cell membrane. In a process called facilitated diffusion, proteins in the cell membrane form channels through which the sugars can pass. The word _facilitate_ means "to make easier." As shown in **Figure 5**, these proteins provide a pathway for the sugars to diffuse. The proteins function much the way downspouts guide water that flows from the roof of a house to the ground. Facilitated diffusion uses no cell energy and is a form of passive transport.

Active Transport During diffusion, molecules move randomly in all directions. A few molecules move by chance from areas of low concentration to areas of high concentration, but most molecules move toward areas of lower concentration. In many cases, cells need the concentration of a molecule inside the cell to be higher than the concentration outside the cell. In order to **maintain** this difference in the concentration of molecules, cells use active transport. Cells supply the energy to do this work—just as you would supply the energy to pedal your bike uphill. Active transport is the movement of materials across a cell membrane using cellular energy. As in facilitated diffusion, proteins within the cell membrane play a key role in active transport. Using the cell's energy, transport proteins "pick up" specific molecules passing by the cell and carry them across the membrane. Calcium, potassium, and sodium are some substances that are carried into and out of cells by active transport.

Crossing the Cell Membrane

Figure 5 Molecules move into and out of a cell by means of passive or active transport.

Interpret Diagrams ✏
Complete the labels. Fill in the missing words.

Academic Vocabulary

To _maintain_ means to keep in an existing state. When have you had to maintain something?

_____

_____

_____

HANDS-ON LAB

ᴜ**Investigate** Model the way that water moves into and out of a cell.

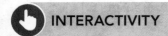

Large Molecules Move Into and Out of Cells

Figure 6 Both endocytosis and exocytosis are forms of active transport. These processes require energy from the cell.

CCC Structure and Function Fill in the blanks by labeling each process shown below.

Moving Large Particles Some materials, such as food particles, are too large to cross the cell membrane. In a process called **endocytosis** (en doh sigh TOH sis), the cell membrane takes particles into the cell by changing shape and engulfing the particles. Once the food particle is engulfed, the cell membrane fuses, pinching off a vacuole within the cell. The reverse process, called **exocytosis** (ek soh sigh TOH sis), allows large particles to leave a cell. This process is shown in **Figure 6**. During exocytosis, the vacuole surrounding the food particles fuses with the cell membrane, forcing the contents out of the cell. Both endocytosis and exocytosis are forms of active transport that require energy from the cell.

☑ **READING CHECK** **Draw Conclusions** Why don't cells use endocytosis to transport all substances across the cell membrane?

....

....

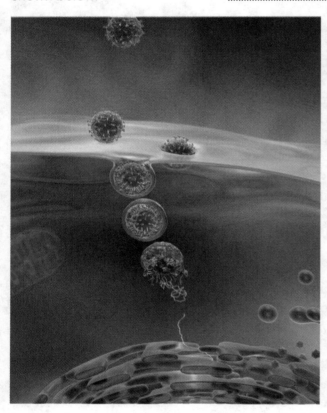

Large Molecules Entering the Cell
Large food particles are close to the cell. In order to bring food into the cell, the membrane wraps itself around a particle and draws it into the cytoplasm.

....

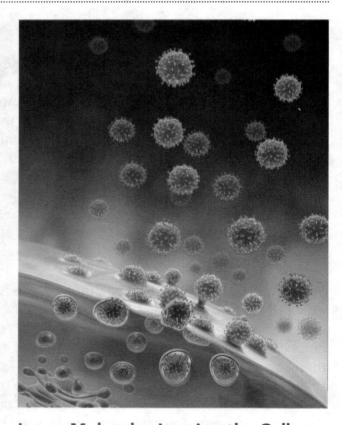

Large Molecules Leaving the Cell
Vacuoles carrying large particles of waste move toward the cell membrane. The vacuoles fuse with the membrane in order to push the waste particles out of the cell.

....

Figure 7 The city of Arcata, California, has a surprising solution for sewage management that also helps protect the environment. They use treated wastewater from their treatment plant to maintain a marsh and wildlife refuge.

SEP Use Models If a city were a model for a cell, would wastewater be more likely part of endocytosis or exocytosis? Explain.

....

....

....

Model It !

Endocytosis and exocytosis may be easier to understand when you compare them to simpler everyday processes. Just as they are regular processes that contribute to a cell's function, there are regular processes that bring needed materials to your household and take away unneeded materials from your household to keep it functioning.

1. **Use an Analogy** Name a process that occurs in your household regularly that is similar to endocytosis, and one that is similar to exocytosis.

....

....

....

2. **SEP Develop Models** Make labeled sketches or flowcharts showing, step-by-step, how each of your chosen processes are similar to endocytosis and exocytosis. Be sure to show how each process contributes to your household's function.

MS-LS1-2

1. Explain Phenomena Why do cells need to maintain homeostasis?

....

....

....

2. Determine Differences How is facilitated diffusion different from diffusion?

....

....

....

....

....

3. CCC Cause and Effect What would happen to a cell placed in extremely salty water?

....

....

....

....

....

4. Compare and Contrast Fill in the Venn diagram below with the following terms: exocytosis, diffusion, endocytosis, osmosis

Into Cell   Out of Cell

5. SEP Construct Explanations How could disease-causing bacteria get inside a cell without damaging the cell membrane?

....

....

....

....

....

Quest CHECK-IN

In this lesson, you learned about the cell membrane and how cells take in the substances they need in order to function. You also learned how cells remove waste products through cellular processes.

CCC Relate Structure and Function Consider which structures of the cell membrane function to help materials move into and out of the cell. How can you best model this information in your animation?

....

....

....

 INTERACTIVITY

Put Your Cells in Motion

Go online to plan an animation that shows the ways materials enter and leave the cell. Then create your animation for the exhibit.

ARTIFICIAL TRANSPORT
Channels

How do you make cell transport more efficient? You engineer it! Scientists at Lawrence Berkeley National Laboratory show us how.

The Challenge: To create an efficient way for large molecules to transport through cells.

Cells transport substances through the cell membrane to maintain homeostasis. The cell membrane is mostly made up of two lipid layers, called a bi-layer. The lipid bi-layer allows small substances, such as oxygen and water, to pass through the membrane. However, some molecules, such as sugar, can only transport through protein channels located on the cell membrane. The selectively permeable nature of the cell membrane will not allow any molecule to enter or exit the cell.

The team of Berkeley Lab scientists engineered nanotubes to create artificial transport channels. The tubes are engineered to allow different molecules to enter the cell. Nanotubes can penetrate and become part of the cell membrane. However, they are not as selective as protein channels. While testing the efficiency of a nanotube, scientists discovered that it can also open or close, similar to a protein channel. The discovery meant that nanotubes could stop unwanted molecules from entering or exiting cells. Scientists are hopeful that the engineering advancement of nanotubes may one-day be used to transport medicine into injured or sick cells.

Nanotubes may one day help transport medicine into cells to correct genetic diseases and deal with other illnesses.

DESIGN CHALLENGE

Can you design a nanotube to help deliver medicine to cells? Go the Engineering Design Notebook to find out!

MS-LS1-2

THE MIGHTY MOLE-RAT

What lives underground in a desert, is as small as a mouse, furless, and able to last for 18 minutes with no oxygen? It's the African naked mole-rat, of course!

To understand what's special about the naked mole-rat's feat, you have to understand a little about how animals process energy. The combination of chemical reactions through which an organism builds up or breaks down materials is called metabolism. Most mammals have a similar metabolism. They break down the sugar glucose and change it into energy their bodies can use. Most animals need oxygen to accomplish this. Without oxygen, animals cannot turn food into energy, so their cells will die. There are times when oxygen levels drop. At this point, their metabolism can usually switch to a form of fermentation. This is a temporary solution. As soon as oxygen levels are back up, the animals' metabolism will return to normal.

A Remarkable Animal

The naked mole-rat is the exception to the rule. Naked mole-rats survive because they use a different method to create energy. This method does not need oxygen or glucose.

When oxygen is plentiful, the Naked mole-rat's metabolism uses glucose to make energy. However, they live in cramped underground colonies with little oxygen. They thrive in these conditions, because they can switch their metabolism. Their blood contains more fructose than other mammals. When oxygen levels are low, they switch their metabolism to use fructose to make energy.

While closely related to mice, naked mole-rats are not so different from humans either. In the human liver, fructose gets changed into other molecules that our bodies use as energy. Think of what you could do if the entire human body could adapt to a fructose-based metabolism, similar to the mole-rats'! In addition to a fructose-based metabolism, the naked mole-rat has developed other remarkable traits, or characteristics. Read the table to learn more.

Use the chart to answer the questions.

1. **Infer** What is one advantage of the naked mole-rat's long life span?

2. **CCC Cause and Effect** What do you think would happen if the naked mole-rats' burrows were exposed to extreme temperatures? Explain.

Remarkable Characteristics of the African Naked Mole-Rat	
Characteristic	**Explanation**
Cold-blooded	Doesn't need to change body temperature because its habitat of underground burrows remains at a constant temperature
Cancer Resistant	Produces a "super sugar" that keeps cells from forming tumors
High Tolerance for Pain	Nerve receptors are less sensitive to pain
Long Life Span	Lives for up to 32 years

3. **SEP Plan Investigations** Scientists determined that naked mole-rats could undergo cellular respiration without oxygen. What sort of investigation do you think they used?

4. **SEP Design Solutions** How might the naked mole-rat's ability to undergo cellular respiration without oxygen be applied to human medicine?

Guiding Questions

- What are the four functions of cell division?
- Which structures in a cell help it to reproduce?

Connections

Literacy Summarize Text

Math Analyze Quantitative Relationships

MS-LS1-2

HANDS-ON LAB

uInvestigate Model how a cell divides.

Vocabulary

cell cycle
interphase
replication
mitosis
cytokinesis

Academic Vocabulary

sequence

Connect It !

✏ **Using the x-ray image as a guide, place a circle on the biker to show where the broken bone is.**

SEP Construct Explanations Where will the bike rider's body get new cells to repair the broken bones?

....

....

The Functions of Cell Division

The bike rider in **Figure 1** really took a tumble! Thankfully, he was wearing a helmet and only suffered a broken arm and a scraped elbow. His body will immediately begin to repair the bones, muscles, and skin. Where will his body get so many new cells to repair the damage? Recall that cells can only be produced by other cells. The new cells will come from older cells that divide in two, over and over again, until there are enough healthy cells to restore full function. Similarly, cell division can replace aging cells and those that die from disease.

Cell division also allows an organism to grow larger. A tiny fertilized egg cell splits into two, two into four, and so on, until a single cell becomes a multicellular organism. Another function of cell division is reproduction. Many single-celled organisms, such as yeasts, reproduce simply through cell division. Other organisms reproduce when cell division leads to the growth of new structures. For example, a strawberry plant can grow new stems and roots. These structures then break away from the parent plant and become a separate plant. Most organisms reproduce when specialized cells from two different parents combine, forming a new cell. This cell then undergoes many divisions and grows into a new organism.

READING CHECK **Determine Central Ideas** What are four functions of cell division?

....

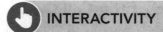
INTERACTIVITY

Reflect on where you think cell division is occurring in your body.

Reflect Think of a time when you injured yourself. In your Science Notebook, describe the appearance and feeling of the injury when it first happened and then how the injured area changed as your body healed.

Cell Division to the Rescue

Figure 1 As soon as you break a bone, your body sets to work repairing it. Many new cells are produced to clean up the mess and produce new tissues.

Phases of the Cell Cycle

Figure 2 The series of diagrams represents an entire cell cycle.

SEP Interpreting Data What happens to the cell's genetic information during the cell cycle?

....

....

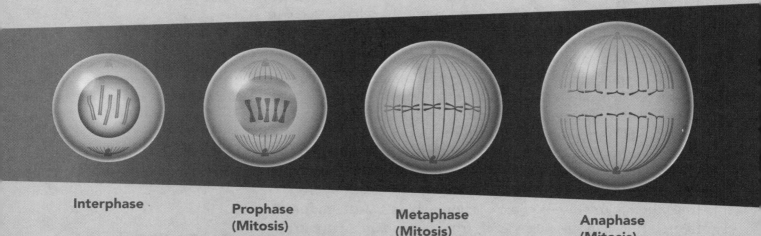

Interphase

Prophase (Mitosis)

Metaphase (Mitosis)

Anaphase (Mitosis)

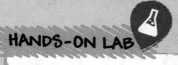

HANDS-ON LAB

Investigate Model how a cell divides.

Academic Vocabulary

Cell division follows a careful sequence of events. Describe the sequence of events on one of your typical school days.

....

....

....

....

....

The Cell Cycle

Most of the time, cells carry out their regular functions, but everything changes when a cell gets the signal to divide. At that point, the cell must accomplish several tasks to be ready for the big division into two "daughter cells." **Figure 2** summarizes those tasks.

First, the cell must grow in size and double its contents. This phase is called interphase. Next, the cell must divide up its contents so that the two daughter cells will have roughly equal contents. This second phase is called mitosis, and it has several stages.

Finally, the cell's cytoplasm physically divides in two in a phase called cytokinesis. The regular **sequence** of events in which the cell grows, prepares for division, and divides to form two daughter cells is known as the **cell cycle**. After the division is complete, each of the daughter cells begins the cycle again.

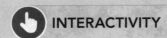

INTERACTIVITY

Explore the cell cycle and learn why living things go through the cell cycle.

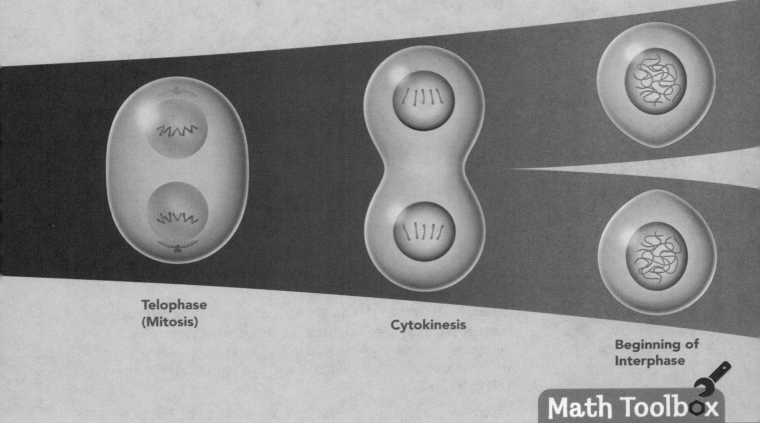

Telophase (Mitosis)

Cytokinesis

Beginning of Interphase

Math Toolbox

Dividing Cells

Every cell division produces two daughter cells. You can see in the diagram that after one division, the single cell has become two cells.

✎ Fill in the last two squares to show the results from two more cell divisions.

| **0 Divisions** | **1 Division** | **2 Divisions** | **3 Divisions** |

1. **Analyze Quantitative Relationships** How does the number of cells increase with each new division of the cells?

....

2. **SEP Use Mathematics** How many cells would there be after five divisions?

....

3. **Hypothesize** Do you think all human cells divide at the same rate throughout life? Explain your reasoning.

....

97

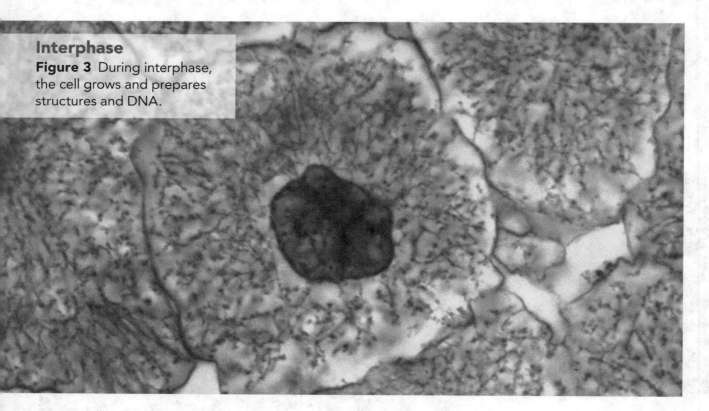

Interphase

Figure 3 During interphase, the cell grows and prepares structures and DNA.

Stage 1: Interphase The first stage of the cell cycle is **interphase**, before cell division begins. During interphase, the cell grows, makes a copy of its DNA, and prepares to divide into two cells. The light microscope image in **Figure 3** shows a cell in interphase.

Growing Early in interphase, a cell grows to its full size and produces the organelles that both daughter cells will need. For example, plant cells make more chloroplasts. All cells make more ribosomes and mitochondria. Cells also make more enzymes, substances that speed up chemical reactions in living things.

Replication Recall that chromatin in the nucleus holds all the genetic information that a cell needs to carry out its functions. That information is in a complex chemical substance called DNA (deoxyribonucleic acid). In a process called **replication**, the cell makes a copy of the DNA in its nucleus before cell division. DNA replication results in the formation of threadlike structures called chromosomes. Each chromosome inside the nucleus of the cell contains two identical sets of DNA, called chromatids.

Preparing for Division Once the DNA has replicated, preparation for cell division begins. The cell produces structures that will help it to divide into two new cells. In animal cells, but not plant cells, a pair of centrioles is duplicated. The centrioles help later with dividing the DNA between the daughter cells. At the end of interphase, the cell is ready to divide.

Stage 2: Mitosis

Once interphase ends, the second stage of the cell cycle begins. During **mitosis** (my TOH sis), the cell's nucleus divides into two new nuclei and one set of DNA is distributed into each daughter cell. Scientists divide mitosis into four parts, or phases: prophase, metaphase, anaphase, and telophase.

During prophase, DNA condenses into separate chromosomes. Recall that during replication, chromosomes formed. The two chromatids that make up the chromosome are exact copies of identical DNA. The nuclear membrane that surrounds the DNA begins to break apart. In metaphase, the chromosomes line up along the center of the cell. The chromatids that will go to each daughter cell are lined up on that side of the cell. Next, in anaphase, fibers connected to the centrioles pull the chromatids apart into each side of the cell. The final phase of mitosis is telophase. During telophase, the chromatids are pulled to opposite ends of the cell. The nuclear membrane reforms around the DNA to create two new nuclei. Each nucleus contains a complete, identical copy of DNA. Test your knowledge of the phases of mitosis in **Figure 4**.

☑ READING CHECK **Summarize Text** What are the three things that a cell has to complete in order to be ready for cell division?

....

....

Literacy Connection

Summarize Text As you read, underline each phase of mitosis. Write a short description of each phase of mitosis.

....

....

....

....

....

....

....

....

....

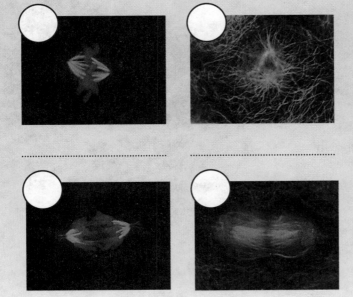

....

....

Scrambled Mitosis

Figure 4 These dividing cells have been marked with a dye that glows under fluorescent light. The dye makes it easy to see the DNA, stained blue, and fibers, stained green. The pictures are in the wrong order.

Identify ✏ Label each phase of mitosis in the space provided. Then, write the numbers 1 to 4 in the circles to show the correct order of the phases in mitosis.

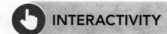
Stage 3: Cytokinesis

The final stage of the cell cycle is called **cytokinesis** (sy toh kih NEE sis). This stage completes the process of cell division. During cytokinesis, the cell's cytoplasm divides, distributing the organelles into each of the two new daughter cells. Cytokinesis usually starts at about the same time as telophase. When cytokinesis is complete, each daughter cell has the same number of chromosomes as the parent cell. Next, each cell enters interphase and the cell cycle begins again.

Cytokinesis in Animal Cells During cytokinesis in animal cells, the cell membrane squeezes together around the middle of the cell. The cytoplasm pinches into two cells. Each daughter cell gets about half of the organelles of the parent cell.

Cytokinesis in Plant Cells Cytokinesis is somewhat different in plant cells. A plant cell's rigid cell wall cannot squeeze together in the same way that a cell membrane can. Instead, a structure called a cell plate forms across the middle of the cell, as shown in **Figure 5**. The cell plate begins to form new cell membranes between the two daughter cells. New cell walls then form around the cell membranes.

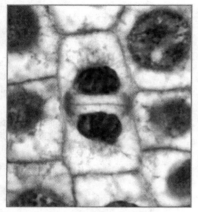

Plant Cytokinesis

Figure 5 One of these plant cells is dividing.

Identify 🖊 Find the cell that is dividing. Place an *X* on each daughter cell and trace the cell plate.

☑ READING CHECK **Determine Conclusions** What would happen if cytokinesis did not occur?

....

....

Question It!

A Two-Celled Organism?

Two students examining a sample of lake water find an unusual-looking organism.

SEP Ask Questions What kinds of questions would you have if you saw the organism shown here? List three questions and two resources you could use to help you to answer them.

....

....

....

....

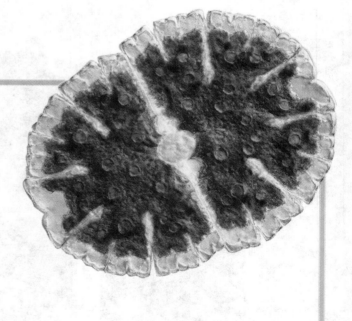

MS-LS1-2

1. **Explain** Why is it important for the cells in your body to go through the cell cycle?

....

....

....

....

2. **SEP Construct Explanations** How does a plant cell accomplish cytokinesis?

....

....

....

....

....

....

3. **SEP Explain Phenomena** Why does the cell need to replicate its DNA during interphase?

....

....

....

....

....

....

4. **SEP Make Observations** What is happening during this part of the cell cycle?

....

....

....

5. **CCC Systems** What would happen to a cell that didn't replicate its DNA before cell division?

....

....

....

6. **SEP Develop Models** ✏ What happens during cytokinesis? Use the space below to sketch and label a diagram of an animal cell undergoing cytokinesis.

Quest CHECK-IN

In this lesson, you learned about cell division. You also explored the four functions of cell division and what cell structures are involved.

SEP Construct Explanations How does cell division and healthy cells contribute to a properly functioning body? Think of ways you can communicate this information in your exhibit.

....

....

....

....

INTERACTIVITY

The Importance of Cells

Go online to find out more about a medical condition that directly involves cells or cell function. Then construct an exhibit that explains to visitors why this topic is important.

☑ TOPIC 2 Review and Assess

1 Structure and Function of Cells

MS-LS1-1, MS-LS1-2

1. Which statement is *not* part of the cell theory?
   A. Cells are the basic unit of structure and function in all living things.
   B. Animal cells are generally more complex than plant cells.
   C. All living things are composed of cells.
   D. All cells are produced from other cells.

2. Reproduction is a function of both
   .... and organisms.

3. **Apply Concepts** How did technology impact the development of the cell theory?

   ....
   ....
   ....
   ....
   ....

4. **Connect to Nature of Science** What were Schleiden, Schwann, and Virchow's contributions to the cell theory?

   ....
   ....
   ....
   ....

5. **SEP Plan an Investigation** Given what you learned about cell theory, how would you conduct an investigation to distinguish between material from a real plant and a fake plant?

   ....
   ....
   ....
   ....

2 Cell Structures

MS-LS1-2, MS-LS1-3

6. Which cell structure breaks down sugars to provide energy for cell activities?
   A. vacuole   B. endoplasmic reticulum
   C. nucleus   D. mitochondrion

7. The outermost layer in a plant cell is the
   .... The outermost layer in an animal cell is the ....

8. **SEP Construct Explanations** Plant cells have a cell wall and cell membranes, but animal cells have only cell membranes. What is a possible reason for this difference?

   ....
   ....
   ....

9. **CCC Relate Structure and Function** What is the relationship among the structures of cells, tissues, and organs?

   ....
   ....

10. **SEP Engage in Argument** Your lab partner just stated that cells, tissues, and organs all have separate functions, and they could not interact to make up a single system. Construct an argument supported with evidence from the text to respond.

    ....
    ....
    ....
    ....
    ....
    ....

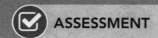
3 **Obtaining and Removing Materials**

MS-LS1-2

11. A cell can bring in a large particle of food using the process of
A. endocytosis.
B. facilitated diffusion.
C. osmosis.
D. exocytosis.

12. The diffusion of water is known as ....

13. CCC Analyze Structures What are the benefits of a selectively permeable membrane?

....

....

....

....

14. CCC Structure and Function From what cell structure are these waste particles being released? What is this process called?

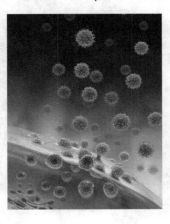

....

....

....

4 **Cell Division**

MS-LS1-2

15. What happens when a cell reproduces?
A. Two similar daughter cells are created.
B. One mother cell and one daughter cell are created.
C. One mother and two similar daughter cells are created.
D. One father and one mother cell are created.

16. SEP Construct Explanations What is the purpose of cell division?

....

....

17. CCC Analyze Properties At what point during the cell division process does one cell become two?

....

....

....

18. SEP Develop Models Draw the stage of the cell cycle in which a cell divides in two new daughter cells. Label it with its name and whether it is a plant or animal cell. Circle the area that shows the separation of the two cells.

MS-LS1-1, MS-LS1-2

Evidence-Based Assessment

Students in a life science class completed an investigation to see what cells really look like. They were given different samples of cells to observe under a microscope. Some cell samples came from animals, while others came from plants. The students were required to draw what they observed and label the organelles and other cell structures. The students found that not all cells look alike, but that they all share common features.

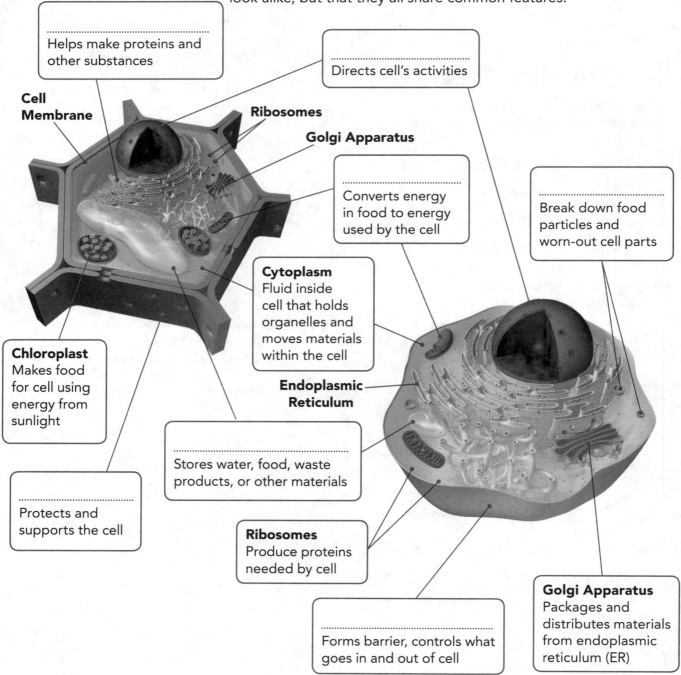

Helps make proteins and other substances

Directs cell's activities

Cell Membrane

Ribosomes

Golgi Apparatus

Converts energy in food to energy used by the cell

Break down food particles and worn-out cell parts

Cytoplasm
Fluid inside cell that holds organelles and moves materials within the cell

Endoplasmic Reticulum

Chloroplast
Makes food for cell using energy from sunlight

Stores water, food, waste products, or other materials

Protects and supports the cell

Ribosomes
Produce proteins needed by cell

Golgi Apparatus
Packages and distributes materials from endoplasmic reticulum (ER)

Forms barrier, controls what goes in and out of cell

1. **SEP Develop Models** 🖊 Use each term to complete the missing labels in the diagrams of the animal cell and the plant cell: Cell Membrane, Cell Wall, Endoplasmic Reticulum, Lysosomes, Mitochondrion, Nucleus, and Vacuole. Then, circle the animal cell.

2. **CCC Structure and Function** What is the mitochondrion's function in the cell?
   A. store genetic information
   B. produce energy
   C. collect the sun's energy
   D. synthesize proteins

3. **SEP Determine Differences** Observe and compare the two types of cells. Complete the table to show three differences between animal cells and plant cells.

Animal Cells	Plant Cells

4. **SEP Distinguish Relationships** Why does the plant cell need both a cell wall and a cell membrane?

   ....
   ....
   ....
   ....
   ....

5. **CCC Scale, Proportion, and Quantity** Plant and animal cells undergo cell division. During the phase of the cell cycle known as interphase, a cell grows in size and doubles its contents. Why does the cell do this?

   ....
   ....
   ....

6. **CCC Cause and Effect** Locate the chloroplast in the plant cell. Based on your understanding of its function, what would happen to a plant if a disease somehow damaged the chloroplasts so that they could not function correctly? Order the following events from 1 to 4, with 1 being the first event and 4 being the last event.

Event	Order
The plant dies.	
A plant disease damages the chloroplast.	
The plant begins to produce less food.	
The plant is unable to obtain energy from sunlight.	

Quest FINDINGS

Complete the Quest!

Phenomenon **Take the time to evaluate your exhibit and add some finishing touches.**

SEP Design Solutions Consider how you want to present your information. What sorts of changes could you make to your exhibit so that it is accessible to people with all sorts of information processing styles.

....
....
....
....

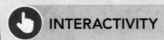

👆 **INTERACTIVITY**

Reflect on Your Museum Exhibit

MS-LS1-1, MS-ETS1-1, MS-ETS1-2,
MS-ETS1-3, MS-ETS1-4

Design and Build a
Microscope

Can you **design** and build your own **microscope** to **examine** small objects?

Background

Phenomenon Have you ever used a magnifying glass to read the date on a small coin more easily? What do you think would happen if you used a second magnifying glass to look through the first magnifying glass?

That's the basic idea behind a compound microscope—using one lens to look through a second lens to get a better view of small objects. This view often gives scientists the ability to understand how the structure of an organism helps with its function. In this activity, you will design and build your own microscope to examine small objects.

Materials

(per group)

- book
- 2 hand lenses; one low-power and one high-power
- metric ruler
- cardboard tubes
- tape
- scissors
- rubber bands
- other common materials for building your microscope

Safety

Be sure to follow all safety guidelines provided by your teacher. The Safety Appendix of your textbook provides more details about the safety icons.

Herald Moth The wings on this Herald moth allow it to fly. Viewing the moth's wings up close could explain how the wing's structure enables the moth to fly.

Procedure

Part 1: Define the Problem

1. **Student Discourse** Work with a partner to discuss and explore how lenses can be used to magnify objects. Using only your eyes, examine words in a book. Then use the high-power lens to examine the same words. Draw your observations in the space provided.

2. Hold the high-power lens 5 to 6 cm above the words in the book. Keep the high-power lens about the same height above the words. Hold the low-power lens above the high power lens.

3. Move the high-power lens up and down until the image is in focus and upside down. Once the image is in focus, experiment with raising and lowering both lenses. Your goal is to produce the highest magnification while keeping the image in clear focus.

4. Measure and record the distance between the book and the high-power lens, and between the two lenses. Draw your observations through both lenses together.

Part 2: Design a Solution

5. Using this information, design your own compound microscope. Think of creative ways to use the available materials. Your microscope should meet all the criteria shown.

6. Sketch your design. Obtain your teacher's approval for your design. Then construct your microscope.

Part 3: Test and Evaluate Your Solution

7. Test your microscope by examining printed words or a printed photograph. Then, examine other objects such as a leaf or onion skin. Record your observations. Did your microscope meet the criteria listed in Step 5?

8. Examine microscopes made by other students. Based on your tests and your examination of other microscopes, identify ways you could improve your microscope.

HANDS-ON LAB

иDemonstrate Go online for a downloadable worksheet of this lab.

Your microscope should:

- contain one low-power lens and one high-power lens
- allow the distance between the two lenses to be easily adjusted
- focus to produce a clear, enlarged, and upside-down image of the object

Part 1: Research and Investigate

Sketch what you observed:

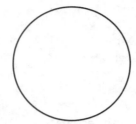
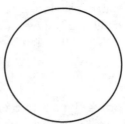

eyes only   high-powered lens   both lenses

Measurements:

....

....

Part 2: Design and Build

Sketch of proposed microscope design:

Part 3: Evaluate and Redesign

Observations: Ideas to improve microscope:

....

....

....

....

....

....

Analyze and Interpret Data

1. **SEP Evaluate Your Solution** When you used two lenses, how did moving the top lens up and down affect the image? What was the effect of moving the bottom lens up and down?

   _____

   _____

   _____

2. **CCC Systems and System Models** Compare the images you observed using one lens with the image from two lenses. What do you think accounts for these differences?

   _____

   _____

   _____

3. **CCC Connect to Technology** How do you think that the compound microscope contributed to the development of the cell theory? Use evidence from your investigation to support the claim.

   _____

   _____

   _____

4. **SEP Use Models** How did modeling a microscope with the two lenses in Part 1 help you determine the design and function of your microscope? What types of limitations did you encounter as you designed and built your prototype?

   _____

   _____

   _____

   _____

5. **SEP Engage in Argument** Imagine you are living in the year 1675. Write a letter to a scientific magazine that will convince scientists to use your new microscope rather than the single-lens variety used by Van Leeuwenhoek. Support your points with evidence from your investigation.

   _____

   _____

   _____

   _____

TOPIC

3

Human Body Systems

NGSS PERFORMANCE EXPECTATIONS

MS-LS1-3 Use argument supported by evidence for
how the body is a system of interacting subsystems
composed of groups of cells.

MS-LS1-8 Gather and synthesize information that
sensory receptors respond to stimuli by sending
messages to the brain for immediate behavior or
storage as memories.

HANDS-ON LAB

ıConnect Use a model to explore
how the human body is organized.

HOW does this person maintain his balance on the slackline?

GO ONLINE to access your digital course

- ▶ VIDEO
- 👆 INTERACTIVITY
- ⚗ VIRTUAL LAB
- ☑ ASSESSMENT
- 📖 eTEXT
- ⚗ HANDS-ON LABS

The Essential Question

How do systems interact in the human body?

CCC Systems and System Models Walking on a slackline requires good balance and coordination. What different actions are taking place in the the body of the person on the slackline?

....

....

....

....

....

Quest KICKOFF

How do your body systems interact when you train for your favorite sport?

Phenomenon Nutritionists and physical trainers study human body systems and how they interact to help athletes maintain peak performance. In this Quest activity, you will develop a training plan for an athlete. In digital activities and labs, you will investigate how body systems interact to supply energy, manage materials, and control processes in order to develop a well-rounded plan. By applying what you have learned, you will produce a training and nutrition presentation for the athlete.

NBC LEARN ▶ VIDEO

After watching the video, which explores a typical day in the life of a teen athlete, think about the requirements of playing a physically demanding sport. List the following in order of importance, with the first being the most important: strength, endurance, flexibility.

1 ....

2 ....

3 ....

 INTERACTIVITY

Peak Performance Plan

MS-LS1-3 Use argument supported by evidence for how the body is a system of interacting subsystems composed of groups of cells.

MS-LS1-8 Gather and synthesize information that sensory receptors respond to stimuli by sending messages to the brain for immediate behavior or storage as memories.

IN LESSON 1
What are the functions of body systems? Think about the body systems that are most important to the athlete's performance.

Quest CHECK-IN

IN LESSON 2
What skills, movements, and processes are involved in the athlete playing the sport? Identify the system interactions that are required by the sport.

 INTERACTIVITY

Training Systems

Quest CHECK-IN

IN LESSON 3
What are the athlete's nutritional needs? Design a nutrition plan for your athlete that maximizes his or her performance.

 INTERACTIVITY

Training Table

A training program designed for this athlete prepared his body to accomplish his personal goal of running through a desert.

Quest CHECK-IN

IN LESSON 4

What effect does the body's demand for more energy have on the circulatory and respiratory systems? Determine how different activities affect heart and respiration rates.

HANDS-ON LAB

Heart Beat, Health Beat

Quest CHECK-IN

IN LESSON 5

What is muscle memory? Consider how training the nervous system can improve the athlete's performance.

INTERACTIVITY

Why Practice Makes Perfect

Quest FINDINGS

Complete the Quest!

Organize your findings about system interactions and nutrition to develop a presentation for your athlete.

INTERACTIVITY

Reflect on Peak Performance Plan

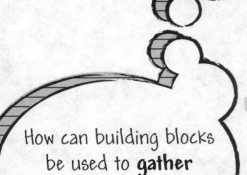

How can building blocks be used to **gather evidence** about how the body is organized?

(per group)
• interlocking plastic blocks

How Is Your Body Organized?

Background

Phenomenon Have you ever had to make a model for a school project? Maybe you had to build a historic monument using craft sticks. As you glued individual craft sticks together, you built a wall. Once the walls were built, you could attach other structures such as a roof. Eventually, you had a complete building. The individual, simple craft sticks became more complex structures as you built your monument.

Your body also has different levels of organization, from simple to complex. You may know that cells are the basic units of structure and function. Other levels of organization include tissues and organs. In this activity, you will devise a model of an organ to observe how the body is a system of interacting subsystems composed of groups of cells.

Develop Your Model

1. **SEP Develop Models** Using interlocking plastic blocks, you and your group will devise a model of an organ that can demonstrate how the body is a system of interacting subsystems made up of cells. As you develop your plan, consider the following criteria:

   • Your model must consist of at least three different tissue groupings.
   • The cells that make up each of the different tissues should be easily identifiable.
   • The different types of tissues should stand out.

2. **SEP Develop Models** After agreeing on a plan, write out the steps that your group will follow to develop the model. Include a sketch of the model. Label the parts and identify what they represent.

Plan and Sketch

HANDS-ON LAB

Connect Go online for a downloadable worksheet of this lab.

Analyze and Interpret Data

1. **CCC System Models** What characteristics does each section of your model have in common? What makes each section different?

   ....

   ....

2. **CCC Systems** How do you think the similarities and differences relate to the function of each part of your model?

   ....

   ....

   ....

3. **SEP Engage in Argument** Based on the evidence from your model, construct an argument that supports or refutes the idea that the body is a system of interacting subsystems.

   ....

   ....

   ....

4. **CCC System Models** Swap your organ model with another group. Examine the model. Are you able to recognize the cells and tissues? How could the other group's model be improved?

   ....

   ....

   ....

   ....

(1) Body Organization

Guiding Questions

- How do groups of cells form interacting subsystems in the body?
- How do the structures of specialized organs relate to their functions in the body?

Connections

Literacy Support Author's Claim

Math Identify Equivalent Expressions

MS-LS1-3

HANDS-ON LAB

uInvestigate Consider how the structures of cells and tissues relate to their functions in the body.

Vocabulary

tissue
organ
organ system

Academic Vocabulary

organized

Connect It !

🖉 **Circle an instrument panel that the co-pilot might control. The co-pilot sits on the right side.**

CCC Structure and Function If an airplane has parts that function like a person's parts, then what part of the body does the pilot represent? Explain your reasoning.

....

....

....

Organization of the Body

Driving a car safely requires constant attention, even in the best road conditions. Controlling an airplane is even more demanding. For a plane to fly safely to its destination, all of its systems must be in good working order. The plane's steering system, brake system, lights, tires, and jet engines are all vital to a safe flight. The pilot and the co-pilot must be skilled at operating the instrument panels shown in **Figure 1**. They have to be able to steer the plane safely through all sorts of conditions. At times, they must fly the plane while relying on the instruments and screens in the cockpit, because they cannot see where the plane is headed.

Like an airplane, your body is **organized** into systems that work together. For example, your digestive and circulatory systems work together to help the cells in your body get the energy they need to function. When you walk up the stairs or ride a bike, your nervous, skeletal, and muscular systems are working together to move your body. Each system is made up of smaller parts, with the smallest being the cells that form the basic units of every living thing. Just as an airplane cannot function properly without its landing gear or its electrical system, the same is true for your body: You need each of your systems so that you can survive and grow.

☑ **READING CHECK** **Support Author's Claim** How is the human body similar to an airplane?

....

....

Academic Vocabulary

What steps do you take to get organized for an upcoming project?

....

....

....

....

All Systems Go
Figure 1 All systems in an airplane, including the pilot and co-pilot, must function properly in order to operate the plane.

Levels of Organization

The smooth functioning of your body depends on its organization. Recall that the levels of organization in the human body are cells, tissues, organs, and organ systems. All tissues are made up of cells. Organs are made of different kinds of tissues. And organ systems are made from organs that work together to perform bodily functions.

Cells and Tissues You are alive because specialized cells are performing their functions throughout your body. When similar cells that perform the same function are grouped together they form a **tissue.** Muscle tissue, for example, contracts, or shortens, to make parts of your body move. Nerve tissue carries electrical signals from the brain all over the body and back again. Connective tissue, such as bone and fat, provides support for your body and attaches all of its parts together. Skin, the largest organ in the human body, has epithelial (ep uh THEE lee ul) tissue that protects your insides from damage. Epithelial tissue covers the inner and outer surfaces of your body.

Math Toolbox

Counting Cells in the Body

Scientists and mathematicians have wondered about the number of cells in the human body for centuries. Estimates of the number of cells have ranged from 100 billion to 1 quadrillion, or a 1 followed by 15 zeros! It's easier to write one quadrillion using exponents: 1×10^{15} where the exponent 15 is the number of zeros.

A team of European scientists recently completed a new estimate of the human cells in an average person. Their estimate is about 37 trillion cells per person.

Name	Number	Written with Power of Ten Exponent
million	1,000,000	1×10^6
billion	1,000,000,000	1×10^9
trillion	1,000,000,000,000	1×10^{12}
quadrillion	1,000,000,000,000,000	1×10^{15}

1. SEP Use Mathematics How do you write 37 trillion as a number and using the power of ten exponent?

....

2. CCC Scale, Proportion, and Quantity How does the new European estimate compare to the smallest and largest estimates of other research groups?

....

....

Organs and Systems Your kidneys, heart, brain, and skin are all organs. An **organ** is a body structure composed of different kinds of tissues that work together. Each organ has a specific function in the body. Because its structure is more complex, the job of an organ is usually more complex than that of a tissue. For example, kidneys remove waste from your blood and form urine. Each kidney contains muscle, connective, and epithelial tissues. In addition, nervous tissue connects to the kidney and helps to control its function. Look at **Figure 2** to see where the different kinds of tissue are found in the kidney. Each tissue contributes in a different way to the kidney's job of filtering blood.

Every organ is part of an **organ system**, which is a group of organs that work together, performing major functions. For example, your kidneys are part of your excretory system. The excretory system also includes the skin, lungs, and liver.

☑ READING CHECK **Summarize Text** What type of cells work together to make a tissue?

....

....

HANDS-ON LAB

и**Investigate** Consider how the structures of cells and tissues relate to their functions in the body.

Many Tissues Make an Organ

Figure 2 Kidneys filter blood to remove waste and excess water.

CCC Structure and Function What might happen to a kidney if the muscle tissue does not function properly?

....

....

....

....

Epithelial tissue in the renal cortex gives the kidney structure and protects the nephrons that filter the blood.

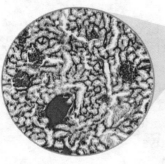

Renal capsule covering connective and fat tissues also protects the kidney.

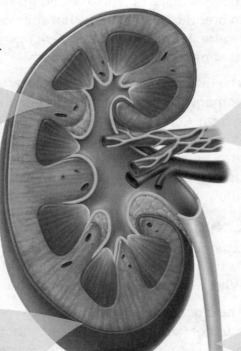

Nerve cells help the kidney pump and filter blood.

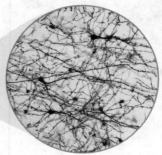

Muscle cells in the ureter drain urine to the bladder.

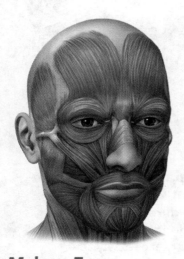

Make a Face

Figure 3 A multitude of facial muscles allows for a variety of expressions.

CCC Structure and Function ✏ Draw an *X* on the muscles involved in blinking your eyes.

▶ **VIDEO**

Find out how your body is like an orchestra.

Human Organ Systems

Eleven major organ systems keep the human body running smoothly. All of the systems work together to support proper functioning.

Control Systems To function properly, each part of your body must be able to communicate with other parts of your body. Your body communicates using the nervous system, which is made up of the brain, spinal cord, and nerves. The nervous system sends information through nerve cells to control your actions.

Many body functions are controlled through the endocrine system, a collection of glands that produces important chemicals. The chemicals in turn affect your energy level, body temperature, digestion, and even your moods!

Structural Systems Three organ systems work to shape, move, and protect your body. The skeletal system includes your bones and connective tissues. The main functions of the skeletal system support your body, protect your organs, make blood cells, and store minerals. Connective tissues cushion the bones and attach bones to muscles.

The muscular system includes 650 muscles that control your movements, help you to stand up straight, and allow you to breathe. The muscles that control your face are shown in **Figure 3**. The muscular system also keeps your blood and your food moving through your body.

The integumentary system protects your body from outside damage. Skin, hair, and nails are all parts of the integumentary system. Oil and sweat glands under the skin help to keep your skin waterproof and your temperature comfortable. Your skin is attached to muscles, which are anchored to bones by connective tissue. Together, these three systems provide your shape and allow you to move your body in many ways.

Oxygen and Transport Systems The respiratory system brings in oxygen and moves out carbon dioxide by way of the lungs. As you breathe in fresh air, oxygen diffuses into the red blood cells. When you breathe out, carbon dioxide diffuses back into the air.

The circulatory system carries oxygen-rich blood to all the parts of your body. Your heart pumps the blood through your blood vessels. Blood cells pass oxygen to your cells and pick up carbon dioxide. Your veins then bring the blood back to your heart and lungs. The circulatory system also transports nutrients, wastes, and disease-fighting cells all over your body through your bloodstream.

Food and Waste Processing Systems Food you put into your mouth begins a journey through your digestive system. Your esophagus squeezes the food down into the stomach, where the food is crushed and broken down by acids. Next, the food travels into the intestines. Useful substances pass through the intestinal walls into the blood. The liver and pancreas produce substances that help to break down food. So do trillions of bacteria that live in your intestines. Some parts of the food cannot be digested. Those parts pass out of your body as waste. You can think of the digestive system as a long tube that runs through your body. Food passes through the tube and back out into the world without ever entering the tissues of your body.

The excretory system gets rid of waste products and toxic substances in your body. Kidneys produce urine, sweat glands in your skin make sweat, and lungs release wastes from the body into the air. Meanwhile, the liver breaks down toxic chemicals into substances that the kidneys can pull out of your blood.

✓ **READING CHECK** **Determine Conclusions** What would happen if your organ systems stopped functioning properly?

....

....

Literacy Connection

Support Author's Claim
Is it true that the human body can make its own chemicals? Cite evidence from the text.

....

....

....

....

Model It!

What? No Bones?
Figure 4 Most of the known animals on Earth are invertebrates. These organisms lack the backbone found in humans, birds, reptiles, and other vertebrates.

SEP Develop Models ✏ Choose a kind of invertebrate— snail, insect, worm, octopus, water bear (shown here), and spider are just a few. Consider how an animal maintains its structure with no bones. Then sketch a diagram to explain how your animal moves with no bones connected to its muscles.

Organ Systems in the Human Body

Figure 5 The structures of different body systems all work together to allow you to grow, obtain energy, move, stay healthy, and reproduce.

CCC Systems and System Models ✏ Use the key on the right to label each body system. There may be more than one function for each system.

	Skeletal	Integumentary	Muscular	Circulatory	Respiratory
BODY SYSTEM	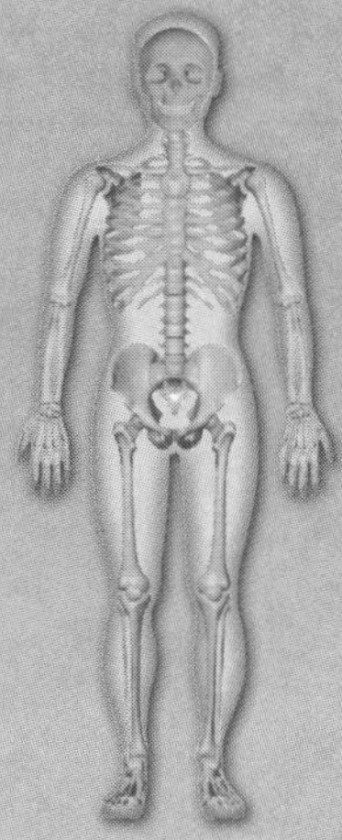	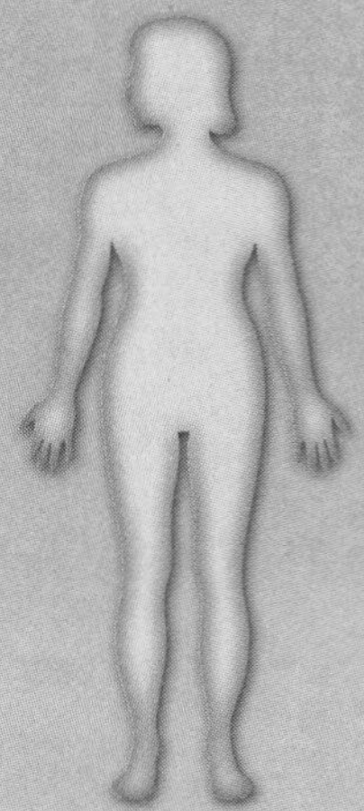	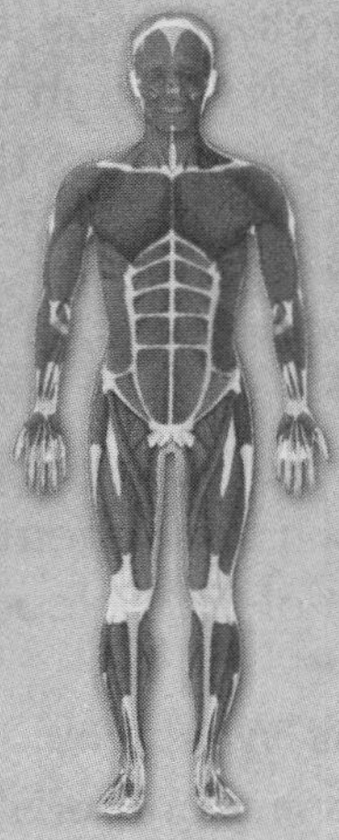	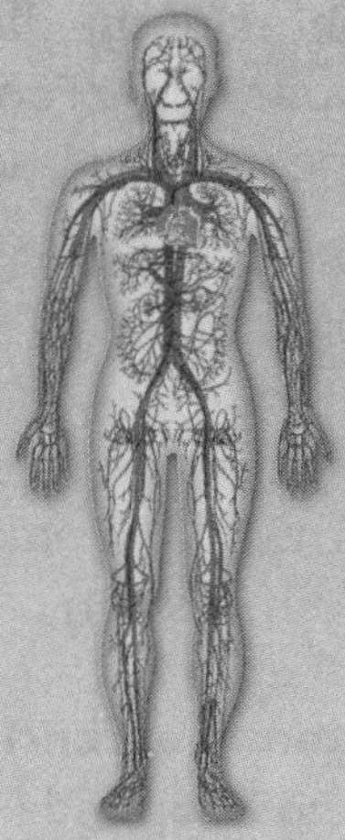	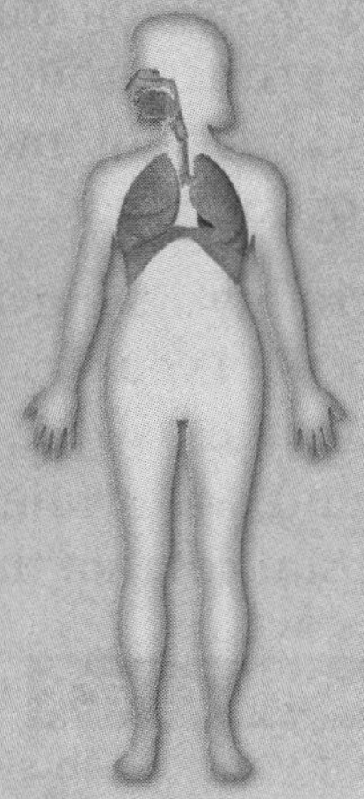
STRUCTURES	Bones, cartilage, ligaments, tendons	Skin, hair, nails, sweat glands, oil glands	Skeletal muscle, smooth muscle, cardiac muscle	Heart, blood vessels	Nose, pharynx, larynx, trachea, bronchi, lungs
FUNCTIONS	Supports body; protects internal organs; allows movement; stores minerals; produces blood cells	Guards against infection and injury; helps regulate body temperature	With skeletal system, produces movement; helps circulate blood and move food through the digestive system	Transports oxygen, nutrients, and wastes; fights infection; helps regulate body temperature	Brings in oxygen needed by cells; removes carbon dioxide from body

👆 **INTERACTIVITY**

Explore the structures and functions of different body systems.

Defense System The immune system is your defense system against infections. Lymph nodes and lymph vessels trap bacteria and viruses. "Swollen glands" are lymph nodes that have grown larger to fight off an infection. White blood cells produced inside your bones also attack and destroy bacteria and other causes of disease. As shown in **Figure 5** above, many different organs work together to help to fight off invading disease organisms.

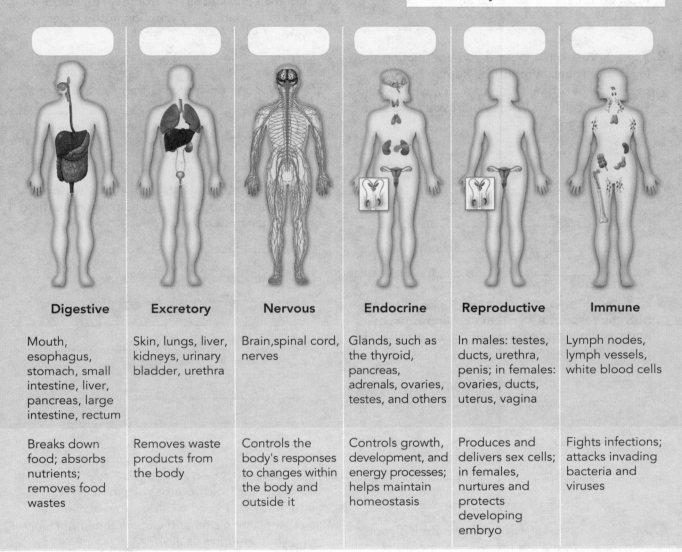

KEY
A Structural Support System
B Oxygen and Transport System
C Food and Waste Processing System
D Defense System
E Reproductive System
F Control System

Digestive	Excretory	Nervous	Endocrine	Reproductive	Immune
Mouth, esophagus, stomach, small intestine, liver, pancreas, large intestine, rectum	Skin, lungs, liver, kidneys, urinary bladder, urethra	Brain, spinal cord, nerves	Glands, such as the thyroid, pancreas, adrenals, ovaries, testes, and others	In males: testes, ducts, urethra, penis; in females: ovaries, ducts, uterus, vagina	Lymph nodes, lymph vessels, white blood cells
Breaks down food; absorbs nutrients; removes food wastes	Removes waste products from the body	Controls the body's responses to changes within the body and outside it	Controls growth, development, and energy processes; helps maintain homeostasis	Produces and delivers sex cells; in females, nurtures and protects developing embryo	Fights infections; attacks invading bacteria and viruses

Reproductive System The reproductive system is responsible for producing sperm and eggs and (in females) for nurturing the fetus until birth. Male reproductive organs include the testes (also known as testicles) and the penis. Female reproductive organs include the ovaries, uterus, and vagina. A cell can reproduce itself to make a new cell, but it takes a whole organ system to create a new human.

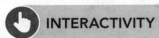 **INTERACTIVITY**

Explain how the human body is organized and how different body systems work together.

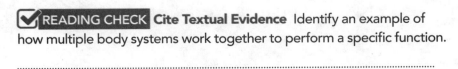 **READING CHECK Cite Textual Evidence** Identify an example of how multiple body systems work together to perform a specific function.

....

....

121

☑ LESSON 1 Check

1. CCC Patterns What is the level of organization in the human body from the least to the most complex?

....

2. SEP Develop Models If you are relating the levels of organization of the human body to the levels of organization of a city, what would you relate cells to? What would you relate the other levels to?

....

....

....

....

....

3. CCC Systems and System Models Explain how the respiratory system exchanges oxygen and carbon dioxide between the air and cells in the body.

....

....

....

....

....

....

4. Apply Concepts How could you tell if your immune system were not functioning well?

....

....

....

5. SEP Construct Explanations If the brain is the control center of the body, why does it have nerves connected to your organs?

....

....

....

....

6. CCC Structure and Function The thin layer of epithelial tissue in the small intestines works somewhat like a cell membrane. How does its structure relate to its function in the digestive system?

....

....

....

....

....

7. CCC Systems and System Models How does learning about organs help us understand how organ systems work?

....

....

....

....

....

....

....

....

....

8. SEP Construct an Argument A younger neighbor just told you that organs are large structures that keep us alive. How would you support their claim, and explain the importance of cells in keeping us alive?

....

....

....

....

....

....

....

....

Artificial SKiN

👆 **INTERACTIVITY**

Identify criteria, constraints, and materials that need to be considered when building an artificial limb.

How do you help people who suffer due to severely damaged skin? You engineer new skin for them! Bioengineers may have solved a big problem.

The Challenge: To grow artificial skin that functions like the real thing.

Phenomenon Until recently, using artificial skin presented doctors with challenges and risks. Without hair follicles and oil glands, the skin could not function properly to help maintain homeostasis, the process that keeps internal conditions in the body stable. But new developments in cell research and bioengineering may have overcome this obstacle.

To make the artificial skin, bioengineers took cells from the mouths of mice. After treating the cells with chemicals, the scientists were able to form random clumps of a mix of cell types that you might find in a newly fertilized egg.

When researchers placed these cells into other mice, the cells gradually changed into specialized tissue. Once this happened, the scientists transplanted them out of those mice and into the skin tissue of other mice. Here the tissues developed normally as integumentary tissue, with hair follicles and oil glands. They also discovered that the implanted tissues made normal connections with the surrounding nerve and muscle tissues, allowing the different body systems to interact normally.

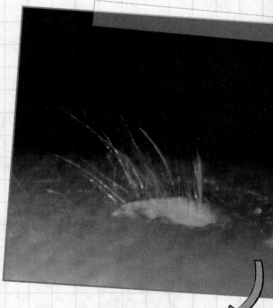

This artificial skin (genetically modified to "glow" green) is able to function just like real skin. It can grow hair and is able to sweat.

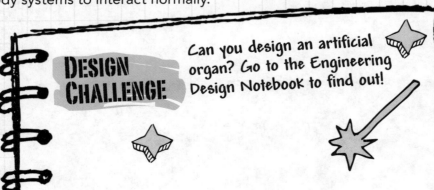

DESIGN CHALLENGE

Can you design an artificial organ? Go to the Engineering Design Notebook to find out!

LESSON

2 Systems Interacting

Guiding Questions

- How do organ systems interact to carry out all the necessary functions for an organism's growth and survival?
- How do organ systems interact to maintain homeostasis?

Connection

Literacy Cite Textual Evidence

MS-LS1-3

HANDS-ON LAB

uInvestigate Identify the body systems used to perform specific actions.

Vocabulary

stimulus
response
gland
hormone
stress

Academic Vocabulary

interactions
stable

Connect It!

In the space provided on the image, list the body systems that you think are involved in skateboarding.

CCC Systems and System Models If one of these body systems were to stop interacting with the other systems, would this activity still be possible? Explain.

....

....

....

Systems Working Together

All the systems in the human body work together to perform all the necessary functions for life. Cells need oxygen provided by the respiratory system and carried by the circulatory system. Organs carry out commands from the nervous system. And every part of the body changes its activities based on signals from the endocrine system.

Movement How is the skateboarder in **Figure 1** able to do what she does? **Interactions** between the skeletal, muscular, and nervous systems make it possible. Skeletal muscles are attached to the bones of the skeleton and provide the force that moves bones. Muscles contract and relax. When a muscle contracts, it shortens and pulls on the bones to which it is attached.

Try standing on one leg and bending the other leg at the knee. Hold that position. You can feel that you are using the muscles at the back of your thigh. Your nervous system controls when and how your muscles act on your bones.

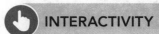

INTERACTIVITY

Explore how joints function in the human body.

Academic Vocabulary

What kinds of interactions are there between people in your neighborhood?

....

....

....

....

Poetry in Motion
Figure 1 We can accomplish impressive feats when all the body's systems are working together properly.

Controlling Body Functions The nervous system has two ways of controlling body functions: electrical signals from nerves and chemical signals from the endocrine system. Both methods help you to respond to your environment.

Transporting Materials

All cells need oxygen and nutrients, and they need to get rid of carbon dioxide and other wastes. But most cells are locked into position with no way to move in search of food. So how can they stay alive? The answer is that blood vessels from the circulatory system carry nutrients to and waste from the cells in the body. Blood vessels divide into smaller and smaller branches until the tiniest, called capillaries, are only as wide as one blood cell. Capillaries, visible in **Figure 2**, pass near every cell in the body.

Blood picks up oxygen from the lungs and food molecules from the intestines and delivers them to needy cells. At the same time, blood collects carbon dioxide and waste from the cells. The carbon dioxide is returned to the lungs to be released into the air. Waste products are filtered from the blood by the kidneys in the excretory system and passed out of the body in urine.

✓ READING CHECK **Determine Meaning** Why do the capillaries have to be so small?

....

....

Special Delivery
Figure 2 Blood cells, like those shown in the inset, travel through a network of blood vessels to transport materials to and from every part of the body.

CCC Structure and Function How do you think a blocked blood vessel would affect an organism?

....

....

....

....

....

....

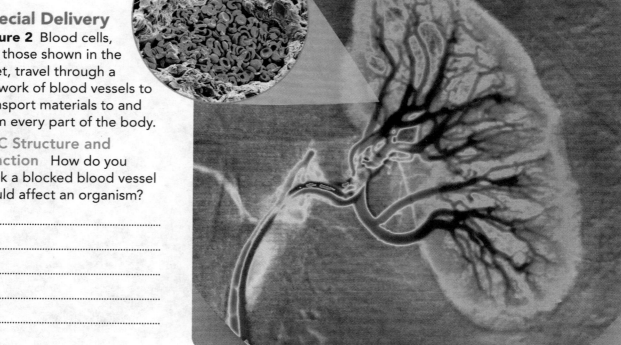

Stimulus and Response Your eyes, ears, skin, nose, and taste buds all send information about your environment to your nervous system. Your senses let you react to loud noises, hot objects, and the odor of your favorite food. Any change or signal in the environment that can make an organism react in some way is called a **stimulus** (plural: stimuli). A **response** is an action or change in behavior that occurs as a result of a stimulus. Responses are directed by your nervous system but often involve other body systems as well. Your muscular and skeletal systems help you reach for food, and your digestive system releases saliva before the food even reaches your mouth. **Figure 3** shows an example of stimulus and response used in an American Sign Language expression.

 **INTERACTIVITY**

Investigate how different body systems work together.

Plan It

Reaction Time

The time that passes between a stimulus and a response is the reaction time. A short reaction time could save you from a fall or a burn, and it might help you beat video games.

SEP Plan an Investigation Plan an investigation to measure reaction times under different conditions. Choose two or three factors that you suspect may influence reaction time, such as time of day, type of stimulus, environmental conditions, or state of mental alertness. How could you display your results?

....
....
....
....
....
....
....
....
....
....
....
....
....
....

Don't Burn Your Mouth

Figure 3 The American Sign Language expression for *hot* shows a reaction to hot food.

Apply Concepts Use the terms *stimulus* and *response* to explain what the sign is expressing.

....

....

....

....

Investigate Identify the body systems used to perform specific actions.

Hormonal Control

The endocrine system uses chemical signals instead of nerves to control body functions. The endocrine system is made up of many **glands**, organs that produce and release chemicals either through tiny tubes called ducts or directly into the bloodstream. For example, when something startles you, your adrenal glands send signals that prepare you to fight or run away. Your heart pumps faster, your lungs let in more air, and your ability to feel pain decreases. The pupils of your eyes even grow larger and allow in more light. You are ready for action.

The chemical produced by an endocrine gland is called a **hormone**. Hormones are carried through your body by the circulatory system. These chemicals affect many body processes. One hormone interacts with the excretory system and the circulatory system to control the amount of water in the bloodstream. Another hormone interacts with the digestive system and the circulatory system to control the amount of sugar in the bloodstream. Hormones also affect the reproductive systems of both males and females. **Figure 4** shows some of the effects of hormones on boys during puberty.

☑ READING CHECK **Cite Textual Evidence** What text on this page supports the idea that the endocrine system functions differently from the nervous system?

....

....

....

Hormones and Puberty

Figure 4 Hormones can have dramatic and long-lasting effects.

CCC Stability and Change Identify some of the changes you see between the before-puberty and after-puberty pictures.

....

....

....

Interacting Systems

Figure 5 This swimmer's body systems work together as she pushes herself to excel.

CCC Systems Read the descriptions of functions happening in the swimmer's body. Then identify the main systems involved.

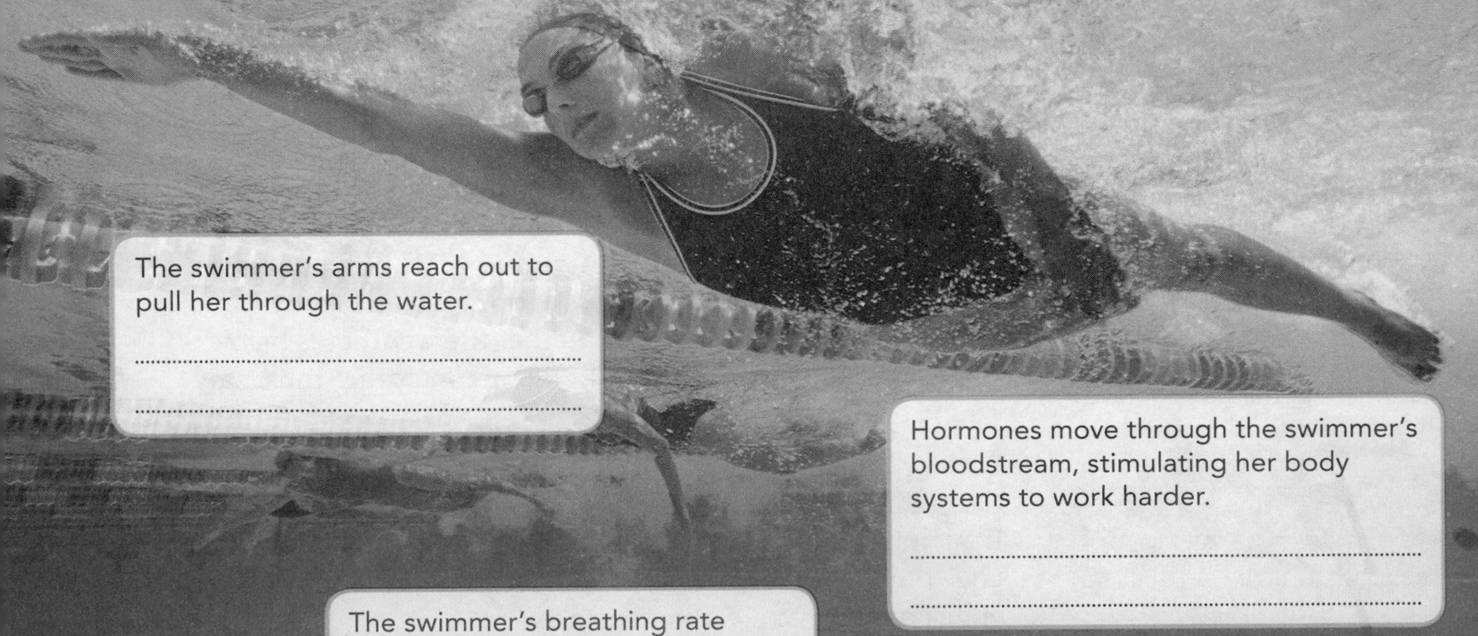

Food from the swimmer's breakfast has been broken down into nutrients and is delievered to cells.

....

....

The swimmer's brain interprets what her eyes see and directs her movements.

....

....

....

Carbon dioxide moves rapidly out of the swimmer's lungs. Cell wastes move into her blood and are filtered by her kidneys.

....

....

....

The swimmer's arms reach out to pull her through the water.

....

....

Hormones move through the swimmer's bloodstream, stimulating her body systems to work harder.

....

....

The swimmer's breathing rate and heart rate increase, supplying more oxygen to her muscle cells.

....

....

Cooling Down

Figure 6 The woman in the first image is using several different ways to warm up.

Apply Concepts Identify some ways the woman in the second drawing might cool her body and maintain a constant body temperature.

....

....

....

Academic Vocabulary

Stable is a common word to describe something that hasn't changed much and isn't expected to change much in the future. Make a list of some things you have heard described as stable.

....

....

....

....

 VIDEO

Find out how a house's heating system is like your body.

Homeostasis

What happens when you go outside in the cold? Does your body temperature fall to meet the outside temperature? It does not, and that's a very good thing! Your body only functions well around 37°C. It is vitally important for your body to maintain that temperature. Whether the weather is below freezing or roasting hot, your body's temperature must stay **stable** and remain close to 37°C.

Each organism requires specific conditions to function. Maintaining those conditions is necessary for life to continue. Remember that the condition in which an organism's internal environment is kept stable in spite of changes in the outside environment is called homeostasis.

Regulating Temperature When your body temperature starts to fall too low, as shown in **Figure 6**, your nervous system sends out signals to your other systems to take action to warm you up. Your skin, which is part of the integumentary system, develops goosebumps. Your muscles cause you to shiver. You tend to move your large muscles to generate heat. All of these actions help to raise your temperature back to normal.

Keeping Balance Structures in your inner ear sense the position of your head. They send this information to your brain, which interprets the signals. If your brain senses that you are losing your balance, then it sends messages to your muscles to move in ways that help you stay steady. **Figure 7** shows the cycle of how your body keeps its balance.

Meeting Energy Needs When the cells in your body need more energy, hormones from the endocrine system signal the nervous system to make you feel hungry. After you eat, other hormones signal your brain to make you feel full.

Maintaining Water Balance All the chemical reactions that keep you alive take place within the watery environment of your cells. If your body needs more water, then your nervous system causes you to feel thirsty. Your senses, muscles, and skeleton take you to a source of water. After you have had enough water, your nervous system causes your thirst to end. Soon after, the water passes through your digestive system to your circulatory system and from there into your cells. Water balance is restored!

INTERACTIVITY

Explain how body systems interact to maintain homeostasis.

Maintaining Homeostasis
Figure 7 Interactions among your ears, brain, and muscular system make up the balance cycle.

SEP Communicate Information 🖉 Fill in the missing steps to create a diagram of the thirst cycle.

✓ **READING CHECK**
Translate Information What role does the nervous system play in maintaining homeostasis? Explain.

....

....

....

....

....

....

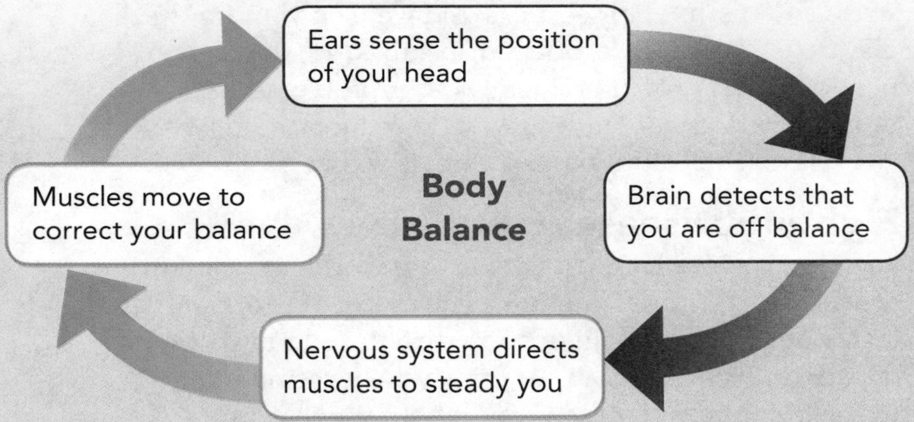

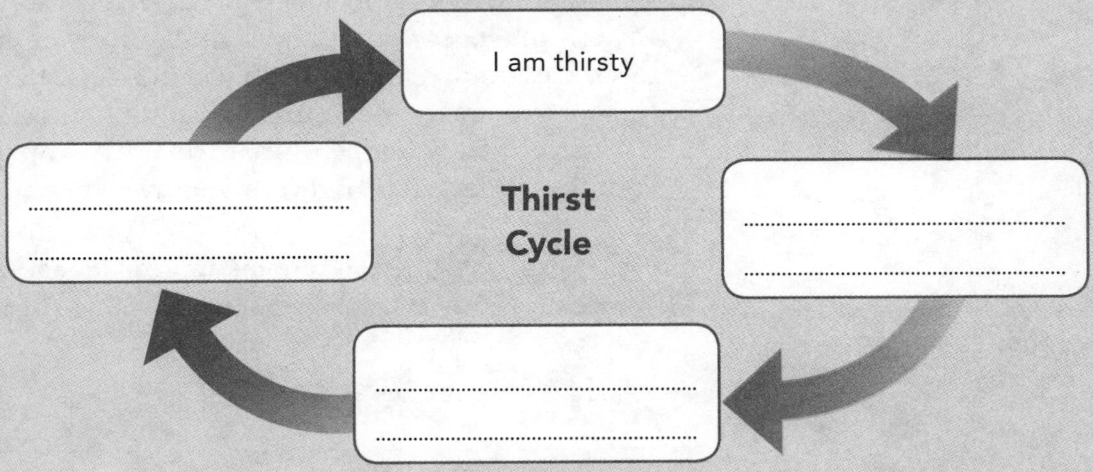

Body Balance

- Ears sense the position of your head
- Brain detects that you are off balance
- Nervous system directs muscles to steady you
- Muscles move to correct your balance

Thirst Cycle

- I am thirsty
- ....
- ....
- ....

Defense Against Disease

Figure 8 The green cell is an immune cell. It engulfs the orange and blue bacteria cells, and destroys them.

Apply Concepts How do you think the immune system is affected by stress?

....

....

....

....

....

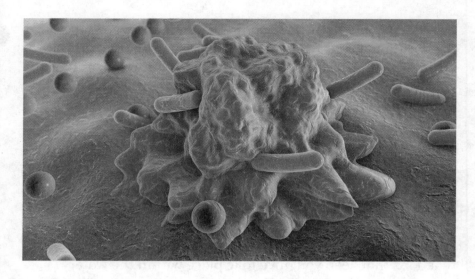

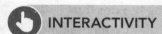

INTERACTIVITY

Analyze symptoms to see what body systems are affected by an illness.

VIDEO

Go inside the world of a medical illustrator.

Managing Stress In general, **stress** is the reaction of a person's body to potentially threatening, challenging, or disturbing events. Each person experiences stress differently. One person may enjoy taking on the challenge of a math test, while someone else might freeze with fear.

Some stress is unavoidable. If stress is over quickly, then the body returns to its normal, healthy condition. However, too much stress for too long a time can be unhealthy. Ongoing stress can disrupt homeostasis and weaken your body's ability to fight disease. Stress also can cause depression, headaches, digestion problems, heart problems, and other health issues. Finding ways to reduce and relieve stress is an important part of a healthy lifestyle.

Fighting Disease When your body systems are in balance, you are healthy. Germs that cause disease can disrupt homeostasis and make you sick. Think about the last time you had a cold or strep throat. You may have had a fever and less energy. Your body was devoting resources to the immune system so it could fight the disease.

The immune system includes specialized cells, such as the one in **Figure 8**, that attack and destroy germs, such as viruses and bacteria. When you are sick, these cells temporarily increase in number. Fighting infection sometimes causes your body temperature to go up. As you get well, your fever goes away and your energy comes back.

✓ READING CHECK **Determine Central Ideas** What role does homeostasis play in helping your body handle stress and fight disease?

....

....

....

MS-LS1-3

1. **Define** What is a hormone?

....

....

2. **Analyze Systems** What are four conditions in the body related to maintaining homeostasis?

....

....

3. **Compare and Contrast** How are chemical signals and electrical signals alike? How are they different?

....

....

....

....

4. **CCC Cause and Effect** Explain how getting sick can affect the body's ability to maintain homeostasis.

....

....

....

....

5. **CCC Matter and Energy** Pick one material that is moved within the body by the organ systems. Describe which systems are involved and how they work together.

....

....

....

....

....

....

6. **Draw Conclusions** Explain how the circulatory system interacts with other body systems to maintain homeostasis.

....

....

....

....

....

7. **SEP Develop Models** ✐ Start with the sentence "I feel hungry." In the space below, draw a cycle diagram to show how your body would respond to this situation.

Quest CHECK-IN

In this lesson, you learned about how body systems interact with one another to carry out functions necessary for growth and survival. You also explored how body systems interact to maintain homeostasis.

CCC Systems Why is it important to understand how different body systems interact when developing a training plan?

....

....

....

👆 INTERACTIVITY

Training Systems

Go online to identify body systems with their functions and use that information to begin a training plan.

MS-LS1-3

AGENTS OF
Infection

Medical professionals and patients need to take safety precautions, such as hand washing, to prevent the spread of infection.

Your immune system is constantly working to fight off infections. Most of the time, the lymph nodes, lymph vessels, and white blood cells that are part of your immune system are able to attack invading viruses and bacteria to fight off infection. But some agents of infection are harder to conquer than others...

There are thousands of living and nonliving things that cause infections. The living ones include bacteria, fungi, worms, and single-celled organisms called protists. A bacterium is responsible for strep throat. Ringworm is caused by a fungus. Dysentery can result from a bacterial infection as well as amoebas. The good news about being infected with one of these organisms is that, for the most part, the infections they cause can be cured with medical treatment. There are also a number of ways that you can protect yourself from infections. For example, you can reduce your chances of getting or spreading an infection by washing your hands and by avoiding touching your face if your hands are not clean.

Nonliving viruses also cause infections. Viruses can cause diseases such as HIV, the common cold, and chicken pox. Only a few medications can treat them. A virus is hard to treat because it uses living cells to make copies of itself. These cells are damaged or destroyed when the new virus particles are released. The virus particles then infect other cells. Depending on the type of infection, people may get better over time. Sometimes a viral infection is so severe that symptoms never go away and conditions worsen.

You may have heard of the Zika virus or the flesh-eating bacterium *Vibrio vulnificus*. Each of these causes serious symptoms in people, often requiring hospitalization. Read about some of these infections in the table.

This bacterium is responsible for causing strep throat.

Infectious Agent	Type of Organism	Cause/Transmission	Symptoms	Treatment
Zika	Virus	Mosquito bites or transmission from infected person	Fever, rash, joint pain	There is no specific medicine or vaccine for Zika virus.
Brain-eating *Naegleria fowleri*	Amoeba	Infection occurs most often from diving, water skiing, or other water sports when water is forced into the nose.	Headache, fever, stiff neck, loss of appetite, seizures, coma	A number of drugs kill *N. fowleri* amoebas in the test tube. But even when treated with these drugs, very few patients survive.
Flesh-eating *Vibrio vulnificus*	Bacterium	It releases a toxin that causes the immune system to release white blood cells that destroy the individual's flesh.	Sweats, fever, and chills with red, swollen, blister-like patches on the body	Either the affected tissue has to be amputated, or antibiotics have to be administered.

Use the text and the table to answer the following questions.

1. Determine Differences How are viruses different from other infectious agents, such as bacteria and fungi?

2. SEP Engage in Argument from Evidence Do you think science and medicine will ever be able to discover a cure for Zika? Explain.

3. Solve Problems What are some steps you can take to protect yourself against an infectious disease?

(3) Supplying Energy

Guiding Questions

- What are the important nutrients your body needs to carry out its processes?
- How does food become the materials your body can use?
- How do your body's systems process the food you eat?

Connections

Literacy Write Arguments

Math Analyze Proportional Relationships

MS-LS1-3

HANDS-ON LAB

µInvestigate Discover how Calories in different foods are measured.

Vocabulary

digestion
nutrients
carbohydrates
peristalsis
saliva
enzyme

Academic Vocabulary

absorption
elimination

Connect It!

✏ **Circle the food choice the runner should make to get the most energy for the race.**

CCC Energy and Matter Consider your daily activities. Which require the most energy? What would happen if you did not eat enough food?

....

....

Make Generalizations Why are your food choices important?

....

....

....

Food and Energy

What have you done so far today? You woke up, got dressed, ate breakfast, and came to school. Later today, you may have karate, dance, or basketball. You may be running in a race like the people in **Figure 1**. All of these activities require energy. In fact, your cells require energy for all the processes that go on inside your body, including breathing, thinking, and growing.

Living things get energy from food. Plants make their own food. Animals and decomposers get their food by eating other organisms and breaking it down into its component parts. **Digestion** is the process by which your body breaks down food into small nutrient molecules.

Nutrients are the substances in food that provide the raw materials the body's cells need to carry out all their essential processes. Some nutrients are broken down and used for energy. Other nutrients are used to repair damaged cells or to help you grow. Your body needs nutrients to perform every function. Therefore, you constantly need nutrients from food to keep up with the body's demand.

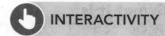

INTERACTIVITY

Learn how our bodies get energized.

Literacy Connection

Write Arguments A classmate claims that an apple and cupcake, both about the same size, give you the same amount of energy. Do you agree or disagree with this statement? Explain.

....

....

....

....

Running Takes Energy
Figure 1 Everything you do in a day takes energy. The cells in your body need a steady supply of energy to keep functioning.

How Sweet It Is

Figure 2 Our bodies can digest simple carbohydrates very quickly so they can give a quick burst of energy.

Form an Opinion ✏ Circle a simple carbohydrate that you think makes a healthy snack. Then, explain why you think that's a better choice than some others.

....

....

....

....

....

....

HANDS-ON LAB

ⁱInvestigate Discover how Calories in different foods are measured.

Main Nutrients The purpose of digestion is the **absorption** of six important nutrients you get from food: carbohydrates, proteins, fats, vitamins, minerals, and water.

Carbohydrates An energy-rich organic compound, such as sugar or a starch, that is made of the elements carbon, hydrogen, and oxygen, is called a **carbohydrate**. They can be quickly broken down and the body can use the energy released in this process. This energy is measured in Calories. High Calorie foods can give you more energy than low Calorie foods.

A carbohydrate can be simple or complex, depending on the size of its molecules. Simple carbohydrates, such as the ones shown in **Figure 2**, are smaller molecules and taste sweet. Complex carbohydrates, such as fiber, are larger molecules. Whole grains, such as brown rice, are considered healthy sources of complex carbohydrates. They are high in fiber and nutrients.

Proteins Your body needs protein for growth and body repair. Proteins are made of smaller components called amino acids. Beans, beef, chicken, eggs, fish, and nuts are all protein sources.

Fats While carbohydrates provide quick energy, fats provide a concentrated energy source and the body also uses fats for long-term energy storage. There are two main types— saturated fat and unsaturated fat. Saturated fats usually come from animal products, such as lard. They are solid at room temperature. Unsaturated fats usually come from plant products and are oils, such as olive oil. They are liquid at room temperature. People should limit saturated fat intake because they are linked to heart disease and other illnesses.

Vitamins Vitamins are nutrients that help your body with chemical reactions. They do not provide any energy or building materials, but without them, you would not be able to function. Your body can make small amounts of some vitamins, such as vitamins D and K, but most have to be taken in through your diet. Vitamins can be fat-soluble or water-soluble. Fat-soluble vitamins, such as A and K, are stored in the fatty tissues of the body and released when needed. Water-soluble vitamins, such as vitamin C, dissolve in water and are not stored in large amounts by the body. Citrus fruits, such as oranges, are high in vitamin C.

Minerals Minerals are nutrients that are not made by the body, but are needed to carry out chemical processes. Calcium for bones and iron for blood are two examples of minerals that are taken in through the diet. Calcium is common in dairy products, such as milk and cheese. Iron is found in meat and leafy green vegetables, such as spinach.

Water Of the six nutrients you need, water is the most important. While the human body can go a few weeks without eating food, it could only survive a few days without water. Survival time without water hinges on both environmental conditions and level of activity. For example, someone hiking in the desert under a blazing sun needs more water than someone in cooler conditions. You get water from much of the food you eat, but you still need to drink water every day.

✓ **READING CHECK** **Cite Textual Evidence** Underline some recommended sources of each of the main nutrients your body needs.

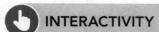

INTERACTIVITY

Discover how food is broken down into bits and pieces in the digestive system.

Reflect Consider the different types of food you eat every day. Are they all equally nutritious?

Plan It!

Nutritionists recommend that people eat a diet that balances the main nutrients while limiting simple carbohydrates, saturated fats, and foods high in salt.

CCC Energy and Matter Describe a dinner you would like to eat that includes all of the main nutrients, but is low in the nutrients that you should limit.

....

....

....

....

....

The Digestive Process

Digestion can be classified into two main types—mechanical and chemical. Mechanical digestion involves the physical breakdown and movement of food. Chemical digestion, as the name suggests, involves the chemical breakdown of food.

Mechanical Digestion The mouth and stomach are the main places where mechanical digestion happens. The movement of the food through the esophagus and the intestines is also part of mechanical digestion. Waves of smooth muscle contractions that move food through the esophagus toward the stomach are called **peristalsis**.

Math Toolbox

Monitoring Sodium Intake

Sodium is a mineral that our bodies need to function. It helps our muscular and nervous systems work and it helps us stay hydrated. However, in certain people too much salt may lead to high blood pressure, which puts people at risk for heart disease, stroke, and other illnesses.

1. **CCC Scale, Proportion, and Quantity** According to the nutrition facts for these potato chips, a serving has 170 mg of sodium, or 7% of the daily recommended value for an average adult. Based on this information, how many milligrams of sodium should an average adult consume in a day? Show your work.

   ....

2. **SEP Use Mathematics** How many servings of potato chips would it take for you reach the maximum amount of sodium you should consume in a day? Show your work.

   ....

   ....

3. **SEP Use Computational Thinking** The American Heart Association recommends that adults consume no more than 1500 mg of sodium a day for optimal heart health. How would this change the percentage of the daily recommended value? How many servings of chips would it take to reach this adjusted maximum daily value?

   ....

   ....

   ....

Nutrition Facts

Serving Size 1 oz (28g/About 15 chips)

Amount Per Serving	
Calories 160	Calories from Fat 90

	% Daily Value*
Total Fat 10g	**16%**
Saturated Fat 1.5g	**8%**
Trans Fat 0g	
Cholesterol 0mg	**0%**
Sodium 170mg	**7%**
Potassium 350mg	**10%**
Total Carbohydrate 15g	**5%**
Dietary Fiber 1g	**5%**
Sugars less than 1g	
Protein 2g	

Vitamin A 0%	•	Vitamin C 10%
Calcium 0%	•	Iron 2%
Vitamin E 6%	•	Thiamin 4%
Niacin 6%	•	Vitamin B_6 10%

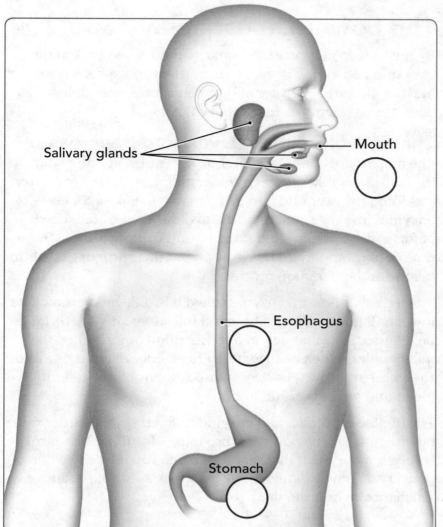

Salivary glands

Mouth

Esophagus

Stomach

Figure 3 The upper digestive system includes the mouth, esophagus, and the stomach.

Synthesize Information
✎ For each part of the digestive system, write M if mechanical digestion takes place and write C if chemical digestion occurs.

Chemical Digestion As shown in **Figure 3**, chemical digestion begins in the mouth. Fluid called **saliva** is released from glands in the mouth and plays an important role in both mechanical and chemical digestion. Your saliva contains chemicals. Some of these chemicals are called enzymes. **Enzymes** are proteins that speed up chemical reactions in the body. Enzymes cause the food to break down faster. Chemical digestion starts in the mouth, which is shown in **Figure 3**, with an enzyme found in saliva. This acts specifically on the carbohydrate starch. Saliva also moistens the food so it can be easily swallowed. Chemical digestion continues in the stomach, where other enzymes and hydrochloric acid further break down food. The partially-digested material then passes into the small intestine, where most chemical digestion takes place.

☑ READING CHECK **Determine Central Ideas** What role do enzymes play on the process of digestion? Explain.

....

....

The Lower Digestive System

By the time food leaves the stomach, it has been broken into very small parts and some of the nutrients have been released. Most of the carbohydrates and proteins have been digested, but fats still remain as large molecules.

The Small Intestine, Liver, and Pancreas

The majority of chemical digestion and nutrient absorption into the blood takes place in the small intestine. Other organs, including the liver and pancreas, shown in **Figure 5**, secrete enzymes into the small intestine to aid with the breakdown of fats and any remaining proteins and carbohydrates. These organs play other roles in the body, but their primary role is to help with the digestion process.

The liver produces an enzyme called bile. Bile breaks down fat into small fat droplets in the small intestine. This allows fat to be digested. Bile is stored in another small organ called the gall bladder. When needed, the gall bladder releases bile into the small intestine. The liver is also responsible for filtering blood and storing certain vitamins.

The pancreas produces an enzyme called trypsin, which breaks down proteins. The pancreas also makes insulin, a chemical involved in a system that monitors blood sugar levels. When a person has Type 1 diabetes, the pancreas does not produce as much insulin as it should.

Got Greens?

Figure 4 Fiber is an important part of a healthy diet. Vegetables are an excellent source of fiber. Because the human body cannot break down fiber, it passes through the digestive system virtually unchanged.

Apply Concepts Why is it important to get plenty of fiber in your diet?

....

....

....

Lower Digestive System

Figure 5 Most chemical digestion takes place in the small intestine.

CCC Structure and Function Why does the gall bladder need to be close to the liver?

....

....

....

....

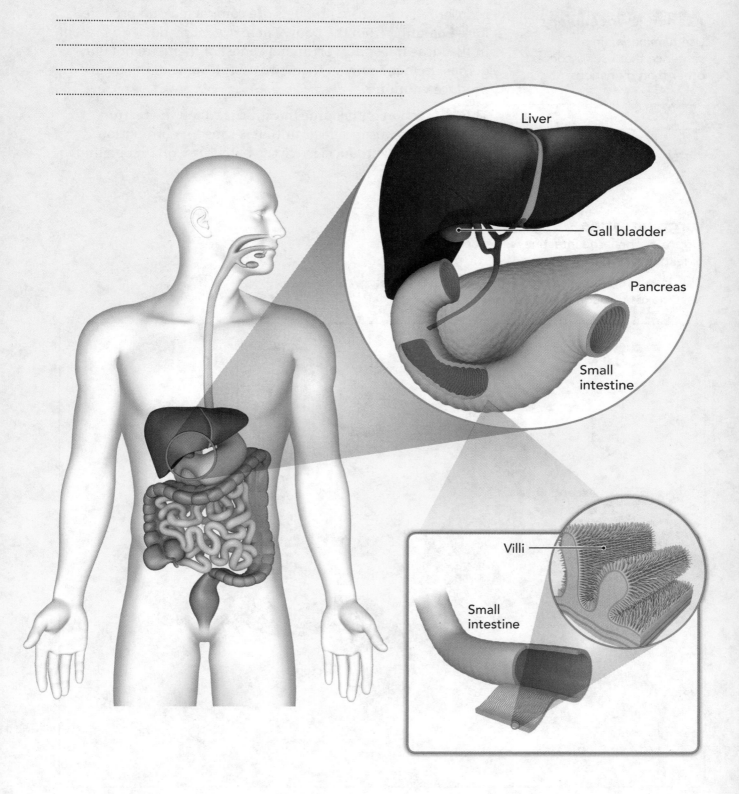

Liver

Gall bladder

Pancreas

Small intestine

Villi

Small intestine

The Large Intestine As shown in **Figure 6**, the last stage of digestion occurs in the large intestine. The large intestine is actually shorter than the small intestine—1.5 m versus 6–8 m. It is in the large intestine that water from food is reabsorbed and waste products are compacted and prepared for **elimination** from the body. There are many bacteria present in the large intestine. Fortunately, most of them are not dangerous. In fact, many of them are useful. Some of the bacteria produce vitamin K.

The last section of the large intestine is called the rectum. This is where waste collects until it is time for elimination. The solid waste products leave the body through an opening called the anus.

Academic Vocabulary

Use *elimination* in a sentence that uses a context other than digestion.

....

....

....

....

Large Intestine

Figure 6 The large intestine is the last section of the digestive system.

SEP Use Models ✏ Draw a line that shows the pathway waste takes through the large intestine.

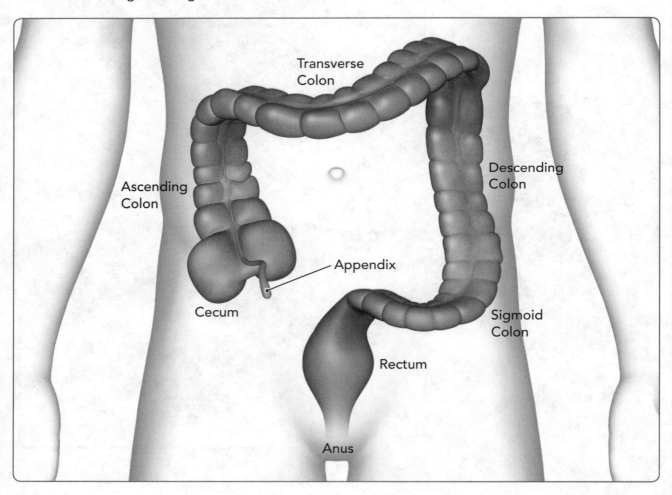

Human Digestive System

Figure 7 Like all body systems, the digestive system relies on many organs working together.

CCC Systems ✏ Circle the names of the organs that provide chemicals for your body to perform chemical digestion. Then, place the pathway of food through the body in sequential order from 1 through 6.

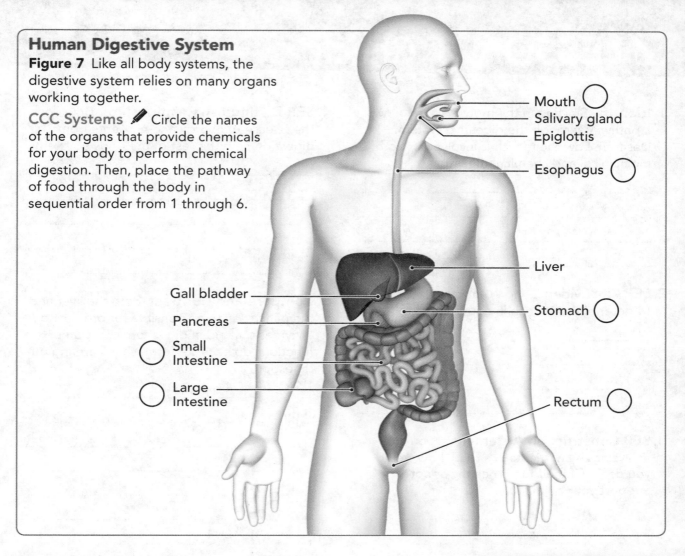

Mouth ◯
Salivary gland
Epiglottis
Esophagus ◯
Liver
Gall bladder
Pancreas
Small Intestine ◯
Large Intestine ◯
Stomach ◯
Rectum ◯

The Digestive System as a Whole You have read about the functions of the different organs that make up the digestive system, which are shown in **Figure 7**. It is important to realize that the digestive system is related to many other systems in the human body. For example, after nutrients are absorbed in the small intestine, they are transported around the body in the blood. The pumping of the heart and the rest of the circulatory system make sure all of your cells get the nutrients they need.

INTERACTIVITY

Find out what a day in the life of a cell is like.

✅ READING CHECK **Write Arguments** Your sister claims that the digestive system works by itself to give your body energy. She states that small branches from the stomach get food to the cells throughout your body. Do you agree with this statement? Why?

....

....

....

....

....

MS-LS1-3

1. **Identify** Starting in the mouth, food follows a pathway through the digestive system. Describe how the mouth is involved in both mechanical and chemical digestion.

....

....

....

....

2. **SEP Cite Evidence** How can you use food labels to determine how rich in nutrients a food is?

....

....

....

....

3. **SEP Construct an Argument** If you are analyzing the nutrients in a food, how would you decide if the food is healthy or not? Support your claim.

....

....

....

....

4. **SEP Distinguish Relationships** How does the release of energy and nutrients from digestion help the rest of the body's systems?

....

....

....

....

....

5. **Compare and Contrast** Both the liver and the pancreas are responsible for producing enzymes that aid in digestion. What other functions do each perform when carrying out digestion?

....

....

....

....

....

....

....

Quest CHECK-IN

In this lesson, you learned about nutrients that are important for maintaining a healthy body. You also learned about the digestive system and how it supports other systems in the body.

SEP Evaluate Reasoning Consider how your dietary needs might differ from someone else's and how you might need to modify your diet based on a day's activities. Why is it important to eat a variety of different foods?

....

....

....

....

👆 INTERACTIVITY

Training Table

Go online to investigate the ideal nutrients for different athletes.

Nutritionist

You Can't Order
OUT IN SPACE

Nutritionists and dieticians promote healthy eating habits and develop nutrition plans tailored to an individual's dietary or medical needs. But what if your client is an astronaut?

Space is a microgravity environment, which means astronauts experience near-weightlessness. While floating around seems like fun, it has serious consequences for the human body. Microgravity affects muscle mass, bone density, and cardiovascular health. It also impacts how the body digests food and processes essential vitamins and minerals.

At NASA, nutritionists work with food scientists to develop meals that counteract the harmful effects of living in space. Nutrients such as iron are added to meals to help deal with bone and muscle loss. The challenge for the nutritionists is creating meals that can be prepared and consumed in microgravity!

 VIDEO

Find out how a nutritionist helps people make healthy diet choices.

MY CAREER

Type "nutritionist" or "dietician" into an online search engine to learn more about these careers.

Space food is often packaged in individual meal pouches, similar to the chicken the astronaut is eating.

Chicken

4 Managing Materials

Guiding Questions

- How are materials transported in the body?
- How does the respiratory system interact with other systems to exchange gases?
- How does the excretory system interact with other systems to remove wastes from the body?

Connections

Literacy Draw Evidence

Math Represent Quantitative Relationships

MS-LS1-3

HANDS-ON LAB

ʊInvestigate Find out how your body's systems work together.

Vocabulary

circulatory system
artery
capillary
vein
lymph
bronchi
alveoli
excretion
nephron

Academic Vocabulary

contract

Connect It !

✏ **Draw an arrow to show in which direction the ants are carrying the food.**

CCC Systems and System Models How do you think actions in the human body might be like the system the ants use to transport food?

....

....

....

....

The Circulatory System

Ants, such as the ones in **Figure 1**, are known for cooperating to transport food to their colonies. Your body has a similar system that transports nutrients and other life-sustaining resources. It is called the **circulatory system**, and it includes the cardiovascular system and the lymphatic system. In addition to bringing nutrients and oxygen to the cells, the circulatory system also removes waste products and helps to fight off diseases and infections.

The main structure of the circulatory system is the heart. This fist-sized organ has the never-ending job of pumping blood around the body. The heart is a muscle that **contracts** and relaxes constantly in order to do its job. Your heart beats around 100,000 times every day. Blood moves from the heart to the lungs and then back to the heart again before it is transported out to the body. Blood moving through the vessels allows for the exchange of gases and brings nutrients to all the cells. For this reason, blood is often called the "river of life."

HANDS-ON LAB

Explore the connection between your heart and breathing.

Academic Vocabulary

What are some other words you can think of that are synonyms for *contracts*?

....

....

Transporting Materials
Figure 1. Just as the circulatory system moves materials in your body, these ants transport food to their colony.

INTERACTIVITY

Explore the highways and byways that make up the body's circulatory system.

Write About It Trace the journey of a molecule of oxygen from the time it enters your body until it reaches a muscle in your fingertip. Describe each step of the process.

The Cardiovascular System

The part of the circulatory system that pumps blood throughout the body is the cardiovascular system. In this system, the heart pumps blood through the body using the various blood vessels. Start on the right side of **Figure 2**.

Blood travels from the lungs to the left atrium down to the left ventricle. It then takes nutrients and oxygen to the cells of the body, where it picks up waste products, such as carbon dioxide. The blood returns through the right atrium. It goes down to the right ventricle, and out to the lungs where gas is exchanged. Then, the process starts all over again.

This continuous process of pumping blood is a double loop system, as shown in **Figure 3**. In loop one, the blood travels from the heart to the lungs and then back to the heart. In loop two, the oxygenated blood moves from the heart out to the body and deoxygenated blood is returned to the heart.

Special cells called red blood cells play a key role in transporting oxygen throughout the body. They take up oxygen in the lungs and deliver it to cells throughout the body. Red blood cells also absorb carbon dioxide in the body and transport it to the lungs, where it is released from the body.

Structure of the Heart

Figure 2 ✏️ The human heart has four main chambers. Each upper chamber is called an atrium and each lower chamber is called a ventricle. The right ventricle has a special collection of cells called the pacemaker that keeps the heart beating in a regular rhythm. Label the four chambers of the heart.

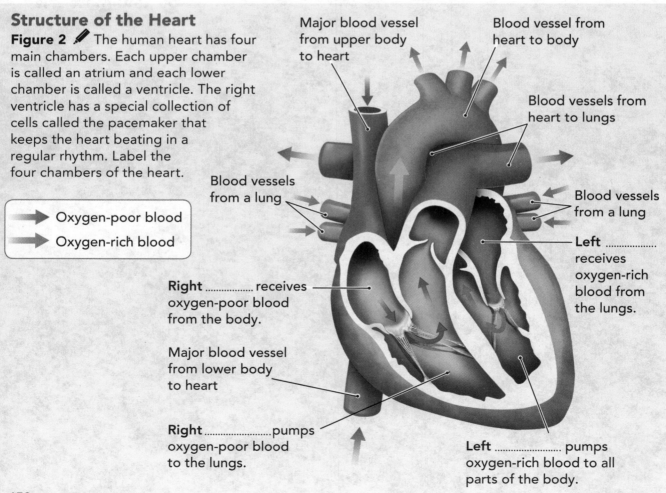

➡️ Oxygen-poor blood
➡️ Oxygen-rich blood

Major blood vessel from upper body to heart

Blood vessel from heart to body

Blood vessels from heart to lungs

Blood vessels from a lung

Blood vessels from a lung

Left .... receives oxygen-rich blood from the lungs.

Right .... receives oxygen-poor blood from the body.

Major blood vessel from lower body to heart

Right .... pumps oxygen-poor blood to the lungs.

Left .... pumps oxygen-rich blood to all parts of the body.

Double Loop System

Figure 3 ✏ Blood flows from the right atrium to the right ventricle and then to the lungs through a special artery called the pulmonary artery. Here it gets oxygenated and then is pumped back to the heart by way of the pulmonary vein. Draw arrows to show the direction of the blood flow.

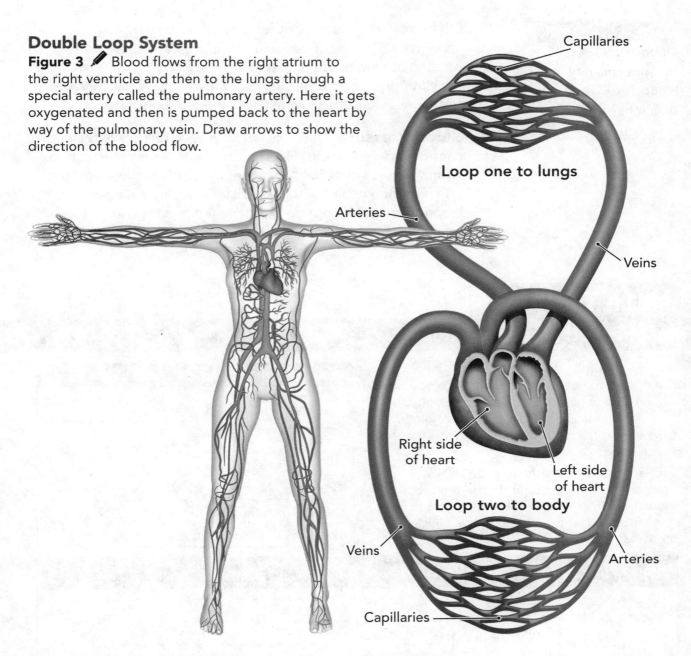

Capillaries

Loop one to lungs

Arteries

Veins

Right side of heart

Left side of heart

Loop two to body

Veins

Capillaries

Arteries

Transport Through the Circulatory System

You know that the main function of the circulatory system is to move materials, such as nutrients and oxygen, to all of the cells of the body. A series of vessels makes this process possible.

Blood Vessels Your heart is connected to the rest of your body through a system of vessels, which are illustrated in **Figure 3**. Not all vessels in the body are the same, Different vessels have different structures and functions. An **artery** carries blood away from the heart. It is a thick-walled and muscular vessel. On the other hand, a **vein** carries blood back to the heart. It has thinner walls than arteries. A **capillary** is a tiny vessel where substances are exchanged between the blood and body cells. Capillaries can be thought of as connecting arteries and veins.

Summarize Text What are the three main types of blood vessels and what are their jobs?

....

....

....

....

....

Diffusion Oxygen and other materials move through capillary walls by diffusion. In diffusion, materials move from an area of high concentration to one of lower concentration. For example, blood contains more glucose than cells do. As a result, glucose diffuses from the blood into body cells.

Blood Pressure The force with which ventricles of the heart contract is what creates blood pressure. This pumping action is what you feel when you are aware of your heartbeat or pulse. The pumping action of the ventricles is strong enough to push blood throughout your body. Without blood pressure, blood would not be able to reach all parts of your body.

Math Toolbox

Exercise and Blood Flow Rate

Your heart pumps more blood through your body when you exercise. The rate of blood flow, however, does not increase in all parts of your body. The table shows how the rate of blood flow changes for different parts of the body during intense exercise.

SEP Communicate Information 🖊 Draw a bar graph to represent the data in the table. Show the difference between the blood flow rate while the body is resting and exercising intensely.

Body Part	Blood Flow Rate, cm³/min	
	Resting	**Intense Exercise**
Brain	750	750
Heart Muscle	250	750
Kidneys	1,100	600
Skeletal Muscle	1,200	12,500
Skin	500	1,800

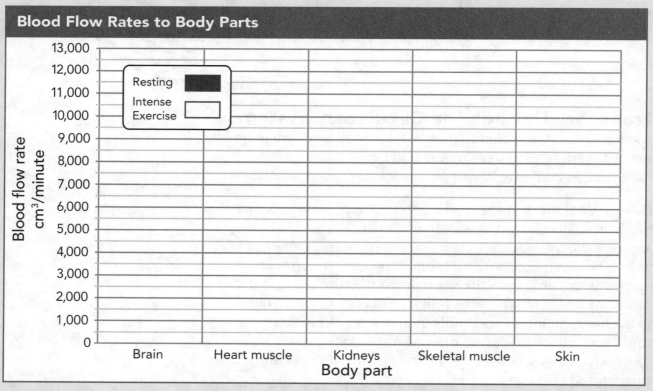

Blood Flow Rates to Body Parts

The Lymphatic System

Figure 4 🖊 The lymphatic system is part of the circulatory system. Its main function is to transport components of blood back into the circulatory system. On the diagram, label the lymph nodes and the lymph vessels.

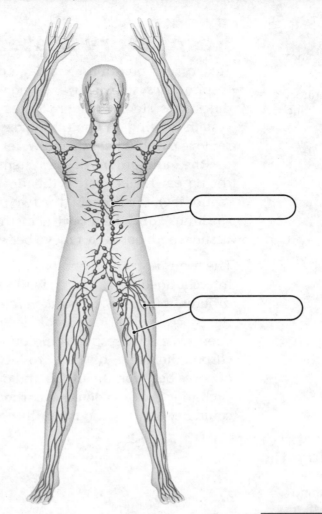

The Lymphatic System

In addition to red blood cells, blood also contains white blood cells, platelets, and plasma. White blood cells fight off diseases. Platelets help clot wounds. Plasma is the liquid part of the blood. As these components of blood move through the cardiovascular system, the fluid moves into the surrounding tissues. From here it needs to move back into the bloodstream. This job is done by the other component of the circulatory system—the lymphatic system. As shown in **Figure 4**, the lymphatic system is a network of vessels that returns fluid to the bloodstream.

Once the fluid is inside the lymphatic system, it is called **lymph** and consists of water, white blood cells, and dissolved materials such as glucose. Lymph flows through vessels called lymph vessels. The vessels connect to small knobs of tissue called lymph nodes, which filter lymph, trapping bacteria and other disease-causing microorganisms in the fluid.

☑️ **READING CHECK** **Determine Central Ideas** The lymphatic system helps to remove bacteria and other microorganisms from the body. Why would this be important for you?

....

....

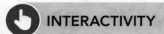
INTERACTIVITY

Investigate how the circulatory and respiratory systems respond to changes in the environment.

Respiratory System

Take a deep breath in. Now let it out. You have just used your respiratory system, shown along with the circulatory and digestive systems in **Figure 5**. It is the job of the respiratory system to bring air containing oxygen into your body and remove carbon dioxide and water from your body. The lungs are the main organs of the system. Other structures include the nose, which moistens the air you breathe, the trachea (windpipe), the **bronchi** (the two passages that direct air into the lungs), and the **alveoli** (tiny thin-walled sacs of lung tissue where gases can move between air and blood).

The terms *respiration* and *breathing* are often used interchangeably. However, while they are related, they are different processes. *Respiration* refers to cellular respiration, the process cells use to break down glucose in order to produce energy. Cellular respiration requires oxygen and produces carbon dioxide as a waste product. Breathing is the exchange of gases between the inside and outside of the body. The gases exchanged are oxygen and carbon dioxide. Cellular respiration could not occur without breathing.

Systems Work Together

Figure 5 ✏ Cellular respiration and breathing both require body systems working together. Circle the body system responsible for the exchange of gases. Complete the labels.

CCC Systems How do you think having a strong respiratory system helps the circulatory system?

....

....

....

....

....

....

....

....

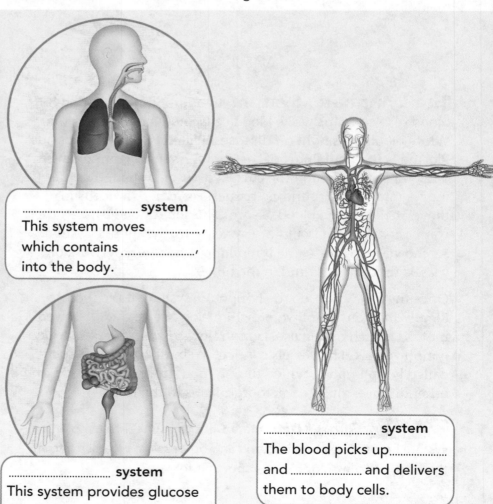

.... **system**
This system moves................,
which contains ....,
into the body.

.... **system**
This system provides glucose
used in ....

.... **system**
The blood picks up..................
and .... and delivers
them to body cells.

Breathing and Gas Exchange

Figure 6 ✏ Complete the diagram labels on the right. In each diagram below, draw an arrow below the diaphragm to show the direction the lungs and diaphragm move when we breathe.

CCC Cause and Effect Pneumonia is an infection people can get in their lungs. It causes the alveoli in your lungs to fill with fluid. How do you think this disease affects breathing?

....

....

....

....

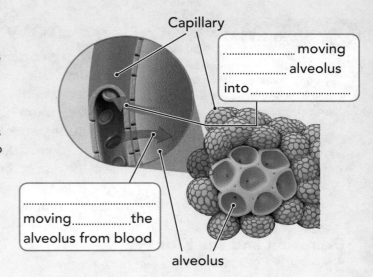

Capillary

.... moving
.... alveolus
into..................................

....
moving...............the alveolus from blood

alveolus

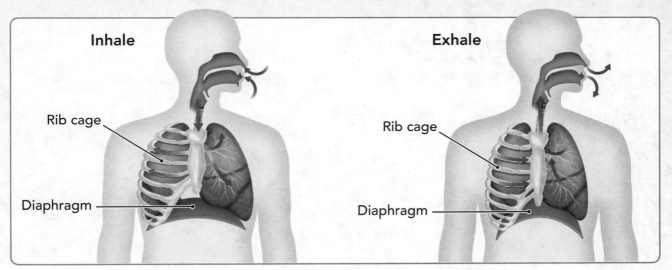

Inhale

Rib cage

Diaphragm

Exhale

Rib cage

Diaphragm

The Breathing Process

When you inhale, your rib muscles and diaphragm contract as shown in **Figure 6**. The chest moves upward and outward as it expands. The air pressure within the lungs lowers, so air moves in. When you exhale, the opposite happens. The muscles relax and the chest lowers. The pressure within the lungs is increased, so air is forced out.

Process of Gas Exchange

Gases move between the alveoli and the blood. After air enters the alveoli, oxygen passes through the capillary walls into the blood. At the same time, carbon dioxide and water pass from the blood into the alveoli. This continual exchange maintains the correct concentrations of gases within the blood.

☑ **READING CHECK** **Draw Evidence** How is the respiratory system interconnected with other systems of the body?

....

....

....

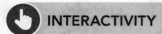

INTERACTIVITY

Investigate how human body systems work together to maintain homeostasis during long-term physical activity.

Excretory System

The process of removing wastes is called **excretion**. The excretory system, which is illustrated in **Figure 7**, removes waste products from the body. The main organs of this system are the kidneys, urinary bladder, urethra, lungs, skin, and liver. All of these organs work together to rid the body of waste. As your cells perform their various functions, they produce waste products. These include carbon dioxide, excess water, and other materials. These wastes need to be removed from the body in order to maintain homeostasis.

Excretion and the Kidneys

Figure 7 🖊 The kidneys are two of the main organs of the excretory system. Label the kidneys and the urinary bladder.

CCC Structure and Function How might a blockage in the ureter impact the excretion of wastes from the body?

....

....

....

....

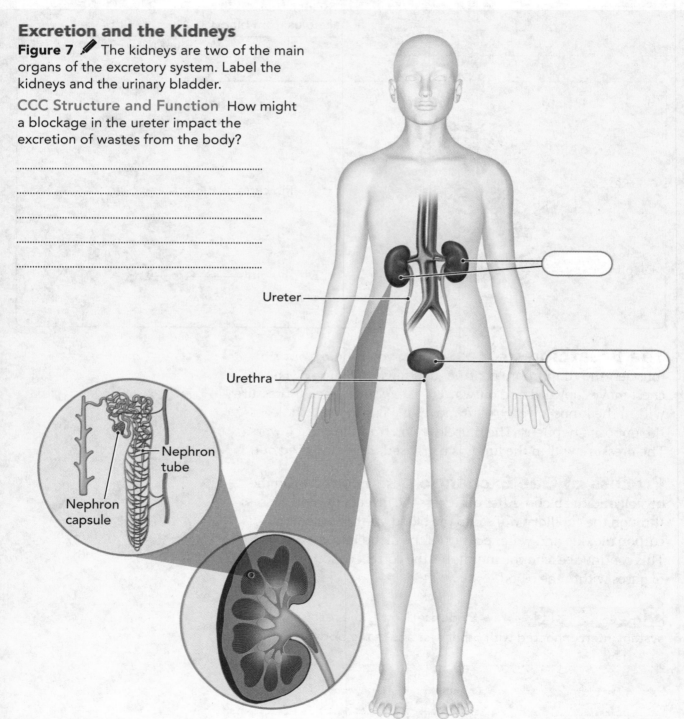

Kidneys The kidneys are two bean-shaped organs that filter blood and regulate the amount of water in the body. The kidneys remove water and urea, a chemical produced from the breakdown of proteins. While the lungs remove some water, most water is excreted from the body in the form of urine, which includes water and urea. Liquid waste collects in the urinary bladder and is expelled through the urethra.

Each kidney is composed of millions of tiny tubes called nephrons. A **nephron** is a small filtering structure in the kidneys that removes wastes from blood and produces urine. This filtration process happens in two stages. First, the nephrons filter both the wastes and the needed materials from the blood. Next, the needed materials are returned to the blood and wastes are excreted.

The Lungs, Skin, and Liver
The respiratory system, digestive system, and integumentary system work with the excretory system to remove wastes from the body. When you exhale, you are not only removing carbon dioxide from the body, but some water as well. Your integumentary system, which includes your skin (**Figure 8**), also removes waste. Sweat glands in your skin release water from your cells to help cool your body. Sweat also contains a small amount of urea. The liver produces urea from proteins and other wastes, including pieces of old red blood cells. Removing waste products from the body helps maintain homeostasis. However, if a disease or some blockage prevents these products from being removed, the body's internal environment can become toxic.

 **READING CHECK** **Read and Comprehend** What are three ways your body excretes waste?

....

....

....

HANDS-ON LAB

☑**Investigate** Find out how your body's systems work together.

HANDS-ON LAB

Revisit the systems of the body and how they work together.

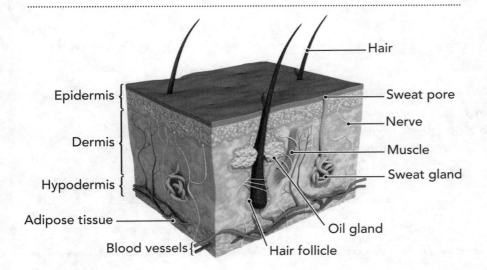

Epidermis
Dermis
Hypodermis
Adipose tissue
Blood vessels
Hair follicle
Oil gland
Hair
Sweat pore
Nerve
Muscle
Sweat gland

Skin and Excretion
Figure 8 ✎ As your body temperature rises, your sweat glands release water to help cool you off. Sweat is a form of excretion. Circle where a bead of sweat would form on the surface of the skin.

Model It

Body's Waste Disposal System

✏️ Complete the table.

Organ	System to which it belongs	How it works in excretion
Lungs		
Skin		
Liver		
Kidneys		

1. Interpret Photos How does the photo of the people, who have exercised, demonstrate excretion?

....

....

2. Explain How else do you think they are removing wastes from their bodies?

....

....

....

3. SEP Analyze and Interpret Data The presence of protein in urine can indicate diabetes or high blood pressure. Which organ is most likely contributing to the presence of proteins in urine? Explain.

....

....

....

☑ LESSON 4 Check

1. Identify What are the major organs of the circulatory system?

....

....

....

....

....

2. Summarize Where does diffusion occur in the circulatory and respiratory systems?

....

....

....

....

....

....

....

....

3. SEP Cite Evidence How do the circulatory and respiratory systems work together to transport gases to all parts of the body?

....

....

....

....

....

....

....

....

....

4. CCC Analyze Systems How does the excretory system remove wastes from the blood of the circulatory system?

....

....

....

....

Quest CHECK-IN

In this lesson, you learned about the structures and functions of the circulatory, respiratory, and excretory systems. You also learned how these systems work together to manage materials that go into and out of your body.

CCC Analyze Systems Consider how your body systems interact when you train for your favorite sport. How does physical exertion impact your heart, lungs, and kidneys?

....

....

....

....

....

HANDS-ON LAB

Heart Beat, Health Beat

Go online and download the lab to explore how physical activity affects heart and perspiration rates.

Controlling Processes

Guiding Questions

- Which systems control processes in the human body?
- How does the body sense and respond to stimuli in the environment?
- How do the cells that make up the nervous system respond to stimuli?

Connection

Literacy Integrate with Visuals

MS-LS1-8

HANDS-ON LAB

uInvestigate Explore the different parts of the nervous system.

Vocabulary

neuron
synapse
brain
spinal cord
gland
negative
  feedback
reflex

Academic Vocabulary

impulse

Connect It!

🖉 **Circle the stimulus in the image that may cause the diver to respond.**

SEP Construct Explanations What senses is the diver using to receive information about this encounter? Explain.

....

....

CCC Cause and Effect Why would the diver know to respond to the stimulus? Explain.

....

....

....

Nervous System

The Internet allows us to communicate quickly with friends near and far. The nervous system is your body's communication network. Your nervous system receives information about what is happening both inside and outside your body. Then it directs how your body responds to this information. For example, in **Figure 1**, the diver's nervous system responds to the information it receives about the sharks. Your nervous system also helps maintain homeostasis, which keeps your internal environment stable. Your nervous system consists of your brain, spinal cord, and nerves.

Like any system, the human nervous system is made up of organs and tissues. A cell that carries information through the nervous system is called a nerve cell, or **neuron**. The structure of a neuron helps it function. Neurons are made up of dendrites and axons. A dendrite is the branched structure that picks up information. The axon receives information from the dendrite and sends it away from the cell.

The nervous system is divided into two systems: the central nervous system (CNS) and the peripheral nervous system (PNS). The brain and spinal cord make up the CNS. The job of the CNS is to control most of the functions of the body and mind. The PNS is a network of nerves that branches out from the CNS and connects to the rest of the body.

HANDS-ON LAB

Test how your knee responds to an external stimulus.

Reflect In your notebook, describe three instances in which your body seems to react to something in the environment, without any thought or conscious decision on your part.

Reacting to the Environment

Figure 1 The diver's encounter with sharks provides stimuli that will result in both immediate reactions and lasting memories.

Neurons The nervous system is made up of three kinds of neurons. A sensory neuron picks up a stimulus from the internal or external environment and converts the stimulus into a message. An interneuron carries this message from one neuron to another. A motor neuron sends the message to a muscle or gland, which reacts accordingly.

Nerve Impulses The function of a neuron is to transmit information. When the dendrite receives information, the neuron sends the information along the cell through the long axon. The message carried by the neuron is called a nerve impulse. The axon transmits the **impulse** to nearby cells.

Synapse As shown in **Figure 2**, the junction where one neuron can transfer an impulse to another neuron is called a **synapse**. At the axon tips, electrical signals change to chemical signals. This allows the signal to bridge the gap and continue to the next neuron. The impulse is converted to an electrical signal again, and travels through the neuron to another neighboring one.

☑ READING CHECK **Interpret Visuals** Identify the path that the nerve impulse will take, starting and ending with the dendrite.

....

....

Academic Vocabulary
Many people say, 'that was an impulse purchase.' Use your understanding of the word *impulse* to explain the context in which the author is using the term in the paragraph.

....

....

....

Signal and Synapse
Figure 2 🖉 Synapses are gaps between neurons where the impulse changes from electrical to chemical and back again. Draw an arrow on the diagram to indicate the direction the nerve impulse is traveling.

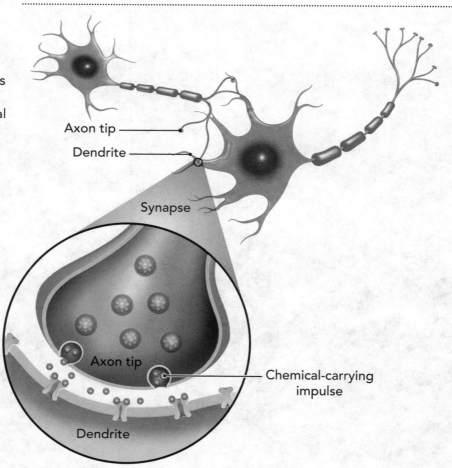

Axon tip

Dendrite

Synapse

Axon tip

Chemical-carrying impulse

Dendrite

Parts of the Nervous System

Figure 3 The brain sits atop the human nervous system, with bundled neurons branching out from the spinal cord.

CCC Cause and Effect What could happen if the brain stem were damaged?

....

....

....

....

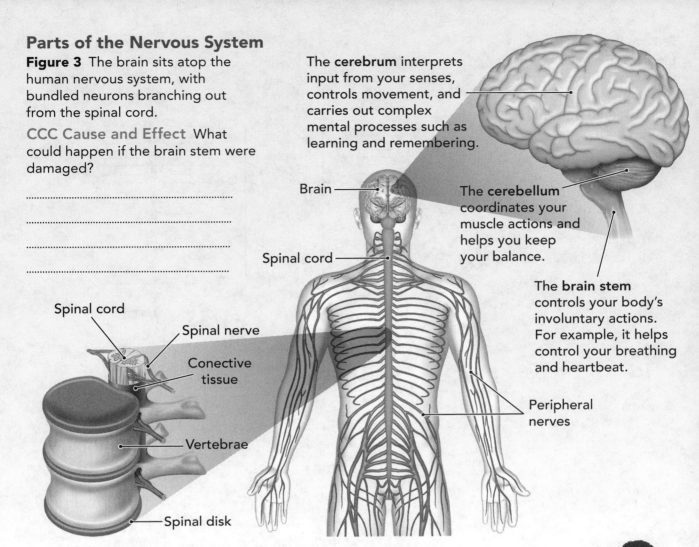

The **cerebrum** interprets input from your senses, controls movement, and carries out complex mental processes such as learning and remembering.

Brain

The **cerebellum** coordinates your muscle actions and helps you keep your balance.

Spinal cord

The **brain stem** controls your body's involuntary actions. For example, it helps control your breathing and heartbeat.

Spinal cord

Spinal nerve

Conective tissue

Vertebrae

Spinal disk

Peripheral nerves

Central Nervous System The central nervous system, which is shown in **Figure 3**, controls the functions of the body. The **brain** is the part of the CNS that is located in the skull and controls most functions of the body. The **spinal cord** is a thick column of nervous tissue that links the brain to most of the nerves that branch out through the body. Most stimuli travel through the spinal cord to the brain. The brain then directs a response, usually back out through the spinal cord.

The Brain The human brain has about 100 billion neurons, all of which are interneurons. These interneurons handle thousands of messages each day. The brain is covered by layers of connective tissue and fluid that help protect the brain from injury. The brain itself has three main components. These control voluntary and involuntary actions such as heart rate, memory, and muscular coordination.

The Spinal Cord The vertebral column that you can feel with your fingers down the length of your neck and back contains the spinal cord. Like the brain, layers of connective tissue surround the spinal cord, along with a layer of fluid.

HANDS-ON LAB

☑ **Investigate** Explore the different parts of the nervous system.

163

Nerve Pairs

Figure 4 Each nerve pair is connected to specific parts of the body.

SEP Analyze and Interpret Data Which parts of the body do you think the thoracic nerve pairs communicate with?

....

....

....

....

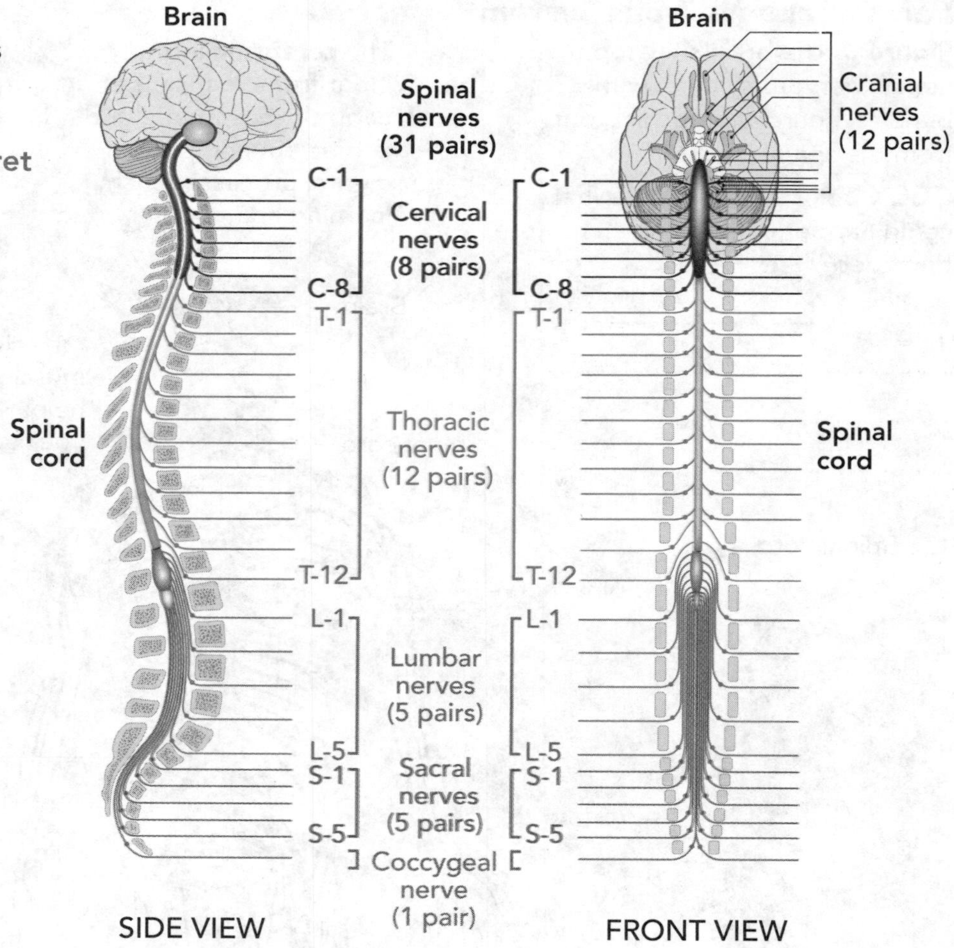

Brain

Spinal cord

Spinal nerves (31 pairs)

C-1

Cervical nerves (8 pairs)

C-8

T-1

Thoracic nerves (12 pairs)

T-12

L-1

Lumbar nerves (5 pairs)

L-5

S-1

Sacral nerves (5 pairs)

S-5

Coccygeal nerve (1 pair)

SIDE VIEW

Brain

Cranial nerves (12 pairs)

Spinal cord

C-1

C-8

T-1

T-12

L-1

L-5

S-1

S-5

FRONT VIEW

Autonomic Response

Figure 5 🖊 One of these pupils is responding to darkness, while the other is responding to light. Circle the eye that is responding bright light.

Contraction of round muscles of the iris constricts pupil.

Contraction of radial muscles of the iris dilates pupil.

Peripheral Nervous System

The network of nerves that connects the central nervous system to the rest of the body is called the peripheral nervous system. It has 43 pairs of nerves, as shown in **Figure 4**, and controls both involuntary and voluntary actions. Twelve pairs of nerves begin in the brain and branch out to parts of the head, while the other pairs begin in the spinal cord and branch out through the torso from the spine. In each nerve pair, one nerve goes to the left side of the body and the other goes to the right. Each spinal nerve has axons of sensory and motor neurons. Sensory neurons bring impulses to the central nervous system. Motor neurons carry impulses from the central nervous system out to the body.

Somatic and Autonomic Systems

The peripheral nervous system has two groups of nerves. The somatic nervous system controls voluntary actions, like typing a text message or throwing a ball. The autonomic nervous system controls involuntary actions, such as digestion or pupil dilation (**Figure 5**).

Reflexes The involuntary reaction of jumping when you hear a loud noise is called a **reflex**. It is an automatic response that occurs without conscious control. While skeletal muscles are largely within your conscious control through the somatic nervous system, some skeletal muscle contractions occur without the brain's involvement.

Pain is one type of stimulus that can trigger what is known as a reflex arc. Sensory neurons detect a pain stimulus, such as sticking your finger on a sharp object (**Figure 6**), and send impulses to the spinal cord. Interneurons in the spinal cord carry the impulses directly to motor neurons in the arm and hand. These motor neurons trigger muscle contractions in the hand to bring the fingertip away from the painful stimulus. At the same time, pain impulses travel to the brain, where they can be interpreted and stored as memories. This is how we learn to not press our fingertips against things like cactus spines and fishhooks.

INTERACTIVITY

Find out how the human brain stacks up against a computer.

☑ READING CHECK **Sequence** What is the sequence of neurons involved in a reflex arc?

Model It !

Learning from Experience

Figure 6 The hooks on this fishing lure would cause pain if you accidentally snagged them on your fingertip.

SEP Develop Models 🖉 In the space, draw a diagram of a brain, spine, arm, and hand. Use arrows and labels to model a reflex arc showing how a person would react to getting snagged by a hook. Also show how pain impulses would reach the brain and result in learning something from the experience.

Figure 7 If a person ends up with too much or too little growth hormone, his or her height will be affected.

CCC Cause and Effect What do you think are some possible health problems of someone with gigantism? Explain.

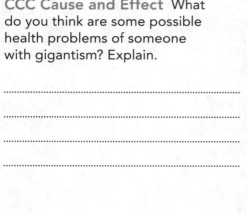

....

....

....

....

Endocrine System

The human body has two systems that maintain homeostasis: the nervous system and the endocrine system. The nervous system maintains homeostasis by sending nerve impulses throughout the body. The endocrine system regulates the body by releasing chemicals called hormones, such as those that regulate height (**Figure 7**). The endocrine system is made up of different glands. A **gland** is an organ that produces and releases chemicals through ducts or into the bloodstream. The hormones of the endocrine system and the glands that regulate them are shown in **Figure 8**.

Regulators One of the links between the nervous system and the endocrine system is the hypothalamus. This gland is located deep inside the brain, just above the spinal cord. Its function is to send out nerve and chemical signals. Its nerve signals control sleep, hunger, and other basic body processes. It produces hormones—chemicals signals that regulate other glands and organs of the endocrine system.

Below the hypothalamus is the pituitary gland. This pea-sized gland receives signals from the hypothalamus and releases hormones. Some of these hormones are signals to other endocrine glands. Others, such as growth hormone, go to work directly on different body tissues.

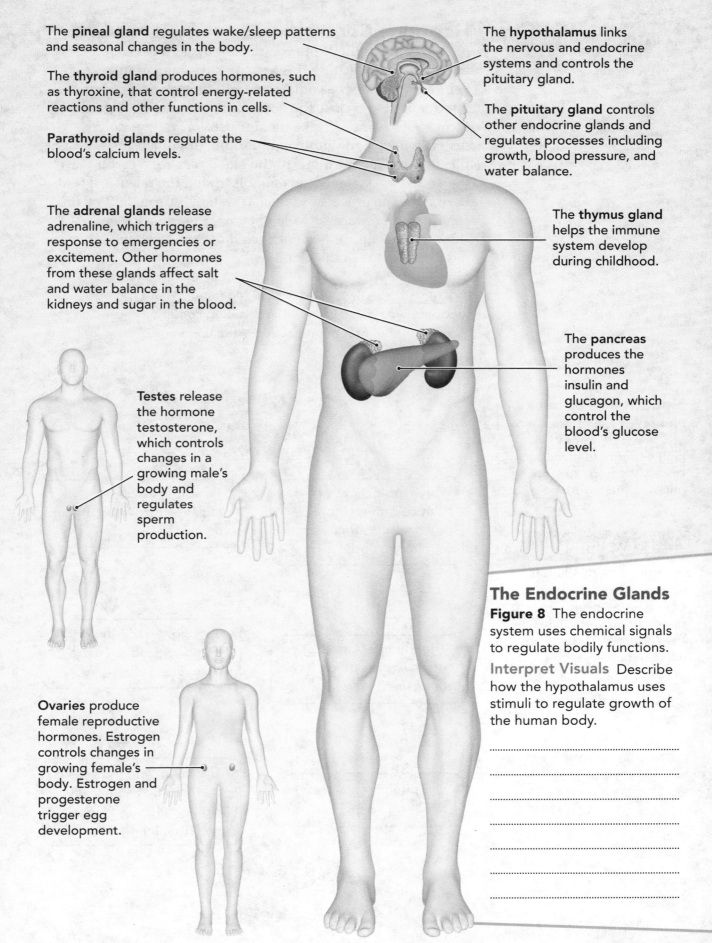

The **pineal gland** regulates wake/sleep patterns and seasonal changes in the body.

The **thyroid gland** produces hormones, such as thyroxine, that control energy-related reactions and other functions in cells.

Parathyroid glands regulate the blood's calcium levels.

The **adrenal glands** release adrenaline, which triggers a response to emergencies or excitement. Other hormones from these glands affect salt and water balance in the kidneys and sugar in the blood.

Testes release the hormone testosterone, which controls changes in a growing male's body and regulates sperm production.

Ovaries produce female reproductive hormones. Estrogen controls changes in growing female's body. Estrogen and progesterone trigger egg development.

The **hypothalamus** links the nervous and endocrine systems and controls the pituitary gland.

The **pituitary gland** controls other endocrine glands and regulates processes including growth, blood pressure, and water balance.

The **thymus gland** helps the immune system develop during childhood.

The **pancreas** produces the hormones insulin and glucagon, which control the blood's glucose level.

The Endocrine Glands

Figure 8 The endocrine system uses chemical signals to regulate bodily functions.

Interpret Visuals Describe how the hypothalamus uses stimuli to regulate growth of the human body.

....
....
....
....
....
....
....

Hormone Control Suppose you open the refrigerator and grab the milk. While you pour yourself a glass, you leave the door open. Because this increases the temperature inside your refrigerator, the compressor will turn on and cool the interior after you close the door. Once it is cool enough, the compressor turns off. Like the refrigerator, your endocrine system works to maintain equilibrium, or homeostasis. When the amount of a hormone in the blood reaches a certain level, the endocrine system sends signals to stop the release of that hormone. The process by which a system is turned off by the condition it produces is called **negative feedback**. **Figure 9** shows how negative feedback regulates the level of the hormone thyroxine in the blood.

READING CHECK Determine Meaning What type of feedback would you call it if the resulting condition caused an increase in the effect that produces the condition?

Negative Feedback

Figure 9 When the level of a released hormone is high enough, the feedback causes the body to stop releasing the hormone.

Literacy Connection

Integrate with Visuals
✏ Underline the names of endocrine glands in the diagram, and circle the caption that describes when negative feedback is provided.

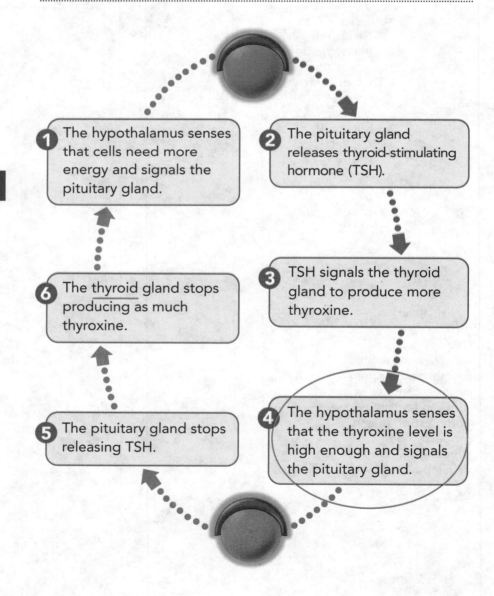

1. The hypothalamus senses that cells need more energy and signals the pituitary gland.

2. The pituitary gland releases thyroid-stimulating hormone (TSH).

3. TSH signals the thyroid gland to produce more thyroxine.

4. The hypothalamus senses that the thyroxine level is high enough and signals the pituitary gland.

5. The pituitary gland stops releasing TSH.

6. The thyroid gland stops producing as much thyroxine.

MS-LS1-8

1. Identify What is the name for the division of the nervous system that handles involuntary actions and processes of the body?

....

2. CCC Analyze Systems What are the two main physical components of the central nervous system?

....

3. CCC Cause and Effect Describe the two signals and pathways that are activated when you touch something and experience pain.

....
....
....
....
....
....
....
....
....

4. CCC Patterns Describe the role chemical signals play a role in both the nervous system and the endocrine system.

....
....
....
....
....
....

5. SEP Construct Explanations Why would it be advantageous to have two separate pathways to react to and learn from pain?

....
....
....
....
....
....
....
....

Quest CHECK-IN

In this lesson, you learned how the nervous system and endocrine system regulate the body and respond to stimuli from the environment.

Evaluate Why are coordination between motor neurons and the brain's ability to learn and make memories essential to improving at a physical activity?

....
....
....
....

INTERACTIVITY

Why Practice Makes Perfect

Go online to explore how athletes develop muscle memory.

☑ TOPIC 3 Review and Assess

1 Body Organization

MS-LS1-3

1. Because its structure is more complex,
    A. a tissue has a more complex function than an organ.
    B. a cell has a more complex function than a tissue.
    C. an organ has a more complex function than a tissue.
    D. a cell has a more complex function than an organ.

2. **CCC Patterns** What is the relationship among organs, cells, and tissues?

    ....
    ....
    ....
    ....

2 Systems Interacting

MS-LS1-3

3. The main purpose of homeostasis is to
    A. fight disease-causing organisms.
    B. keep internal conditions stable.
    C. produce offspring.
    D. replicate DNA.

4. **SEP Construct Explanations** Suppose you sit in the same position so long that your leg starts to hurt. How do the body's different parts interact to stop the pain?

    ....
    ....
    ....
    ....
    ....

3 Supplying Energy

MS-LS1-3

5. The liver helps the circulatory system by
    A. filtering blood of harmful substances.
    B. helping blood vessels to absorb nutrients.
    C. storing bile that is released into the bloodstream.
    D. releasing chemicals that begin to break down food in the mouth.

6. .... in the stomach are responsible for the mechanical digestion that takes place there.

7. **SEP Develop Models** ✏ Draw a flow chart to show how the digestive, circulatory, and excretory systems work together to process food and supply nutrients to the body.

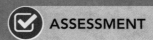
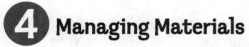 **Managing Materials**

MS-LS1-3

8. Which of the following organs function as both a respiratory organ and an excretory organ?
  A. liver   **B.** skin
  C. kidneys   **D.** lungs

9. Organs such as the kidneys, lungs, skin, and liver work together to
  A. remove carbon dioxide.
  B. eliminate excess water.
  C. help maintain homeostasis.
  D. filter out urea.

10. One role of rib bones in the .... system is to protect the heart from physical injury.

11. **CCC Relate Structure and Function** How does the structure of the alveoli in the lungs help with their function in the respiratory system?

....

....

....

....

....

12. **SEP Construct Explanations** Explain how the respiratory and circulatory systems work together to manage materials in the body.

....

....

....

....

....

....

....

5 **Controlling Processes**

MS-LS1-8

13. The spinal cord is a thick column of
  A. blood vessels that helps to support and hold up the body.
  B. bony discs that protects nervous tissue.
  C. muscle tissue that connects nerve cells in the brain with nerve cells in the body.
  D. nervous tissue that connects the brain to the body's nerves.

14. The .... system releases hormones that .... processes in the body.

15. **CCC Analyze Systems** How does the nervous system regulate basic body processes?

....

....

....

....

....

....

16. **SEP Construct Explanations** Suppose a child reaches for a hot pan on the stove and burns himself. Explain how the child's brain functions to protect his body from injury both at that moment as well as in the future.

....

....

....

....

....

....

....

....

MS-LS1-3, MS-LS1-8

Evidence-Based Assessment

Crigler-Najjar syndrome is a rare inherited disorder with about 100 confirmed cases worldwide. Children born with the syndrome do not produce a certain liver enzyme. As a result, a toxic substance builds up in the body, which causes damage to other body systems.

The diagram below details some of the major effects of this disorder.

2 As the bilirubin level increases, it enters the bloodstream and builds up in the eyes and skin. This causes them to become yellow, a condition known as jaundice.

1 After about 115 days in the bloodstream, red blood cells are broken down in the liver. This produces a toxic substance called bilirubin. Without the enzyme, the liver cannot convert the bilirubin into a form that can be safely removed from the body.

3 Eventually, bilirubin builds up in the brain and nervous tissue and causes neurological damage.

4 Children with acute cases can also suffer from difficulty in coordination, muscle weakness, and muscle spasms.

1. **CCC Cause and Effect** Which of the following body systems does not seem to be directly affected by the syndrome?
   A. circulatory system
   B. nervous system
   C. skeletal system
   D. muscular system

2. **SEP Use Models** Why would a child with Crigler-Najjar syndrome suffer from muscle weakness and spasms?
   A. Red blood cells attack the liver, causing it to release bilirubin, which attacks the muscular system.
   B. The brain does not function properly, so it signals the body to produce excess bilirubin, which damages muscle tissue.
   C. Red blood cells die and build up in muscle tissue, which interferes with their proper functioning.
   D. Bilirubin builds up in the body and causes damage to the nervous system, which affects the muscular system.

3. **SEP Construct Explanations** How are cells and tissue in the liver affected by Crigler-Najjar syndrome?

....

....

....

....

....

....

....

....

4. **CCC Analyze Systems** How does Crigler-Najjar syndrome affect the circulatory system?

....

....

....

....

....

....

....

5. **SEP Engage in Arguments** How does Crigler-Najjar syndrome demonstrate that the body depends on many interactions among different body systems in order to function properly?

....

....

....

....

....

....

....

....

....

Quest FINDINGS

Complete the Quest!

Phenomenon Organize your data and determine the best way to present your training and nutrition plan.

CCC Cause and Effect Why is it important to consider how one body system impacts other body systems when designing a successful training plan?

....

....

....

....

....

....

👆 **INTERACTIVITY**

Reflect on Peak Performance Plan

Reaction Research

How can you **design** and **conduct** an **investigation** about **reaction times?**

Materials

(per group)

- meter stick (with centimeters marked)
- calculator

Safety

Be sure to follow all safety guidelines provided by your teacher. The Safety Appendix of your textbook provides more details about the safety icons.

Background

Phenomenon You've been hired by a video game company to do some research and gather data on reaction times. Reaction time refers to the amount of time it takes for a person to recognize a stimulus and then direct the body to respond with an action. The developers are working on a new rhythm game in which the player presses buttons on the controller in time with visuals and music. They want to know how quickly a player might react to different stimuli, such as a shape changing color on the screen, a musical beat, or a vibration or rumble in the controller.

You will design and conduct an investigation to explore how different factors affect reaction times. Then you will analyze the data you have collected and draw some conclusions to share with the game developers.

Design Your Investigation

1. You and your partner can test reaction times with the meter stick. The subject sits at a table with a hand extended beyond the edge of the table as shown. The researcher holds up the meter stick so that the 0 lines up with the top of the subject's hand. The meter stick is dropped and the subject grabs it as quickly as possible. Measure the distance the meter stick falls by recording the centimeter mark closest to the top of the subject's hand.

2. You can use an equation to calculate how long it takes an object to fall based on how far an object falls. In the following equation, t is time, d is distance, and a is acceleration. To calculate the reaction time, use a calculator to solve the equation. (Note: A falling object accelerates due to gravity at a rate of 980 cm/s^2.)

$$t = \sqrt{(2d/a)}$$

3. Based on the data that the developers want, identify the three types of stimuli that you will test in your investigation.

   - ....
   - ....
   - ....

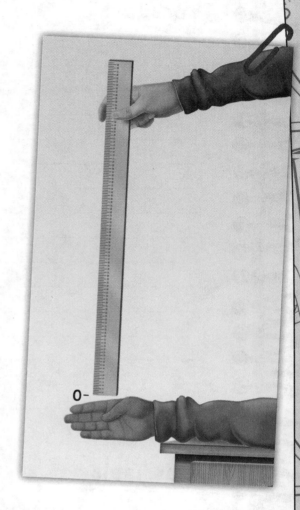

4. Develop a procedure for your investigation based on the three stimuli you identified.
   Write your procedure in the space provided.
   As you plan your investigation, consider these questions.

   - How will you use the meter stick to determine reaction times?
   - What tests will you perform to collect data about reaction times for each type of stimulus?
   - How many trials of each test will you perform?
   - What data will you record?

5. After getting your teacher's approval, carry out the investigation. Make a table in the space provided to record your data.

HANDS-ON LAB

uDemonstrate Go online for a downloadable worksheet of this lab.

Procedure

_____

_____

_____

_____

_____

_____

_____

_____

_____

_____

_____

_____

Data Table

Analyze and Interpret Data

1. **SEP Reason Quantitatively** Show the equations you used to calculate average reaction times to the visual, auditory, and tactile stimuli.

....

....

....

....

2. **SEP Defend Your Claim** Based on the trends or patterns you notice in the data, what claims can you make about reaction times to different stimuli? Explain.

....

....

....

....

3. **SEP Evaluate Evidence** Choose one stimulus that you tested in the investigation. Identify the body systems that are involved in responding to that stimulus. Then, draw a flow chart to diagram the process and explain how the systems interact.

....

4. **SEP Communicate Information** What conclusions would you share with the game developers? Which types of cues in the game would likely increase the chances of a player doing better? Explain.

....

....

....

....

....

Reproduction and Growth

NGSS PERFORMANCE EXPECTATIONS

MS-LS1-4 Use argument based on empirical evidence and scientific reasoning to support an explanation for how characteristic animal behaviors and specialized plant structures affect the probability of successful reproduction of animals and plants respectively.

MS-LS1-5 Construct a scientific explanation based on evidence for how environmental and genetic factors influence the growth of organisms.

MS-LS3-2 Develop and use a model to describe why asexual reproduction results in offspring with identical genetic information and sexual reproduction results in offspring with genetic variation.

HANDS-ON LAB

uConnect Use a model to investigate how parental care can influence the survival of offspring.

Why does this tree have such a strange shape?

GO ONLINE to access your digital course

▶ VIDEO

👆 INTERACTIVITY

⚗ VIRTUAL LAB

☑ ASSESSMENT

📖 eTEXT

⚗ HANDS-ON LABS

The Essential Question

What factors influence the growth of organisms and their ability to reproduce?

CCC Cause and Effect Only found on Socotra Island, off the coast of Yemen, the cucumber tree grows in a hot and dry climate. How do you think the tree's shape helps it to survive?

....

....

....

....

Quest KICKOFF

How can we reduce the impact of construction on plants and animals?

Phenomenon Environmental scientists study habitats and the organisms that live there. They investigate how the availability of resources—such as water, food, and space—affects the ability of plants and animals to survive and reproduce. In this Quest activity, you will consider how to build a basketball court on school grounds, with minimal impact on local plants and animals. In digital activities, you will explore the factors that affect plant and animal growth and reproduction. By applying what you have learned, you will develop a construction proposal for the basketball court.

NBC LEARN ▶ VIDEO

After watching the video, which explores how construction impacts habitats and organisms, consider the issue on a local level. Choose a plant or animal, and then explain how human activity in your town or city affects the organism.

....

....

....

....

....

....

....

....

....

....

 INTERACTIVITY

Construction Without Destruction

MS-LS1-5 Construct a scientific explanation based on evidence for how environmental and genetic factors influence the growth of organisms.

IN LESSON 1

How do different organisms reproduce? Think about how the court's impact on the habitat might affect the ability of organisms to survive and reproduce there.

Quest CHECK-IN

IN LESSON 2

What effect might tree removal and construction work have on plants in the area? Assess the environmental impact on the ability of the plants to survive and reproduce.

 INTERACTIVITY

Protect the Plants

Quest CHECK-IN

IN LESSON 3

How does construction work impact animals? Think about how construction noise might interfere with the ability of an organism to reproduce successfully.

 INTERACTIVITY

The Mating Game

Before construction begins for a facility, such as a basketball court, professionals complete a construction proposal. It often outlines how organisms may be impacted once the construction is complete.

Quest CHECK-IN

IN LESSON 4

STEM How can the impact of the court's location and construction be minimized? Develop a plan that ensures the successful survival and reproduction of plants and animals.

 INTERACTIVITY

Make Your Construction Case

Quest FINDINGS

Complete the Quest!

Present your construction plan using the information and data that you have collected as evidence to support your recommendations.

 INTERACTIVITY

Reflect on Your Basketball Court Plans

To Care or Not To Care

How can you use a model to **make an argument** about how parenting affects the chance of offspring survival?

Background

Phenomenon A female sea turtle will lay over 100 eggs on a beach. Before the eggs hatch, she returns to the sea. Once her offspring hatch, they rush to the sea without any protection from a parent. Few of the offspring make it to adulthood. A female grizzly bear will give birth to one or two cubs. She will stay with the cubs and protect them until they reach adulthood. While some may not make it to adulthood, many grizzly cubs do. Why do so few sea turtles survive to adulthood as compared to grizzly cubs? In this activity, you will develop a model to show how parental care can influence the survival of offspring.

Materials

(per group)
• pop beads
• plastic tweezers
• stopwatch
• strip of cardboard

Safety

Be sure to follow all safety procedures provided by your teacher. The Safety Appendix of your textbook provides more details about the safety icons.

Develop a Model

☐ 1.  Think about how sea turtles and grizzly bears interact with their offspring. Develop a model that shows both of these interactions. Keep the following criteria in mind as you develop your model.

   • Use the materials provided.
   • Identify what each material will represent.
   • Consider the number of offspring of each species.
   • Collect data that will help you determine the percentage of offspring that survives.

☐ 2. **SEP Develop Models** Develop a plan to model sea turtle survival without parental care.

....

....

....

....

3. SEP Develop Models Develop a plan to model grizzly bear survival with parental care.

....

....

....

....

4. Show your plans to your teacher before you begin.

HANDS-ON LAB

Connect Go online for a downloadable worksheet of this lab.

Observations

Analyze and Interpret Data

1. **Compare and Contrast** Describe the similarities and differences between your two models.

....

....

....

2. **CCC Cause and Effect** How did modeling parental care affect the survival of the offspring?

....

....

....

3. **SEP Construct Arguments** Animals that do not provide parental care often have large numbers of offspring at once. Use the results from your models to explain why.

....

....

....

(1) Patterns of Reproduction

Guiding Questions

- How do organisms reproduce and transfer genes to their offspring?
- How do offspring produced by asexual reproduction and sexual reproduction compare?
- Why do different offspring of the same parent usually look different?

Connections

Literacy Cite Textual Evidence

Math Summarize Distributions

MS-LS3-2

HANDS-ON LAB

u**Investigate** Explore traits in an imaginary organism.

Vocabulary

asexual reproduction
sexual reproduction
fertilization
trait
gene
inheritance
allele

Academic Vocabulary

dominant

Connect It!

✏️ **The pictures show offspring with their mothers. Circle the offspring you think might look like the father.**

SEP Construct Explanations Summarize what you already know about how the three kinds of animals in the picture produce offspring.

....

....

....

....

....

....

Asexual and Sexual Reproduction

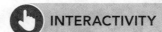

INTERACTIVITY

Consider the traits that make you unique.

Living things reproduce. Giraffes make more giraffes, hermit crabs make more hermit crabs, and bald eagles make more bald eagles. Some animals produce offspring that look exactly like the parent. Others, such as humans and the animals in **Figure 1,** produce offspring that look different from the parents.

Animals use one of two main methods—asexual or sexual reproduction—to produce offspring. Reproduction guarantees that a species' genes are passed on to the next generation.

Reflect What do you think is the benefit of reproducing asexually? In your science notebook, explain how asexual reproduction could give some animals an advantage.

Asexual Reproduction
A reproductive process that involves only one parent and produces offspring that are genetically identical to the parent is called **asexual reproduction**. It is the simplest form of reproduction. Animals such as sponges, corals, and certain jellyfish reproduce asexually.

One form of asexual reproduction is fragmentation. During fragmentation, a new organism forms from a piece of the original. For example, a whole new sea star can develop from a single arm that breaks off (see **Figure 2**). Another method of asexual reproduction is called budding. In this process, a new animal grows out from the parent until it fully matures and breaks off. Sponges and some sea anemones reproduce in this way.

Reproduction Results in Offspring
Figure 1 All living things have the ability to reproduce.

Sexual Reproduction

Sexual Reproduction Consider the variety of trees, birds, fish, and plants in the world around you. Clearly, many life forms are unique. When organisms reproduce sexually, their offspring display a variety of traits. Even members of the same species are not exact copies of each other. Sexual reproduction is responsible for the variety of life you see.

In **sexual reproduction**, two parents combine their genetic material to produce a new organism which differs from both parents. Sexual reproduction involves an egg cell and a sperm cell joining to form a new cell in a process called **fertilization**. Sperm cells are from the father and contain half of the father's chromosomes. Egg cells are from the mother and contain half the mother's chromosomes. When fertilization occurs, a full set of chromosomes is present in the new cell.

Because offspring receive roughly half their genetic information from each parent, they receive a combination of specific characteristics. A specific characteristic that an organism can pass to its offspring through its genes is called a **trait**. A **gene** is a sequence of DNA that determines a trait and is passed from parent to offspring. As a result, offspring may look very similar to their parents, or they may look very different, like the wild dogs in **Figure 2**. These differences are known as variations, and they are what make you different from your siblings. Individual variations depend on which genes were passed on from each parent.

Sexual vs. Asexual Reproduction

Figure 2 (top) A new sea star, identical to its parent, is developing from a single arm. (bottom) The fur patterns of the African wild-dog pups are different from their mother's.

Classify Which offspring resulted from sexual reproduction?

....

Model It!

SEP Develop Models ✏ Suppose a sea star produces offspring through asexual reproduction and two neighborhood dogs produce offspring through sexual reproduction. Draw a picture that shows how genetic information is passed down in each method of reproduction. Label the traits passed on to each offspring from the parent(s). Use your model to explain to a partner how genetic information is passed down in both types of reproduction.

Comparing Types of Reproduction Both

methods of reproduction have advantages and disadvantages. Organisms that reproduce asexually do not have to find a mate. They can also produce many offspring fairly quickly. The downside is that all of the offspring have exactly the same genetic makeup as the parent. This can be a problem if the environment changes. If one individual organism is unable to tolerate the change, then chances are the rest of the identical offspring will not be able to handle it either.

Organisms that reproduce sexually pass on genes with greater genetic variation. This variation may increase their chances of surviving in a changing environment. It is possible that they received a gene from a parent that helps them adapt to the changing environment. One potential downside of sexual reproduction is that the organism needs to find a mate. This can sometimes be a problem for animals, such as polar bears, that live in remote areas.

☑ READING CHECK Cite Textual Evidence What are some advantages of wild dogs reproducing sexually?

....

....

....

VIDEO

Compare asexual reproduction and sexual reproduction.

HANDS-ON LAB

ᴎInvestigate Develop and use models of asexual and sexual reproduction to compare how genetic information is passed from parent(s) to offspring.

Math Toolbox

Sexual Reproduction

Gestation is the time period between fertilization and birth. The data in the table are based on recorded observations from hundreds of pregnant individuals in each species.

Animal	Gestation Range (days)	Median Gestation Time (days)	Bottom Quartile Median (days)	Top Quartile Median (days)
Hamster	16–23	20	17	22
Red Fox	49–55	52	50	53
Gerbil	22–26	24	23	25
Leopard	91–95	93	92	94

1. **CCC Proportion** What is the relationship between the size of the animal and how long it takes for its offspring to develop?

....

....

2. **SEP Communicate Information** ✏ Choose two species from the table and construct a box plot for each one.

▶ **VIDEO**

Explore the relationship between inheritance and alleles.

Inherited Traits

When sperm and egg cells come together, genetic information from the mother and father mix. **Inheritance** is the process by which an offspring receives genes from its parents. Genes are located on chromosomes and describe the factors that control a trait. Each trait is described by a pair of genes, with one gene from the mother and one from the father. Sometimes the pair of genes are the same. At other times, there are two different genes in the pair.

For example, imagine a mouse with white fur and a mouse with brown fur have offspring. The genes for fur color from each parent are different. As shown in **Figure 3,** some of the offspring produced may be brown, some may be white, and others may be combinations of more than one color. Each offspring's fur color depends on how its inherited genes combine.

Academic Vocabulary
Describe a situation in which you have been dominant.

....
....
....
....
....
....

An **allele** is a different form of the same gene. One allele is received from each parent, and the combination of alleles determines which traits the offspring will have. In the simplest case, alleles are either dominant or recessive. If an offspring inherits a **dominant** allele from either parent, that trait will always show up in the offspring. But, if the offspring inherits recessive alleles from each parent, a recessive trait will show. This relationship allows parents with two dominant alleles to pass on recessive alleles to their offspring. For example, two brown-eyed people may have a blue-eyed child. However, most genetic traits do not follow these simple patterns of dominant and recessive inheritance.

Incomplete Dominance

Sometimes intermediate forms of a dominant trait appear. This means that mixing of colors or sizes occurs. Incomplete dominance may occur when a dominant allele and recessive allele are inherited. The offspring will have a mixture of these two alleles. For example, in some species of sheep, gray fleece results from a dominant white-fleece allele and a recessive black allele. Incomplete dominance also occurs in petal color in some species of plants. **Figure 4** shows how petal color can result in the blending of two colors.

Codominance

Unlike incomplete dominance, which shows blending of traits, codominance results in both alleles being expressed at the same time. In cattle, horses, and dogs, there is a color pattern called roan. This color pattern appears when a dominant white-hair allele and a dominant solid-color allele is inherited. The offspring has hairs of each color intermixed, giving the solid-color a more muted or mottled look.

Incomplete Dominance Figure 4 ✏ Circle the flowers that demonstrate incomplete dominance in petal color.

Model It !

CCC Cause and Effect ✏ Draw the parents of this flower in the box. Assume that the flower's color is determined by codominance.

187

		Father's blood type				
		A	B	AB	O	Child's blood type must be
Mother's blood type	A	A or O	A, B, AB, or O	A, B, or AB	A or O	
	B	A, B, AB, or O	B or O	A, B, or AB	B or O	
	AB	A, B, or AB	A, B, or AB	A, B, or AB	A or B	
	O	A or O	B or O	A or B	O	

Human Blood Types

Figure 5 A gene with multiple alleles is expressed as one of four blood types: A, B, AB, and O.

Multiple Alleles

Every offspring inherits one allele from each parent for a total of two alleles. However, sometimes one trait has more than two alleles. For example, there are three alleles for blood type—A, B, and O. The A and B blood types are codominant and O is recessive. As you see in **Figure 5**, you receive two of the multiple alleles from each parent, but each possible combination of alleles results in one of four different blood types. Multiple alleles are not found only in blood types. **Figure 6** shows how fur color in some rabbits is the result of multiple alleles.

Multiple Alleles

Figure 6 These rabbits all came from the same litter.

SEP Engage in Argument from Evidence What evidence from the picture demonstrates that the fur color of these rabbits results from multiple alleles?

....

....

....

....

Polygenic Inheritance

Some traits are controlled by more than one gene. In polygenetic inheritance, these different genes are expressed together to produce the trait. Human height is an example of this. If the mother is 5 feet 2 inches tall and the father is 6 feet tall, then you might think that all of the offspring would be 5 feet 7 inches. However, there can be a large variation among the heights of the children. This fact is due to multiple genes working together to produce the trait.

✓ **READING CHECK** **Determine Central Ideas** How do alleles influence inherited traits? Explain with an example of incomplete dominance.

....

....

....

Genes and the Environment

What kinds of things have you learned in your life? Maybe you know how to paint. Maybe you can ride a unicycle. Or maybe you know how to solve very complicated math problems. Whatever your abilities, they are acquired traits that are the result of learned behaviors.

Acquired Traits The traits you inherited can be affected by your experience. For example, humans are born with teeth, vocal cords, and tongues—all of which enable us to speak. The language you learn to use depends on your environment. You were not born speaking a particular language, but you were born with the capacity to learn languages, whether a spoken language or sign language. The ability for language is an inherited trait. The language or languages you use, however, are acquired traits.

The combination of inherited traits and acquired traits helps many organisms to survive in their environment. The fox squirrel in **Figure 7** has inherited traits from its parents that help it survive in its environment. The squirrel also acquired traits that help it survive, by learning behaviors from its parents and by interacting with its environment.

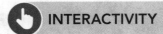

INTERACTIVITY

Find out how we learn about genes and traits from studying twins.

HANDS-ON LAB

Investigate Explore traits in an imaginary organism.

Acquired Traits

Figure 7 This fox squirrel has traits that were inherited as well as traits that were acquired through learning.

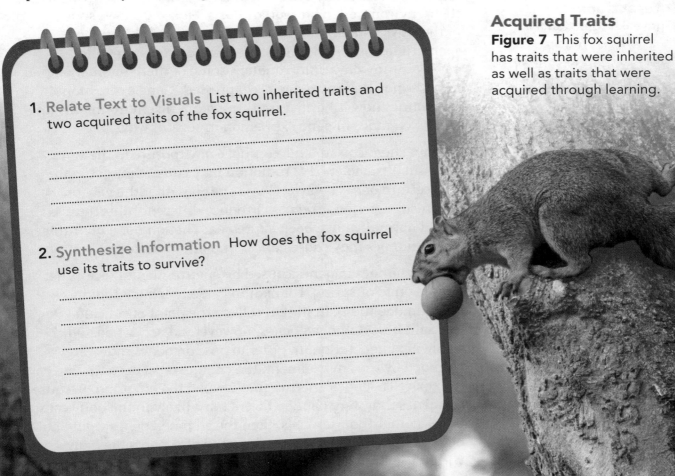

1. **Relate Text to Visuals** List two inherited traits and two acquired traits of the fox squirrel.

....

....

....

....

2. **Synthesize Information** How does the fox squirrel use its traits to survive?

....

....

....

....

....

....

189

Environmental Interactions

Figure 8 Protection from the sun when you are outside all day is important.

Implement a Solution List three acquired behaviors that people have learned to protect themselves from ultraviolet light.

....

....

....

....

....

Literacy Connection

Cite Textual Evidence Underline two sentences that tell how changes to genes in body cells differ from changes to genes in sex cells.

Environmental Factors Organisms interact with their environment on a regular basis. **Figure 8** shows some of the ways you interact with your environment. You may spend time with friends, breathe fresh air, exercise, and enjoy a sunny day. Unfortunately, some of these interactions may change the way a gene is expressed. Gene expression determines how inherited traits appear. The environment can lead to changes in gene expression in several ways.

Certain chemicals in tobacco smoke or exposure to the sun's harmful ultraviolet (UV) radiation may cause changes in the way certain genes behave. These changes alter the way an organism functions and may produce different traits than would normally have been expressed. Though not a guarantee, these changes may cause cancer and other diseases.

Not all changes in genes caused by environmental factors get passed on to offspring. For example, too much UV radiation can damage the DNA in skin cells to the point of causing cancer. These damaged genes, however, do not get passed to the next generation. In order to pass on genes that were changed by the environment, the change must occur in one of the sex cells—egg or sperm—that formed the offspring. Because the genes that were changed were most likely in the body cells, or cells other than sex cells, then the changed genes would not be passed on to you, and would instead affect only the individual with the changed genes.

1. Distinguish Relationships What does inheritance mean in terms of reproduction?

....
....
....

2. Determine Differences ✎ Indicate whether each of the listed traits is acquired from the environment or has been inherited.

Trait	Acquired	Inherited
Brown fur in rabbits		
Length of an elephant's trunk		
Having a spiked haircut		
An overweight horse		
Feather patterns of a parrot		

3. CCC Cause and Effect What happens if an offspring inherits a dominant allele from one of its parents?

....
....
....

4. SEP Construct Explanations What is a possible benefit to an organism expressing codominant or incomplete dominant traits?

....
....
....
....
....
....

5. Support Your Explanation How does sexual reproduction differ from asexual reproduction?

....
....
....
....
....
....
....

6. SEP Construct Explanations A species of butterfly has alleles for wing color that are either blue or orange. But, when a blue butterfly and an orange butterfly mated, the wings of the offspring were blue and orange. Explain the process through which wing color was expressed.

....
....
....
....

7. SEP Evaluate Evidence Human hair color is a trait with very broad variation. Which pattern of inheritance could account for human hair color? Explain your answer.

....
....
....
....
....
....

Plant Structures for Reproduction

Guiding Questions

- How do plants reproduce?
- How do seeds become new plants?
- Which specialized plant structures affect the probability of successful reproduction?

Connection

Literacy Cite Textual Evidence

MS-LS1-4

HANDS-ON LAB

uInvestigate Demonstrate how flower structures relate to successful reproduction.

Vocabulary

zygote
pollination
cones
ovule
fruit
germination

Academic Vocabulary

disperse

Connect It

✏️ **Circle the fruits shown here.**

CCC Structure and Function Where in the fruit are seeds found and what is their purpose?

....

....

Plant Reproduction

Have you ever run from a bee buzzing around a garden? Have you taken the time to appreciate the pleasant scent and beautiful colors of a rose? Have you challenged a friend to see who could spit a watermelon seed the farthest? If you have done any of these things, you are already familiar with some of the methods plants use to reproduce.

When a seed, like ones from the fruits and vegetables in **Figure 1**, is planted in healthy soil and gets plenty of water and sunlight, it can grow into an adult plant. But this is just one part in the process of how plants reproduce. A lot must first happen in a plant's life before it can produce a seed that can grow into a plant. Surprisingly to some, plants are like animals in that reproduction requires a sperm cell fertilizing an egg cell for a new organism to begin.

To ensure successful reproduction, plants have evolved specialized structures over time. Different types of plants have different structures and methods that help them reproduce. But the goal is the same: to produce new generations of life.

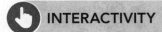

INTERACTIVITY

Explore the relationship between seeds and the food we eat.

Find the Fruit
Figure 1 Fruits may not look alike, but they function just the same. Inside a seed is a partially developed plant.

193

Plant Life Cycles

Figure 2 ✏ Complete the diagrams. Identify the sporophyte and gametophyte stage in each diagram.

The Life Cycle of a Moss Plant

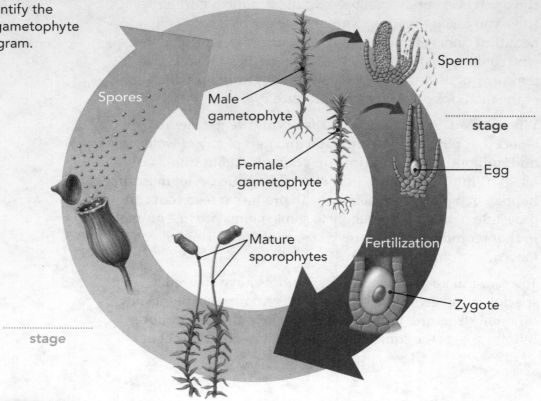

Spores

Male gametophyte

Female gametophyte

Sperm

stage

Egg

Mature sporophytes

Fertilization

Zygote

.... **stage**

Spore Production

Figure 3 Fern sporophytes are the recognizable parts of the plant.

Identify What is the purpose of the sporophyte stage?

....

....

....

....

....

Plant Life Cycles

Plants have complex life cycles that include two different stages: the sporophyte (SPOH ruh fyt) and gametophyte (guh MEE tuh fyt) stages. During the sporophyte stage, a plant produces the spores that will eventually develop into gametophytes. During the gametophyte stage, male and female gametophytes produce sex cells that will eventually be involved in the process of fertilization, which occurs when a sperm cell unites with an egg cell to produce a new organism.

Nonvascular and Seedless Vascular Plants

Mosses and other nonvascular plants produce sporophytes that resemble small trees or flowers. The sporophytes release spores that grow into male and female gametophytes. These gametophytes produce the sperm and egg cells that are needed for a **zygote**, or fertilized egg, to form and develop into a new sporophyte as is shown in **Figure 2**.

The life stages of seedless vascular plants, such as ferns, are similar to nonvascular plants in some ways. Sporophytes produce spores that develop into gametophytes. But fern gametophytes have both male and female structures that produce sex cells. When a sperm cell fertilizes an egg cell, a new sporophyte begins to develop.

The Life Cycle of an Angiosperm

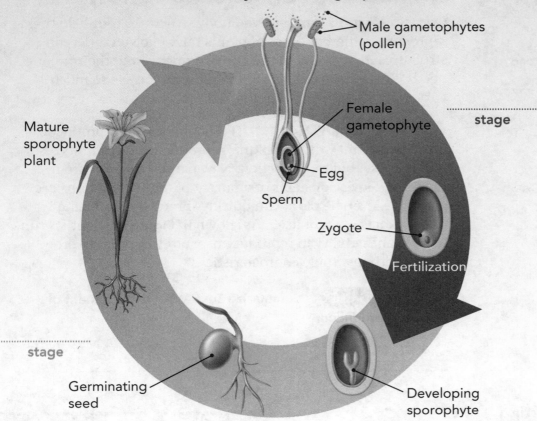

Male gametophytes (pollen)

Female gametophyte

Egg

Sperm

stage

Mature sporophyte plant

Zygote

Fertilization

stage

Germinating seed

Developing sporophyte

Other Vascular Plants The two other types of vascular plants are gymnosperms and angiosperms. Unlike both ferns and mosses, gymnosperm and angiosperm gametophytes actually develop inside structures within a larger sporophyte. In gymnosperms, they develop inside cones, and in an angiosperm like the one shown in **Figure 2**, they develop inside flowers.

The male gametophyte in these types of plants is called pollen. Pollen contains cells that will mature into sperm cells. For reproduction to occur, pollen must travel to the female gametophyte so it can fertilize egg cells. This process of transferring pollen from male reproductive structures to female reproductive structures in plants is called **pollination**. Pollination must occur in these plants before fertilization can occur.

☑ READING CHECK **Determine Central Ideas** How do the sporophyte stage and gametophyte stage make a cycle?

....

....

....

....

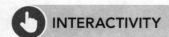

INTERACTIVITY

Explore how plant structures help plants reproduce asexually and sexually.

Structures for Reproduction

Over time, plants have evolved body structures that help them reproduce. Different types of plants have evolved different structures in response to their environments and their unique needs. Reproduction is one of the reasons you see so much variety in the different plant types.

Asexual Reproduction Though sexual reproduction is the dominant way that plants reproduce, many plants also undergo asexual reproduction. New plants can grow from the roots, leaves, or stems of a parent plant. If conditions are favorable, a single plant can quickly spread by producing many exact copies of itself. As shown in **Figure 4**, scientists can use a plant's ability to reproduce asexually in order to grow plants with favorable characteristics.

☑ **READING CHECK** **Summarize Text** What is the benefit of asexual reproduction?

....

....

Apple Tree Grafting

Figure 4 Grafting is one way that humans can reproduce plants. Part of a plant's stem is cut and then attached to another plant. These apple trees have been grafted in order to ensure that the desired characteristics from the original tree are maintained in future trees.

Apply Concepts Is grafting a form of sexual or asexual reproduction?

....

Male and Female Cones

Figure 5 Male cones, such as the ones to the right, hold pollen. Female cones, such as the two shown below, open when the weather is warm and dry. They close when conditions are cold and wet.

CCC Structure and Function How do you think the cone's ability to open and close helps with reproduction?

....

....

....

....

....

Gymnosperms Trees such as pines, redwoods, firs, cedars, and hemlocks are all classified as gymnosperms. Many gymnosperms have needle-like leaves and deep roots. However, all have cones and unprotected seeds. These two characteristics set them apart from other vascular plants.

The structures in **Figure 5** are **cones** , which are the reproductive structures of gymnosperms. Male cones hold pollen, whereas the female cone has an **ovule**, the structure holding the egg. The female cone also makes a sticky substance on the outside of the cone, needed for pollination. Pollen from the male cone is light enough to be carried by the wind. When the wind blows, pollen may land on the sticky female cone. When this happens, the egg may become fertilized. The ovule seals off and the zygote develops into a plant embryo in the seed. Seeds can remain in the female cone for a few years, until they mature.

The seeds of gymnosperms are "naked," meaning they are unprotected. Once the female cone matures, the scales open, exposing the seeds. As wind blows, the exposed seeds are blown out of the cone and spread by the wind.

Literacy Connection

Cite Textual Evidence Which detail in the text helped you understand what gymnosperms are?

....

....

....

....

....

....

....

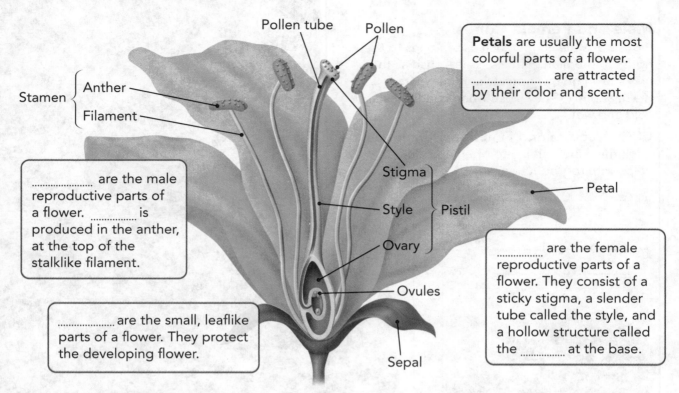

Pollen tube

Pollen

Petals are usually the most colorful parts of a flower. .... are attracted by their color and scent.

Stamen { Anther

Filament

.... are the male reproductive parts of a flower. .... is produced in the anther, at the top of the stalklike filament.

Stigma

Style

Pistil

Ovary

Petal

.... are the female reproductive parts of a flower. They consist of a sticky stigma, a slender tube called the style, and a hollow structure called the .... at the base.

Ovules

.... are the small, leaflike parts of a flower. They protect the developing flower.

Sepal

Flower Parts and Their Jobs

Figure 6 Flowers contain the reproductive structures of angiosperms. Complete the diagram by filling in the missing words.

CCC Structure and Function What is the purpose of the flower's petals? Why is their function important?

....
....
....
....
....

HANDS-ON LAB

Investigate
Demonstrate how flower structures relate to successful reproduction.

Angiosperms All angiosperms share two important characteristics. They all produce flowers and fruits that contain seeds. The angiosperm life cycle begins when pollen forms in the flower's anthers. These structures are found at the end of the stamens, which are the male reproductive structure. The female reproductive structure is the pistil and has three parts: the stigma, style, and ovary. When pollen falls on the stigma, pollination may occur, which can lead to fertilization.

Some angiosperms are pollinated by the wind, but most rely on animals called pollinators, such as bees and hummingbirds. When an organism enters a flower to obtain food, it becomes coated with pollen. Some of the pollen can drop onto the flower's stigma as the animal leaves. The pollen can also be brushed onto the stigma of the next flower the animal visits. If the pollen falls on the stigma of a similar plant, fertilization can occur. A sperm cell joins with an egg cell inside an ovule within the ovary at the base of the flower. The zygote then begins to develop into the seed's embryo. Other parts of the ovule develop into the rest of the seed.

Additional structures help a flowering plant to reproduce successfully. Colorful, often pleasantly-scented petals surround the plant's reproductive organs and attract pollinators. Green sepals protect the growing flower. The flower is what develops the **fruit**—the ripened ovary and other structures of an angiosperm enclosing one or more seeds.

Seed Dispersal Fruits are the means by which angiosperm seeds are **dispersed**. Often the scent and color of fruit attracts animals to the plant. Animals eat the fruit and then the seeds in it pass through the animal's digestive system. As the animal moves around, seeds are deposited in different areas in the animal's dung, or droppings. The droppings have an added benefit of providing nutrients and moisture for the seed.

In other cases, seeds disperse by falling into water or being carried by the wind. Seeds with barbs attach to fur or clothing and are carried away. Others are ejected by the seed pods and scattered in different directions. Seeds dispersed far from the parent plant have a better chance of surviving. Distance keeps the new plant from competing with the parent plant for light, water, and nutrients. When a seed lands in a spot with suitable conditions, germination may occur. **Germination** occurs when the embryo sprouts out of the seed.

☑ READING CHECK **Cite Textual Evidence** How do the examples of seed dispersal given in the text help you understand the role of seed dispersal in plant reproduction?

....

....

....

Academic Vocabulary
Use *dispersed* in another sentence that uses a context other than seeds and plants.

....

....

....

....

👆 **INTERACTIVITY**

Explore the relationship between plants and pollinators.

Model It !

Flower to Fruit
The male and female flower parts enable reproduction to take place. They contain structures to form the egg and sperm that will join to create the zygote.

SEP Develop and Use Models ✏️ Draw a sequence of pictures to show the steps that must take place for a flowering plant to reproduce and form a new seedling.

MS-LS1-4

1. Define What is a fruit?

....

....

....

2. CCC Structure and Function Why do flowers have brightly-colored petals and attractive scents?

....

....

....

....

....

3. Determine Differences How does seed dispersal in angiosperms differ from seed dispersal in gymnosperms?

....

....

....

....

....

....

4. CCC Patterns In what ways are sexual and asexual production in plants similar, and in what ways do they differ?

....

....

....

....

....

....

....

....

....

....

5. SEP Construct Explanations Tell how seeds are produced and spread in gymnosperms.

....

....

....

....

....

....

Quest CHECK-IN

In this lesson, you learned about plant structures that help them reproduce successfully.

SEP Design Solutions How might knowing about the ways the local plants reproduce help in the planning and design of the basketball court?

....

....

....

....

....

....

INTERACTIVITY

Protect the Plants

Go online to assess the impact of the construction project on plants.

GARDENING in Space

▶ **VIDEO**

Learn more about growing plants in space.

Do you know how to grow plants in space? You engineer it! NASA engineers and astronauts show us how.

The Challenge: To grow plants on long space flights.

Phenomenon Future space-flight missions will take months, years, and eventually multiple lifetimes, to reach their distant destinations. These missions will rely on growing plants in space as a source of food for astronauts, a method for recycling carbon dioxide into breathable oxygen, and potentially as part of the process that recycles, filters, and purifies water.

Plant structures and their functions are adapted to life on Earth. Leaves grow toward sunlight and roots grow down, due to gravity. In space, with no sunlight and very little gravity, plants do not grow easily. Because water floats away without gravity, watering plants in space is also tricky. Astronauts grow some plants directly in water. Other plants grow in a spongy clay-like material that allows water to reach all the roots.

NASA engineers have designed plant growth chambers used on the International Space Station (ISS) to investigate the effects of space on plant growth. The systems use LED lights and have multiple sensors to track data on temperature, moisture, and oxygen levels.

This is not a picture taken from above. These plants are growing sideways!

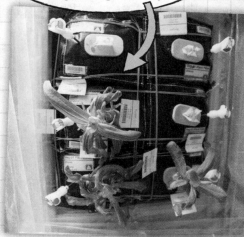

The Veggie System was installed in 2014. It allows the astronauts to grow their own food aboard the ISS.

DESIGN CHALLENGE Can you design and build a model of a lunar growth chamber for plants? Go to the Engineering Design Notebook to find out!

Animal Behaviors for Reproduction

Guiding Questions

- What causes animals to behave in certain ways?
- What are some different ways in which animals reproduce?
- How can the behavior of animals increase their chances of reproducing?

Connections

Literacy Summarize Text

Math Draw Comparative Inferences

MS-LS1-4

HANDS-ON LAB

uInvestigate Explore how salmon migrate from the ocean back to their home river.

Vocabulary

behavior
instinct
pheromone
mating system
migration

Academic Vocabulary

typically

Connect It!

✏ **Circle the most vulnerable member of this elephant herd.**

Make Observations What do you notice about where the young elephants are in relation to the older ones?

....

....

SEP Construct Explanations Why do you think the elephants travel this way?

....

....

Animal Behavior

Have you ever noticed how busy animals are? Most are constantly looking for food or trying to avoid other animals that think of them as food. Many also spend a lot of time looking for mates and caring for their young. All of these actions are examples of an animal's behavior. The way an organism reacts to changes in its internal conditions or external environment is **behavior**. Like body structures, the behaviors of animals are adaptations that have evolved over long periods of time.

Some behaviors are learned while others are known without being taught. An **instinct** is a response to a stimulus that is inborn and that an animal performs correctly the first time. For example, when sea turtles hatch from their eggs, they know by instinct to travel to the ocean. Other behaviors are learned. Learning is the process that leads to changes in behavior based on practice or experience.

The goal of most animal behaviors is to help them survive or reproduce (**Figure 1**). When an animal looks for food or hides from a predator, it is doing something that helps it stay alive. When animals search for mates and build nests for their young, they are behaving in ways that help them reproduce.

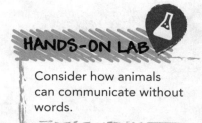
HANDS-ON LAB

Consider how animals can communicate without words.

Elephant Behavior
Figure 1 The adult elephants stay close to the baby for its protection. Many animals instinctively risk their own safety to protect their young from danger.

INTERACTIVITY

Find out more about animal behavior.

Literacy Connection

Summarize Text After reading each section of text, briefly summarize the key ideas from that section to a family member or classmate or make an audio recording of yourself. Later, go back and listen to the recording or play it for someone else. Clarify any ideas that may be confusing.

Mating Behaviors When animals mate, a male animal fertilizes a female animal's egg cells with his sperm cells. The fertilized egg will eventually develop into a new organism. This process is an important part of ensuring the continued survival of the species. Scientists believe that the drive to reproduce evolved in animals over time as a way to ensure the success of their species and their own individual genes.

The behavior patterns related to how animals mate are called **mating systems**, and they vary from species to species. Some species of animals are monogamous. That means that they only mate with one other organism for a period of time, which can range from just a season or to their entire lives. In other animal species, such as baboons, a male has multiple female mates at one time. There are other species in which females have multiple male mates. Honeybees use this mating system. In still other species, males and females both have multiple mates during any one period of time. Scientists believe that these different mating systems evolved over time to best meet the needs of each particular species.

Model It

The terms defined below are used to describe the different mating systems that are observed in animal species.

monogamy: one female mates with one male
polygyny: one male mates with multiple females
polyandry: one female mates with multiple males
polygynandry: females mate with multiple males and males mate with multiple females

SEP Develop Models ✏ Use the information above and the symbols for male and female, which are shown to the right, to model the four types of mating systems in the space provided. Monogamy has been completed for you.

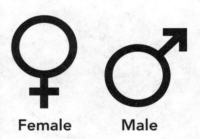

Female   Male

Monogamy

Courtship Behaviors
Figure 2 This male peacock shows off his elaborate feathers to attract females that he hopes to mate with.

CCC Structure and Function How do you think this peacock's feathers help him to attract mates?

....
....
....
....
....
....
....

Imagine a male walrus swimming in the icy water making a series of whistling and clacking sounds. A group of females looks on from the floating ice pack. One joins the male in the water and they dive together in a dance-like ritual. This courtship behavior is an activity that prepares males and females of the same species for mating. These behaviors are ways for animals to attract the attention of potential mates.

Communication Animals communicate in many ways, using sounds, scents, and body movements. Often, the goal of communication is reproduction.

One way animals communicate is with sound. You have probably heard birds singing outside. Birds sing for many reasons, but one of the reasons they sing is to attract mates. Many animals also use chemical scents to send messages. A chemical released by one animal that affects the behavior of another animal of the same species is called a **pheromone** (fehr uh mohn). In many species of moths, for example, females release a pheromone into the air that is a signal to males that she is ready to mate.

Competition Animals compete for resources, such as food and water. They also compete for access to mates, which may involve displays of aggression. Aggression is a threatening behavior that one animal uses to intimidate or dominate another animal. Another competitive behavior that is often observed in animals is establishing and maintaining a territory. A territory is an area that is occupied and defended by an animal or group of animals. An animal that is defending its territory will drive away other animals that may compete with it for mates.

Reflect As you learn about animal behaviors related to reproduction, spend some time observing animals in the area around your neighborhood and school. Record notes and observations in your science notebook. Explain what type of behavior you think you were observing and why.

Reproductive Strategies

Different animal species have different ways of caring for their young. Some species have no contact with their offspring, while others spend many years caring for them. For example, most amphibian larvae, or tadpoles, develop into adults without parental help. Similarly, the offspring of most reptiles, such as snakes, are independent from the time they hatch. Offspring that do not receive parental care must be able to care for themselves from the time of birth. Generally, animals that provide no parental care release many eggs at a time. Although many will not survive, the sheer number of potential offspring ensures that at least some will make it.

Parental Investment The offspring of most birds and all mammals **typically** spend weeks to years under the care and protection of a parent. Most bird species lay eggs in nests that one or both parents build. Then one or both parents sit on the eggs, keeping them warm until they hatch. After hatching, one or both parents will feed and protect their young until they are able to care for themselves. Young mammals, such as the infant chimpanzee in **Figure 3**, are usually quite helpless for a long time after they are born. After birth, mammals are fed with milk from the mother's body. One or both parents may continue caring for their offspring until the young animals are independent. Typically, animals that provide parental care have only a few offspring at a time. Many only have one. Scientists believe that these animals work harder to care for their young because they have fewer or no other offspring to take their place.

Academic Vocabulary

What are some synonyms, or words and phrases that have a similar meaning, for the term *typically*?

....

....

....

Parenting Behavior

Figure 3 This female chimpanzee carries her infant on her back until it is old enough to better care for itself.

Distinguish Relationships What are the benefits and drawbacks of this behavior for the mother chimpanzee?

....

....

....

....

....

....

....

Survivorship Curves

To show how the probability of death changes with age for different species, scientists use graphs called survivorship curves. In a Type I survivorship curve, individuals are most likely to live a full life. In a Type III survivorship curve, individuals are most likely to die when they are young. In a Type II survivorship curve, an individual's chance of dying remains constant.

SEP Interpret Data What can you infer about the role of parental care for the three species represented in the graph?

....

....

....

....

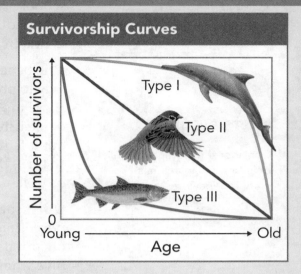

Survivorship Curves

Type I

Type II

Type III

Number of survivors

0

Young ——→ Old

Age

Fertilization Strategies

For animals that reproduce sexually, a new organism begins when a sperm cell and an egg cell are joined in the process of fertilization. Fertilization may occur in one of two ways: externally or internally. **External fertilization** occurs when eggs are fertilized outside of a female's body, and **internal fertilization** occurs when eggs are fertilized inside a female's body.

The male fish in **Figure 4** are fertilizing the females' eggs by releasing their sperm into a cloud of eggs the female just released. The fertilized eggs will develop outside the female's body. Not all the eggs will become fertilized but the huge number of potential offspring means that many will.

When fertilization occurs internally, a male animal releases sperm directly into a female's body where the eggs are located. The fertilized eggs may develop inside or outside the mother's body. Many animals, such as reptiles and birds, lay eggs in which offspring develop until they hatch. For others, including most mammals, offspring develop inside the mother's body until they are ready to be born.

✓ READING CHECK Determine Central Ideas How are internal and external fertilization alike and different?

....

....

....

External Fertilization
Figure 4 Male fish release sperm in a cloud over the eggs.

Make Observations What makes the image an example of external fertilization?

....

....

HANDS-ON LAB

Investigate Explore how salmon migrate from the ocean back to their home river.

 INTERACTIVITY

Consider the impact of light pollution on an animals' mating behaviors.

Cooperative Behaviors

In some cases, animals increase their chances for surviving and reproducing when they live and work together. For example, some fish form schools, and some insects live in large groups. Hoofed mammals, such as bison and wild horses, often form herds. Living in a group helps these animals stay alive.

One benefit of living in a large group is that it is an effective way to protect young animals from predators. Elephants like those in **Figure 1** protect the offspring of the group by forming a defensive circle around them. By working together, each adult female helps to protect the offspring of the other females. In turn, the other members of the group protect her offspring as well.

Other species of animals that live in groups may take on parenting responsibilities of animals that are not their offspring (**Figure 5**). For example, there are worker bees in a hive whose sole job is providing food and protection for the bee larvae. They may not be the parents of the offspring, but they still work hard to care for the hive's young.

✓ **READING CHECK** **Summarize Text** How can cooperative behaviors help animals that are raising offspring?

....

....

....

....

Working Together

Figure 5 Orcas live in a pod. All adult members of the pod help parent any offspring in the pod. Likewise, some spiders live in a nest and work together to raise their young.

Integrate Information What is the benefit of shared responsibility when raising young? Explain.

....

....

....

....

....

....

....

....

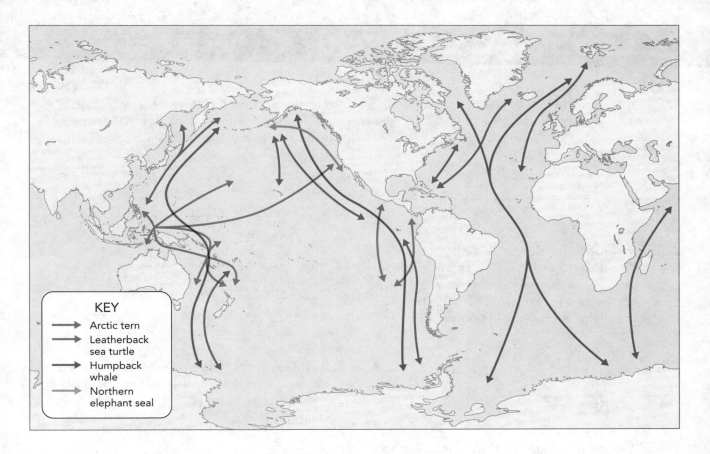

KEY
→ Arctic tern
→ Leatherback sea turtle
→ Humpback whale
→ Northern elephant seal

Migratory Behaviors
Many animals spend their entire lives in a relatively small area. But there are many others that migrate. **Migration** is the regular, seasonal journey of an animal from one place to another and back again. Animals have different reasons for migration. Some migrate to an area that provides plenty of food or a more comfortable climate during a harsh season. Others, such as the animals whose migratory routes are shown in **Figure 6**, migrate to a better environment for reproduction. In some cases, large groups of animals of the same species gather together in the same place at the same time so they can mate. They may also stay there to begin the process of raising their young. By migrating every year, these animals increase their chances of finding a mate and producing offspring in conditions that will be favorable to their survival.

Animal behaviors related to mating and raising offspring are often tied to Earth's cycles. Polar bears, for example, mate in the spring and give birth in the winter. Other animals reproduce with more or less frequency, but almost all follow some kind of predictable cycle. Following these patterns ensures that offspring are born when they have the best chances of survival.

Migratory Routes
Figure 6 Many animals travel thousands of miles every year to mate and raise their young.

SEP Use Models ✏️
A friend took a road trip across the United States from the west coast to the east coast. Draw an arrow on the map showing the trip. How does your friend's trip compare to the animal trips represented in the map?

....

....

....

....

☑ LESSON 3 Check

1. **Determine Differences** What is the difference between learned behaviors and instincts?

....
....
....
....

2. **SEP Evaluate Evidence** Male birds of paradise are known for having bright markings that they flash while making complex movements when females are nearby. What is this behavior an example of and what is its purpose?

....
....
....
....

3. **SEP Construct Explanations** Describe how animals use pheromones to attract potential mates.

....
....
....
....
....

4. **Compare and Contrast** Describe two different parenting strategies that animals use and explain why they are both effective.

....
....
....
....
....
....
....
....

5. **SEP Develop Models** ✏ Draw a picture showing how animals that use cooperative behaviors might be able to protect offspring from predators.

Quest CHECK-IN

In this lesson, you learned how animal behaviors can help individuals find mates. You also learned how animal parenting behaviors can affect how likely their offspring are to survive.

Explain Phenomena Consider various ways a male bird might attract a female mate. Suppose the male bird is of a species that does not display colorful feathers, the way peacocks do. What sort of behaviors could the male birds use to attract female birds?

....
....
....

☝ INTERACTIVITY

The Mating Game

Go online to explore different techniques and behaviors that animals use to increase their odds of reproductive success.

MS-LS1-4

Avian Artists

As male birds go, the Vogelkop bowerbird is rather plain. It doesn't have the bright feathers of a cardinal or the fancy plumage of a peacock. But what the bowerbird lacks in color, it makes up for in engineering and decorating skills.

The Vogelkop bowerbird displays some of the most complex courtship behavior observed in birds. To attract a mate, the male builds an elaborate structure out of twigs, called a bower. After completing the bower, the male bowerbird collects brightly colored flowers and berries to decorate the bower. Males compete to build the most magnificent bowers and amass the most beautiful collections in the hopes of impressing female bowerbirds.

When a female comes by to inspect the bower and collection, the male will strut and sing inside the bower. If the female likes the male's decorating expertise, then they will mate. The female will leave to build a nest and raise the young on her own.

MY DISCOVERY

What other animal species display extraordinary behavior when it comes to courtship? Do some research to find out more.

Male Vogelkop bowerbirds spend years making their bowers.

The Vogelkop bowerbird lives on the island of New Guinea in the Pacific Ocean.

Factors Influencing Growth

Guiding Questions

- How do environmental and genetic factors influence an organism's growth?
- What stimulates plant growth?
- Which factors control plant and animal growth?

Connections

Literacy Analyze Text Structure

Math Represent Quantitative Relationships

MS-LS1-5

HANDS-ON LAB

uInvestigate Observe how environmental factors such as pollution affect plant growth.

Vocabulary

hormone
auxin
tropism
photoperiodism
dormancy
metamorphosis

Academic Vocabulary

stimuli
essential

Connect It !

✎ Vines are plants that can use other structures, such as trees, for support. Circle a vine in the picture and draw an arrow to show the direction of its growth.

CCC Structure and Function How do you think the vine was able to grow up the tree?

....

....

SEP Construct Explanations Why do you think the vine used the tree to grow?

....

....

Growth and Development of Organisms

The way organisms grow and develop, and the size they reach, varies from species to species.

Several factors influence how organisms grow. Some are determined by the genetic characteristics that are passed from parent to offspring during reproduction. Other factors occur outside of the organism and can be related to their access to needed resources, the conditions in their environment, and their responses to other **stimuli**. Healthy plants inherit traits that determine successful growth, but if the conditions around them are not ideal, the plants may not grow or develop normally.

To increase their odds for survival, plants and animals have changed over time. These changes are a result of adapting to stimuli in the environment. The vines in **Figure 1**, for example, grow in response to their environment. Vines have evolved to grow around larger trees and other structures as a means of accessing sunlight and gaining space for further growth.

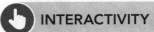

INTERACTIVITY

Explore the conditions required for living things to grow and thrive.

HANDS-ON LAB

Investigate Analyze and explain how genetic factors affect the growth of adult plants.

Academic Vocabulary

Often, a dog barks when someone rings the doorbell and knocks on the door. What are the stimuli in this situation?

....

....

....

Plant Growth
Figure 1 These vines have evolved the adaptation of growing up and around other trees.

Plant Responses and Growth

If you've ever grown a garden, you've probably witnessed how plants grow over time. As with all living things, plant growth is controlled by responses to stimuli. For plants, these responses are controlled by **hormones**, chemicals that affect growth and development. One important plant hormone is called **auxin** (AWK sin). It speeds up the rate at which plant cells grow and controls a plant's response to light.

Tropisms In animals, a typical response to a stimulus is to move toward or away from it. But plants cannot move in the same way that animals do, so they often respond by growing either toward or away from a stimulus. A plant's growth response toward or away from a stimulus is called a **tropism** (TROH piz um). Touch, gravity, and light are three stimuli that trigger tropisms in plants.

The stems of some plants, such as the vines in **Figure 1**, show a response to touch called thigmotropism. As a vine grows, it coils around any object it touches. This is an example of positive thigmotropism, because the vine grows toward the stimulus. Plants also know which direction to grow, because they respond to gravity. This response is called gravitropism. Roots show positive gravitropism if they grow downward. Stems, on the other hand, show negative gravitropism (**Figure 2**). Plants' response to light is called phototropism. The leaves, stems, and flowers of plants grow toward light.

How Plants Respond

Figure 2 Plants respond to stimuli from the environment in a variety of ways.

Negative Gravitropism The stems of plants respond to the stimulus of gravity by growing upward, away from gravity.

Positive Phototropism When stems and leaves grow toward sources of light, it shows positive phototropism.

CCC Patterns ✏ Place a circle where the sun would be in the picture above.

Seasonal Change Depending on where you live, you may have noticed flowers blooming in the spring and the leaves of trees changing color in autumn. These changes are caused by changing conditions brought on by the seasons.

In many plants, the amount of darkness it experiences determines when it blooms. A plant's response to seasonal changes in the length of night and day is called **photoperiodism**. As shown in **Figure 2**, plants respond differently to the length of nights. Other plants are not affected at all by the lengths of days and nights.

Have you ever wondered why some trees lose their leaves in the fall? As winter draws near, many plants prepare to go into a state of **dormancy**. Dormancy is a period when an organism's growth or activity stops. Dormancy helps plants survive freezing temperatures and the lack of liquid water. With many trees, the first visible change is that the leaves begin to turn color. Cooler weather and shorter days cause the leaves to stop making chlorophyll. As chlorophyll breaks down, yellow and orange pigments become visible. This causes the brilliant colors of autumn leaves like the ones shown in **Figure 2**. Over the next few weeks, sugar and water are transported out of the tree's leaves. When the leaves fall to the ground, the tree is ready for winter.

Literacy Connection

Analyze Text Structure
Text structure describes how a text is organized. Section headings can give you clues about how a text is organized. What do you notice about the text structure on this page?

....

....

....

....

....

....

....

....

Photoperiodism Irises, left, bloom when days are getting longer and nights are getting shorter. Chrysanthemums, above, bloom when the lengths of the day and night reaches a certain ratio.

Dormancy Some species of trees go into a state or dormancy every winter.

Analyze Benefits Why do you think some trees evolved to go into a state of dormancy during the winter months?

....

....

....

Plant Diseases

Figure 3 Insects, worms, and other pests can cause disease in plants and have an impact on their growth.

Make Observations ✏ Circle the diseased parts of the plant.

📓 **Write About It** Locate two plants in or around your home, school, or neighborhood: one that appears healthy and one that does not. Explain which factors you think are helping the healthy plant grow and which factors are keeping the unhealthy one from growing to its full size.

Environmental Conditions

In ideal conditions, a plant will reach a certain maximum size that is normal for its species. However, in some cases, plants do not get enough of the resources they need, so they do not grow as large as they normally would. A lack of sunlight, for instance, may keep a plant from growing to full size or weaken its structure.

In addition to sunlight, plants need nutrient-rich soil and water to grow. Soil contains the nutrients a plant needs to carry out its life processes. Nutrient-poor soil may result from an area being overly crowded with plants. Competition for the nutrients in the soil may mean that few plants get the nutrients they need. Similarly, if a plant does not receive enough water, it will not grow to a healthy size. Diseases like the one shown in **Figure 3** can impact plant growth as well.

Plan It !

Water Needs and Plant Growth

SEP Plan Investigations You want to find out how the amount of water you give plants affects their growth. In the space below, describe a plan for an investigation that can help you answer this question.

....
....
....
....
....
....
....

Animal Growth

Like plants, animals grow and develop starting at the beginning of their lives. Also like plants, their growth is affected by both internal and external stimuli to which they are constantly responding.

Embryo Development After fertilization, the offspring of animals develop in different ways. The growing offspring, or embryo, may develop outside or inside the mother's body.

One way animal embryos develop is inside an egg that is laid outside the parent's body. Most invertebrates lay eggs. Many fish, reptiles, and birds do, too. The contents of the egg provide the nutrients a developing embryo needs. The eggs of land vertebrates, such as reptiles and birds, are called amniotic eggs. When inside the parent's body, amniotic eggs are covered with membranes and a leathery shell.

In other cases, an embryo develops inside an egg that is kept, or retained, within the parent's body. The developing embryo gets its nutrients from the egg's yolk, just like the offspring of egg-laying animals. The egg hatches either before or after being released from the parent's body. This type of development is found in some species of fish, amphibians, and reptiles.

In placental mammals, which include elephants, wolves, and humans, the embryo develops inside the mother's body. The mother provides the embryo with everything it needs during development. As is shown in **Figure 4**, **essential** nutrients and gases are exchanged between the embryo and the mother through an organ called the placenta. The embryo develops inside its mother's body until its body systems can function on their own.

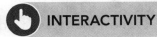

INTERACTIVITY

Observe how animals grow and develop over time.

INTERACTIVITY

Find out how cows are being bred to be bigger and bigger.

Academic Vocabulary

What does it mean when someone describes something as being essential? Use *essential* in a sentence.

....

....

....

....

....

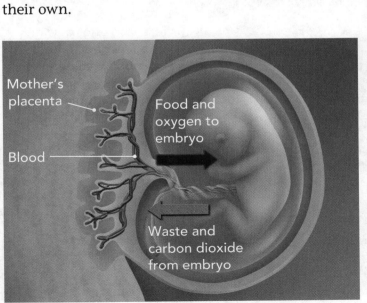

Mother's placenta

Food and oxygen to embryo

Blood

Waste and carbon dioxide from embryo

Placental Mammal Development
Figure 4 The embryos of placental mammals develop inside their mothers' bodies.

Draw Conclusions What would be some of the advantages of this type of embryo development compared to an amniotic egg laid outside the mother's body?

....

....

....

....

....

Life Cycles

Figure 5 Different animals go through different life cycles. Unlike you, both of these animals go through metamorphosis.

Sequence ✏ Add arrows to the diagram to show the order in which these stages occur.

Egg

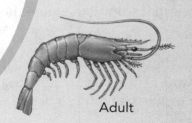
Adult

Larval stages

Crayfish and other crustaceans, such as crabs and shrimp, begin their lives as tiny, swimming larvae. The bodies of these larvae do not resemble those of adults. Eventually, crustacean larvae develop into adults.

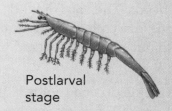
Postlarval stage

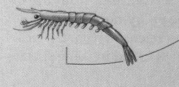

Adult frogs reproduce sexually.

Eggs are fertilized outside the female's body.

Frogs begin their life cycle as fertilized eggs in water. After a few days, tadpoles wriggle out of the eggs and begin swimming. Over time, tadpoles develop into adult frogs.

Front legs develop and the tail is absorbed.

A tadpole hatches from an egg.

Hind legs develop.

Comparing Life Cycles Many young animals, including most vertebrates, look like small versions of adults from the time they are born. Other animals go through the process of **metamorphosis**, or major body changes, as they grow and develop into adults (**Figure 5**).

External and Internal Factors

Animal growth and development are affected by both internal and external factors. Internal factors include genetic and hormonal characteristics that are part of an organism's life processes. External factors, on the other hand, are the environmental conditions that an animal may or may not have any control over.

Environmental Conditions Access to resources and exposure to diseases and parasites can also affect the growth and development of animals. If animals do not receive the nutrition they need during development or if they become sick, they may not reach their full adult size. Space is another resource that can affect animal growth. For example, the growth of some species of fish, such as goldfish like the one in **Figure 6**, is affected by how large a body of water they live in. If its living space is not large enough, it will not reach its full adult size.

☑ READING CHECK **Determine Meaning** How is your life cycle different from animals that undergo metamorphosis?

....

....

....

👆 **INTERACTIVITY**

Construct an explanation with evidence for how environmental and genetic factors influence the growth of organisms.

Figure 6 If a goldfish's tank is too small, its growth may be restricted.

CCC Cause and Effect In ideal conditions, a goldfish will grow to be about 10 to 20 cm long. But most people think of goldfish as very small fish that only grow to be a few centimeters long. What conclusion can you draw from this information?

....

....

....

....

....

INTERACTIVITY

Observe the effects that water and food have on the growth and production of crop plants.

Genes The genes an offspring inherits from its parents are a major factor in how it develops and grows. In your own classroom, you can probably observe how students' heights vary. Part of these differences is due to the genes your classmates inherited from their parents. Children usually grow up to be about the same height as their parents.

Hormones Another internal factor that influences growth and development are the hormones that are naturally produced by animals' bodies. For instance, male animals produce greater amounts of testosterone than female animals. In many animal species, the production of testosterone in male animals results in males growing to be larger than females.

Math Toolbox

Human Malnutrition and Height

In 1945, after World War II, the Korean Peninsula was divided into two nations: North Korea and South Korea. The two countries had different forms of government and economic systems. The data table shows the average heights in the two countries from 1930 to 1996.

1. **SEP Communicate Information** 🖋 Use the data in the table to make a bar graph in the space below.

2. **SEP Interpret Data** Are the height differences in these two countries likely the result of genetics, hormones, or environmental conditions? Explain why.

....
....
....
....
....
....
....
....
....
....

Years	Average height of North Koreans (cm)	Average height of South Koreans (cm)
1930–1939	159.4	158.9
1940–1949	160.6	161.1
1950–1959	161.8	163.1
1960–1969	162.7	165
1970–1979	163.5	166.7
1980–1989	164.5	167.8
1990–1996	165.2	168.4

Source: NCD Risk Factor Collaboration, 2017

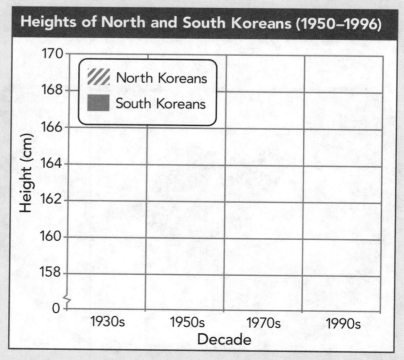

Heights of North and South Koreans (1950–1996)

MS-LS1-5

1. Distinguish Relationships Describe three types of stimuli that cause plants to exhibit tropism.

....
....
....
....
....
....

2. CCC Cause and Effect What causes plants to bloom in different seasons?

....
....
....
....
....

3. SEP Construct Explanations Why might soil have an effect on plant growth?

....
....
....

4. Distinguish Differences How does offspring development in egg-laying animals and placental mammals differ?

....
....
....
....
....
....

5. SEP Develop Models ✏ Draw diagrams showing three different ways that animal embryos develop. Include labels.

Quest CHECK-IN

In this lesson, you learned about some of the factors that affect the growth and development of plants and animals. You also learned about some of the different stages that animals go through as they develop.

SEP Design Solutions Consider the environmental impact of new construction near a wildlife habitat. At what point during the year do you think construction would have the least impact? Explain.

....
....
....
....

👆 INTERACTIVITY

Make Your Construction Case

Go online to consider the criteria and constraints involved in your construction project.

Warmer Waters, FEWER FISH

Atemperature increase of a few degrees does not seem like much cause for concern. But it turns out that even small increases in water temperature are having a big impact.

The increased warmth of the water is affecting the growth of certain species of fish. Atlantic cod, which are used to very cold water, can adapt to higher temperatures. In fact, populations of cod exposed to warmer waters ranging from 12 to 15 degrees Celsius (53.6°F to 59.0°F) tend to benefit. The cod grow larger and reproduce more. But as soon as the water warms barely one degree Celsius beyond that high range, to 15.9°C (60.6°F), the growth and development of the fish suffers.

Temperature–Size Rule

In Norway, every fall for over a century, scientists have measured and recorded the size of Atlantic cod. These annual surveys have included well over 100,000 cod so far. Recently, scientists made a key observation. As soon as the temperature in the Atlantic cod's habitat rose above 15 degrees Celsius, the Atlantic cod suffered from stunted growth.

Water is a heat sink—it readily absorbs heat from everything around it. The researchers found that in years with very high summer temperatures, the ocean's surface waters were much warmer, too. And the juvenile cod raised in these warmer waters were smaller than usual. The young fish simply did not grow as large as they could. This small difference may not seem significant at first. But there is a consequence to consider: Size determines an individual's success at survival and reproduction. The smaller individuals tend to have fewer offspring.

An Atlantic cod can grow quite large, up to 1.2 meters, and weigh as much as 40 kilograms. The largest cod ever captured was a whopper, weighing over 96 kg (211 lb)!

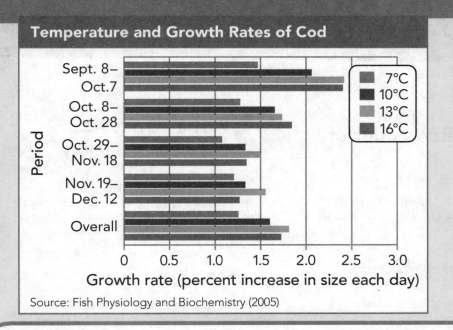

Temperature and Growth Rates of Cod

Growth rate (percent increase in size each day)

Period

Legend:
- 7°C
- 10°C
- 13°C
- 16°C

Source: Fish Physiology and Biochemistry (2005)

Answer the following questions.

1. **Analyze Data** Refer to the graph. At what temperature does the Atlantic cod grow most slowly? Which temperature seems to be ideal for growth? Explain.

2. **Cite Evidence** What is the evidence that warmer water temperature is an environmental factor influencing the growth of a species?

3. **Apply Scientific Reasoning** Why are some scientists concerned about the Atlantic cod population as the air temperature increases? Explain.

4. **Connect to Society** One out of seven people on Earth depends on fish as a protein source. What could happen if warming waters have a similar effect on other stocks of fish?

1 Patterns of Reproduction

MS-LS3-2

1. Asexual reproduction is different from sexual reproduction in that the offspring of asexual reproduction

A. are identical to the parent.

B. contain half the chromosomes of the parent.

C. have no genetic material.

D. have more variety in their traits.

2. Different forms of a gene are called

A. alleles.

B. offspring.

C. recessive.

D. traits.

3. Which example best describes incomplete dominance?

A. humans with blood type AB

B. flowers with red petals

C. horses with roan color pattern

D. sheep with gray fleece

4. .... inheritance refers to any trait that is controlled by more than one gene.

5. CCC Patterns Explain why sexual reproduction results in offspring with more genetic variation than asexual reproduction.

....

....

....

....

....

....

....

....

2 Plant Structures for Reproduction

MS-LS1-4

6. A maple tree produces male and female flowers. Which term best describes the maple?

A. gymnosperm   B. angiosperm

C. sporophyte   D. non-vascular

7. Both ferns and cedar trees rely on .... to successfully fertilize themselves.

8. CCC Structure and Function What are two specialized structures of an apple tree that increase the chances that it will reproduce and have offspring that survive? Explain.

....

....

....

....

....

....

9. SEP Engage in Argument from Evidence Coconut palms are tropical trees usually found growing on shorelines. The tree produces fruit in a hard shell that can float on water. How does this help ensure the tree's successful reproduction?

....

....

....

....

....

....

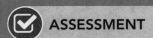
 Animal Behaviors for Reproduction

MS-LS1-4

10. What are mating systems?
  A. threatening behaviors that animals use to gain control over other animals
  B. behavior patterns that are related to how animals reproduce
  C. chemicals released by one animal that affect the behavior of another animal of the same species
  D. behaviors related to the movement of animals from one place to another and back again

11. Which statement about fertilization strategies is true?
  A. Internal fertilization mostly occurs in fish and amphibians.
  B. Internal fertilization results in eggs that develop outside the female's body.
  C. External fertilization is common for animals that live in water.
  D. External fertilization occurs in all land animals.

12. Cooperative behaviors can .... (increase/decrease) an animal's chances of surviving to reproduce.

13. CCC Patterns In general, how is the number of offspring produced by an animal related to the amount of time and energy it invests in caring for its young?

....

....

....

....

....

....

....

 Factors Influencing Growth

MS-LS1-5

14. Which is *not* a stimulus that can trigger tropisms in plants?
  A. light
  B. gravity
  C. touch
  D. temperature

15. An insect such as the butterfly goes through the process of .... as it grows and develops into an adult.

16. CCC Cause and Effect Oak trees go into a state of dormancy during the winter. Suppose that a forest of oaks grows in an area that begins to experience warmer winters due to climate change. What effect do you think this will have on the oak trees? Explain.

....

....

....

....

....

17. CCC Cause and Effect How do environmental conditions affect the growth of an animal?

....

....

....

....

....

....

....

....

MS-LS1-4, MS-LS1-5

Evidence-Based Assessment

A team of researchers investigated how climate change and warming temperatures affected animals in the Colorado Rocky Mountains. One of the animals they studied was the yellow-bellied marmot. This large rodent lives in small colonies and survives the harsh winters by hibernating for eight months. The marmots forage for grasses and seeds, which only grow once the winter snow has melted.

Because the ground is bare of snow for such a brief time each year, the marmots have a very short breeding season. It begins as soon as they come out of hibernation. Not long after, the snow melts and more food becomes available to the marmots.

However, the researchers discovered that warming temperatures were disrupting marmot hibernation patterns. They compiled data about the first marmot sighted coming out of hibernation each year for over 20 years. The data is summarized in the graph.

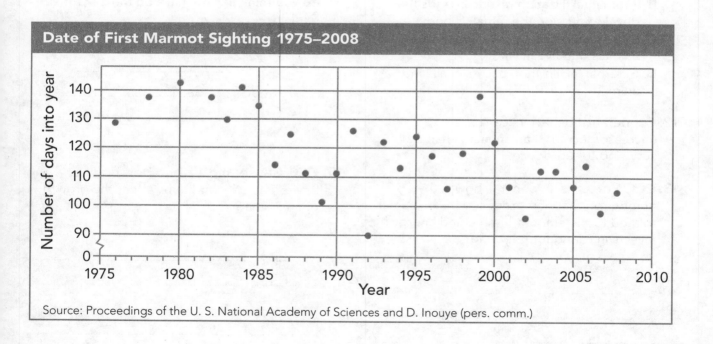

Date of First Marmot Sighting 1975–2008

Source: Proceedings of the U. S. National Academy of Sciences and D. Inouye (pers. comm.)

1. **SEP Analyze Data** What trend is shown by the data in the graph?
   - A. The first marmot coming out of hibernation tends to be sighted earlier and earlier.
   - B. The first marmot coming out of hibernation was sighted later each year.
   - C. The date the first marmot came out of hibernation fluctuated randomly.
   - D. There was little or no change in the date the first marmot was sighted each year.

2. **SEP Engage in Argument from Evidence** What environmental factor do you think influences when marmots wake from hibernation? Support your response with details or data from the researchers' investigation.

   ....

   ....

   ....

   ....

   ....

   ....

   ....

   ....

   ....

   ....

3. **CCC Cause and Effect** How does the marmot's behavior after coming out of hibernation help to ensure that it will successfully reproduce?

   ....

   ....

   ....

   ....

   ....

   ....

   ....

   ....

   ....

4. **SEP Construct Explanations** The researchers found that while the air temperature was increasing earlier each year, the snow was not melting at a faster rate. Explain what effect an earlier breeding season will have on the growth of young marmots if the snow melts the same time year to year.

   ....

   ....

   ....

   ....

   ....

   ....

   ....

   ....

   ....

   ....

Quest FINDINGS

Complete the Quest!

Phenomenon Finalize and present your construction plan using the information you have gathered as evidence to support your recommendations.

SEP Design Solutions Is there a way your town or city could ensure that the wild plants and animals that live there have the resources they need to grow and reproduce?

....

....

....

....

👆 **INTERACTIVITY**

Reflect on Your Basketball Court Plans

Clean and Green

How can you evaluate **claims** about laundry **detergents** that are marketed as **safe** for the environment?

Background

Phenomenon Many businesses promote products, such as soaps and detergents, that are environmentally friendly. Greenwashing, which is a combination of the terms *green* and *whitewashing*, is the practice of claiming that a product is more environmentally safe than it really is. You are a budding botanist working with an environmental watchdog group. You must evaluate the biological effects of "natural" detergents that claim to be safer for the environment than regular detergents.

In this investigation, you will design and conduct an experiment to determine the effects of "eco-friendly" laundry detergents on plant growth. It will probably take several days for the seeds to germinate. Keep in mind that the factors for healthy plant growth include height, color, and general appearance.

Materials

(per group)

- 3 plastic Petri dishes with lids
- potting soil
- graduated cylinder
- 30 radish seeds
- masking tape
- day-old tap water
- metric ruler
- wax pencil
- "regular" detergent solution
- "eco-friendly" detergent solution
- scale or balance

Safety

Be sure to follow all safety guidelines provided by your teacher. The Safety Appendix of your textbook provides more details about the safety icons.

Design Your Investigation

☐ 1. With your group, discuss how you will investigate the effects of the detergents on plant growth. Also, discuss the types of data you will need to collect in order to determine how environmental factors affect plant growth.

☐ 2. Work together to identify the factors you will control and the variables you will change. Think about what a plant normally needs from its environment in order to live and grow. Decide what measurements and observations you will need to make and how often you will need to make them. To make these decisions, consider the following questions:

   • How many different groups of seeds will you use?
   • How will you determine the number of seeds that germinate in each group?
   • How will you determine the health of the shoots in each group of seeds?
   • What qualitative observations will you make?

☐ 3. Write a detailed procedure for your experiment in the space provided. Make sure you describe the setup for your investigation, the variables you will measure, a description of the data you will collect, and how you will collect the data. Before proceeding, obtain your teacher's approval.

☐ 4. In the space provided, construct a data table to organize the data you will collect. When constructing your data table, consider the following questions:

   • How many seeds will you put in each petri dish?
   • How many times will you collect data?
   • Will you collect data at the same time each day, or at different times?
   • What qualitative observations will you record?

☐ 5. Carry out your procedure for investigating the effect of your pollutant on plant growth. You will need to make observations once a day over several days. Make your measurements each day and record the data you collect.

uDemonstrate Lab

Procedure

....
....
....
....
....
....
....
....
....
....
....

Data Table and Observations

Analyze and Interpret Data

1. **SEP Use Mathematics** Identify the dependent variables you measured in this investigation. Calculate the percentage of seeds that had germinated each day in each dish. Then, calculate the mean length of the shoots for each day you collected data. Make this calculation for the seeds in each dish.

....

....

....

....

2. **CCC Cause and Effect** Describe any patterns you see in the data for the seedlings grown under the three conditions in the Petri dishes. Summarize the data by writing a cause-and-effect statement about the effects of the detergents on the growth of the plants.

....

....

....

....

....

3. **Make Generalizations** Based on the results of your experiment, do you think the manufacturer's claim is valid? Is the product is safe for the environment? Explain.

....

....

....

....

....

4. **SEP Analyze Data** Share your results among the groups that tested the other "natural" detergents. Look for similarities and differences in the data. What do you think might account for any differences?

....

....

....

....

....

SEP.1, SEP.8

The Meaning of Science

Science Skills

Science is a way of learning about the natural world. It involves asking questions, making predictions, and collecting information to see if the answer is right or wrong.

The table lists some of the skills that scientists use. You use some of these skills every day. For example, you may observe and evaluate your lunch options before choosing what to eat.

Skill	Definition
classifying	grouping together items that are alike or that have shared characteristics
evaluating	comparing observations and data to reach a conclusion
inferring	explaining or interpreting observations
investigating	studying or researching a subject to discover facts or to reveal new information
making models	creating representations of complex objects or processes
observing	using one or more of your senses to gather information
predicting	making a statement or claim about what will happen based on past experience or evidence

Scientific Attitudes

Curiosity often drives scientists to learn about the world around them. Creativity is useful for coming up with inventive ways to solve problems. Such qualities and attitudes, and the ability to keep an open mind, are essential for scientists.

When sharing results or findings, honesty and ethics are also essential. Ethics refers to rules for knowing right from wrong.

Being skeptical is also important. This means having doubts about things based on past experiences and evidence. Skepticism helps to prevent accepting data and results that may not be true.

Scientists must also avoid bias—likes or dislikes of people, ideas, or things. They must avoid experimental bias, which is a mistake that may make an experiment's preferred outcome more likely.

Scientific Reasoning

Scientific reasoning depends on being logical and objective. When you are objective, you use evidence and apply logic to draw conclusions. Being subjective means basing conclusions on personal feelings, biases, or opinions. Subjective reasoning can interfere with science and skew results. Objective reasoning helps scientists use observations to reach conclusions about the natural world.

Scientists use two types of objective reasoning: deductive and inductive. Deductive reasoning involves starting with a general idea or theory and applying it to a situation. For example, the theory of plate tectonics indicates that earthquakes happen mostly where tectonic plates meet. You could then draw the conclusion, or deduce, that California has many earthquakes because tectonic plates meet there.

In inductive reasoning, you make a generalization from a specific observation. When scientists collect data in an experiment and draw a conclusion based on that data, they use inductive reasoning. For example, if fertilizer causes one set of plants to grow faster than another, you might infer that the fertilizer promotes plant growth.

Make Meaning

Think about a bias the marine biologist in the photo could show that results in paying more or less attention to one kind of organism over others. Make a prediction about how that bias could affect the biologist's survey of the coral reef.

Write About It

Suppose it is raining when you go to sleep one night. When you wake up the next morning, you observe frozen puddles on the ground and icicles on tree branches. Use scientific reasoning to draw a conclusion about the air temperature outside. Support your conclusion using deductive or inductive reasoning.

SEP.1, SEP.2, SEP.3, SEP.4, CCC.4

Science Processes

Scientific Inquiry

Scientists contribute to scientific knowledge by conducting investigations and drawing conclusions. The process often begins with an observation that leads to a question, which is then followed by the development of a hypothesis. This is known as scientific inquiry.

One of the first steps in scientific inquiry is asking questions. However, it's important to make a question specific with a narrow focus so the investigation will not be too broad. A biologist may want to know all there is to know about wolves, for example. But a good, focused question for a specific inquiry might be "How many offspring does the average female wolf produce in her lifetime?"

A hypothesis is a possible answer to a scientific question. A hypothesis must be testable. For something to be testable, researchers must be able to carry out an investigation and gather evidence that will either support or disprove the hypothesis.

Scientific Models

Models are tools that scientists use to study phenomena indirectly. A model is any representation of an object or process. Illustrations, dioramas, globes, diagrams, computer programs, and mathematical equations are all examples of scientific models. For example, a diagram of Earth's crust and mantle can help you to picture layers deep below the surface and understand events such as volcanic eruptions.

Models also allow scientists to represent objects that are either very large, such as our solar system, or very small, such as a molecule of DNA. Models can also represent processes that occur over a long period of time, such as the changes that have occurred throughout Earth's history.

Models are helpful, but they have limitations. Physical models are not made of the same materials as the objects they represent. Most models of complex objects or processes show only major parts, stages, or relationships. Many details are left out. Therefore, you may not be able to learn as much from models as you would through direct observation.

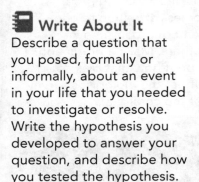

📓 Write About It
Describe a question that you posed, formally or informally, about an event in your life that you needed to investigate or resolve. Write the hypothesis you developed to answer your question, and describe how you tested the hypothesis.

📓 Reflect Identify the benefits and limitations of using a plastic model of DNA, as shown here.

Science Experiments

An experiment or investigation must be well planned to produce valid results. In planning an experiment, you must identify the independent and dependent variables. You must also do as much as possible to remove the effects of other variables. A controlled experiment is one in which you test only one variable at a time.

For example, suppose you plan a controlled experiment to learn how the type of material affects the speed at which sound waves travel through it. The only variable that should change is the type of material. This way, if the speed of sound changes, you know that it is a result of a change in the material, not another variable such as the thickness of the material or the type of sound used.

You should also remove bias from any investigation. You may inadvertently introduce bias by selecting subjects you like and avoiding those you don't like. Scientists often conduct investigations by taking random samples to avoid ending up with biased results.

Once you plan your investigation and begin to collect data, it's important to record and organize the data. You may wish to use a graph to display and help you to interpret the data.

Communicating is the sharing of ideas and results with others through writing and speaking. Communicating data and conclusions is a central part of science.

Scientists share knowledge, including new findings, theories, and techniques for collecting data. Conferences, journals, and websites help scientists to communicate with each other. Popular media, including newspapers, magazines, and social media sites, help scientists to share their knowledge with nonscientists. However, before the results of investigations are shared and published, other scientists should review the experiment for possible sources of error, such as bias and unsupported conclusions.

Write About It

List four ways you could communicate the results of a scientific study about the health of sea turtles in the Pacific Ocean.

SEP.1, SEP.6, SEP.7, SEP.8

Scientific Knowledge

Scientific Explanations

Suppose you learn that adult flamingos are pink because of the food they eat. This statement is a scientific explanation— it describes how something in nature works or explains why it happens. Scientists from different fields use methods such as researching information, designing experiments, and making models to form scientific explanations. Scientific explanations often result from many years of work and multiple investigations conducted by many scientists.

Scientific Theories and Laws

A scientific law is a statement that describes what you can expect to occur every time under a particular set of conditions. A scientific law describes an observed pattern in nature, but it does not attempt to explain it. For example, the law of superposition describes what you can expect to find in terms of the ages of layers of rock. Geologists use this observed pattern to determine the relative ages of sedimentary rock layers. But the law does not explain why the pattern occurs.

By contrast, a scientific theory is a well-tested explanation for a wide range of observations or experimental results. It provides details and describes causes of observed patterns. Something is elevated to a theory only when there is a large body of evidence that supports it. However, a scientific theory can be changed or overturned when new evidence is found.

Write About It
Choose two fields of science that interest you. Describe a method used to develop scientific explanations in each field.

SEP Construct Explanations Complete the table to compare and contrast a scientific theory and a scientific law.

	Scientific Theory	Scientific Law
Definition		
Does it attempt to explain a pattern observed in nature?		

Analyzing Scientific Explanations

To analyze scientific explanations that you hear on the news or read in a book such as this one, you need scientific literacy. Scientific literacy means understanding scientific terms and principles well enough to ask questions, evaluate information, and make decisions. Scientific reasoning gives you a process to apply. This includes looking for bias and errors in the research, evaluating data, and identifying faulty reasoning. For example, by evaluating how a survey was conducted, you may find a serious flaw in the researchers' methods.

Evidence and Opinions

The basis for scientific explanations is empirical evidence. Empirical evidence includes the data and observations that have been collected through scientific processes. Satellite images, photos, and maps of mountains and volcanoes are all examples of empirical evidence that support a scientific explanation about Earth's tectonic plates. Scientists look for patterns when they analyze this evidence. For example, they might see a pattern that mountains and volcanoes often occur near tectonic plate boundaries.

To evaluate scientific information, you must first distinguish between evidence and opinion. In science, evidence includes objective observations and conclusions that have been repeated. Evidence may or may not support a scientific claim. An opinion is a subjective idea that is formed from evidence, but it cannot be confirmed by evidence.

Write About It

Suppose the conservation committee of a town wants to gauge residents' opinions about a proposal to stock the local ponds with fish every spring. The committee pays for a survey to appear on a web site that is popular with people who like to fish. The results of the survey show 78 people in favor of the proposal and two against it. Do you think the survey's results are valid? Explain.

Make Meaning

Explain what empirical evidence the photograph reveals.

SEP.3, SEP.4

Tools of Science

Measurement

Making measurements using standard units is important in all fields of science. This allows scientists to repeat and reproduce other experiments, as well as to understand the precise meaning of the results of others. Scientists use a measurement system called the International System of Units, or SI.

For each type of measurement, there is a series of units that are greater or less than each other. The unit a scientist uses depends on what is being measured. For example, a geophysicist tracking the movements of tectonic plates may use centimeters, as plates tend to move small amounts each year. Meanwhile, a marine biologist might measure the movement of migrating bluefin tuna on the scale of kilometers.

Units for length, mass, volume, and density are based on powers of ten—a meter is equal to 100 centimeters or 1000 millimeters. Units of time do not follow that pattern. There are 60 seconds in a minute, 60 minutes in an hour, and 24 hours in a day. These units are based on patterns that humans perceived in nature. Units of temperature are based on scales that are set according to observations of nature. For example, 0°C is the temperature at which pure water freezes, and 100°C is the temperature at which it boils.

Write About It

Suppose you are planning an investigation in which you must measure the dimensions of several small mineral samples that fit in your hand. Which metric unit or units will you most likely use? Explain your answer.

Measurement	Metric units
Length or distance	meter (m), kilometer (km), centimeter (cm), millimeter (mm) 1 km = 1,000 m $\quad$ 1 cm = 10 mm 1 m = 100 cm
Mass	kilogram (kg), gram (g), milligram (mg) 1 kg = 1,000 g $\quad$ 1 g = 1,000 mg
Volume	cubic meter (m³), cubic centimeter (cm³) 1 m³ = 1,000,000 cm³
Density	kilogram per cubic meter (kg/m³), gram per cubic centimeter (g/cm³) 1,000 kg/m³ = 1 g/cm³
Temperature	degrees Celsius (°C), kelvin (K) 1°C = 273 K
Time	hour (h), minute (m), second (s)

Math Skills

Using numbers to collect and interpret data involves math skills that are essential in science. For example, you use math skills when you estimate the number of birds in an entire forest after counting the actual number of birds in ten trees.

Scientists evaluate measurements and estimates for their precision and accuracy. In science, an accurate measurement is very close to the actual value. Precise measurements are very close, or nearly equal, to each other. Reliable measurements are both accurate and precise. An imprecise value may be a sign of an error in data collection. This kind of anomalous data may be excluded to avoid skewing the data and harming the investigation.

Other math skills include performing specific calculations, such as finding the mean, or average, value in a data set. The mean can be calculated by adding up all of the values in the data set and then dividing that sum by the number of values.

Hour	Number of Ducks Observed at a Pond
1	12
2	10
3	2
4	14
5	13
6	10
7	11

SEP Use Mathematics The data table shows how many ducks were seen at a pond every hour over the course of seven hours. Is there a data point that seems anomalous? If so, cross out that data point. Then, calculate the mean number of ducks on the pond. Round the mean to the nearest whole number.

Graphs

Graphs help scientists to interpret data by helping them to find trends or patterns in the data. A line graph displays data that show how one variable (the dependent or outcome variable) changes in response to another (the independent or test variable). The slope and shape of a graph line can reveal patterns and help scientists to make predictions. For example, line graphs can help you to spot patterns of change over time.

Scientists use bar graphs to compare data across categories or subjects that may not affect each other. The heights of the bars make it easy to compare those quantities. A circle graph, also known as a pie chart, shows the proportions of different parts of a whole.

Write About It
You and a friend record the distance you travel every 15 minutes on a one-hour bike trip. Your friend wants to display the data as a circle graph. Explain whether or not this is the best type of graph to display your data. If not, suggest another graph to use.

SEP.1, SEP.2, SEP.3, SEP.6

The Engineering Design Process

Engineers are builders and problem solvers. Chemical engineers experiment with new fuels made from algae. Civil engineers design roadways and bridges. Bioengineers develop medical devices and prosthetics. The common trait among engineers is an ability to identify problems and design solutions to solve them. Engineers use a creative process that relies on scientific methods to help guide them from a concept or idea all the way to the final product.

Define the Problem

To identify or define a problem, different questions need to be asked: *What are the effects of the problem? What are the likely causes? What other factors could be involved?* Sometimes the obvious, immediate cause of a problem may be the result of another problem that may not be immediately apparent. For example, climate change results in different weather patterns, which in turn can affect organisms that live in certain habitats. So engineers must be aware of all the possible effects of potential solutions. Engineers must also take into account how well different solutions deal with the different causes of the problem.

Reflect Write about a problem that you encountered in your life that had both immediate, obvious causes as well as less-obvious and less-immediate ones.

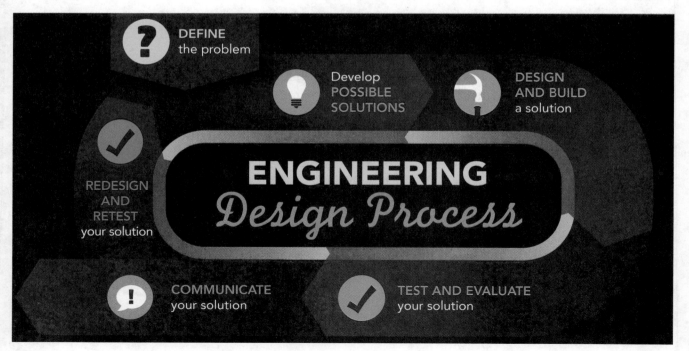

DEFINE the problem

Develop POSSIBLE SOLUTIONS

DESIGN AND BUILD a solution

REDESIGN AND RETEST your solution

ENGINEERING Design Process

COMMUNICATE your solution

TEST AND EVALUATE your solution

As engineers consider problems and design solutions, they must identify and categorize the criteria and constraints of the project.

Criteria are the factors that must be met or accomplished by the solution. For example, a gardener who wants to protect outdoor plants from deer and rabbits may say that the criteria for the solution are "plants are no longer eaten" and "plant growth is not inhibited in any way." The gardener then knows the plants cannot simply be sealed off from the environment, because the plants will not receive sunlight and water.

The same gardener will likely have constraints on his solution, such as budget for materials and time that is available for working on the project. By setting constraints, a solution can be designed that will be successful without introducing a new set of problems. No one wants to spend $500 on materials to protect $100 worth of tomatoes and cucumbers.

Develop Possible Solutions

After the problem has been identified, and the criteria and constraints identified, an engineer will consider possible solutions. This often involves working in teams with other engineers and designers to brainstorm ideas and research materials that can be used in the design.

It's important for engineers to think creatively and explore all potential solutions. If you wanted to design a bicycle that was safer and easier to ride than a traditional bicycle, then you would want more than just one or two solutions. Having multiple ideas to choose from increases the likelihood that you will develop a solution that meets the criteria and constraints. In addition, different ideas that result from brainstorming can often lead to new and better solutions to an existing problem.

Make Meaning
Using the example of a garden that is vulnerable to wild animals such as deer, make a list of likely constraints on an engineering solution to the problem you identified before. Determine if there are common traits among the constraints, and identify categories for them.

Design a Solution

Engineers then develop the idea that they feel best solves the problem. Once a solution has been chosen, engineers and designers get to work building a model or prototype of the solution. A model may involve sketching on paper or using computer software to construct a model of the solution. A prototype is a working model of the solution.

Building a model or prototype helps an engineer determine whether a solution meets the criteria and stays within the constraints. During this stage of the process, engineers must often deal with new problems and make any necessary adjustments to the model or prototype.

Test and Evaluate a Solution

Whether testing a model or a prototype, engineers use scientific processes to evaluate their solutions. Multiple experiments, tests, or trials are conducted, data are evaluated, and results and analyses are communicated. New criteria or constraints may emerge as a result of testing. In most cases, a solution will require some refinement or revision, even if it has been through successful testing. Refining a solution is necessary if there are new constraints, such as less money or available materials. Additional testing may be done to ensure that a solution satisfies local, state, or federal laws or standards.

Make Meaning Think about an aluminum beverage can. What would happen if the price or availability of aluminum changed so much that cans needed to be made of a new material? What would the criteria and constraints be on the development of a new can?

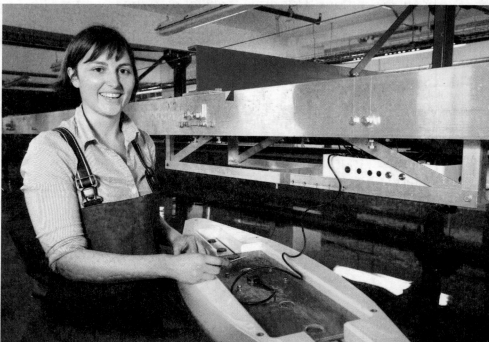

A naval architect sets up a model to test how the the hull's design responds to waves.

Communicate the Solution

Engineers need to communicate the final design to the people who will manufacture the product. This may include sketches, detailed drawings, computer simulations, and written text. Engineers often provide evidence that was collected during the testing stage. This evidence may include graphs and data tables that support the decisions made for the final design.

If there is feedback about the solution, then the engineers and designers must further refine the solution. This might involve making minor adjustments to the design, or it might mean bigger modifications to the design based on new criteria or constraints. Any changes in the design will require additional testing to make sure that the changes work as intended.

Redesign and Retest the Solution

At different steps in the engineering and design process, a solution usually must be revised and retested. Many designs fail to work perfectly, even after models and prototypes are built, tested, and evaluated. Engineers must be ready to analyze new results and deal with any new problems that arise. Troubleshooting, or fixing design problems, allows engineers to adjust the design to improve on how well the solution meets the need.

SEP Communicate Information Suppose you are an engineer at an aerospace company. Your team is designing a rover to be used on a future NASA space mission. A family member doesn't understand why so much of your team's time is taken up with testing and retesting the rover design. What are three things you would tell your relative to explain why testing and retesting are so important to the engineering and design process?

....

....

....

....

....

....

....

....

Safety Symbols

These symbols warn of possible dangers in the laboratory and remind you to work carefully.

 Safety Goggles Wear safety goggles to protect your eyes in any activity involving chemicals, flames or heating, or glassware.

 Lab Apron Wear a laboratory apron to protect your skin and clothing from damage.

 Breakage Handle breakable materials, such as glassware, with care. Do not touch broken glassware.

 Heat-Resistant Gloves Use an oven mitt or other hand protection when handling hot materials, such as hot plates or hot glassware.

 Plastic Gloves Wear disposable plastic gloves when working with harmful chemicals and organisms. Keep your hands away from your face, and dispose of the gloves according to your teacher's instructions.

 Heating Use a clamp or tongs to pick up hot glassware. Do not touch hot objects with your bare hands.

 Flames Before you work with flames, tie back loose hair and clothing. Follow your teacher's instructions about lighting and extinguishing flames.

 No Flames When using flammable materials, make sure there are no flames, sparks, or other exposed heat sources present.

 Corrosive Chemical Avoid getting acid or other corrosive chemicals on your skin or clothing or in your eyes. Do not inhale the vapors. Wash your hands after the activity.

 Poison Do not let any poisonous chemical come into contact with your skin, and do not inhale its vapors. Wash your hands when you are finished with the activity.

 Fumes Work in a well-ventilated area when harmful vapors may be involved. Avoid inhaling vapors directly. Test an odor only when directed to do so by your teacher, and use a wafting motion to direct the vapor toward your nose.

 Sharp Object Scissors, scalpels, knives, needles, pins, and tacks can cut your skin. Always direct a sharp edge or point away from yourself and others.

 Animal Safety Treat live or preserved animals or animal parts with care to avoid harming the animals or yourself. Wash your hands when you are finished with the activity.

 Plant Safety Handle plants only as directed by your teacher. If you are allergic to certain plants, tell your teacher; do not do an activity involving those plants. Avoid touching harmful plants such as poison ivy. Wash your hands when you are finished with the activity.

 Electric Shock To avoid electric shock, never use electrical equipment around water, when the equipment is wet, or when your hands are wet. Be sure cords are untangled and cannot trip anyone. Unplug equipment not in use.

 Physical Safety When an experiment involves physical activity, avoid injuring yourself or others. Alert your teacher if there is any reason you should not participate.

 Disposal Dispose of chemicals and other laboratory materials safely. Follow the instructions from your teacher.

 Hand Washing Wash your hands thoroughly when finished with an activity. Use soap and warm water. Rinse well.

 General Safety Awareness When this symbol appears, follow the instructions provided. When you are asked to develop your own procedure in a lab, have your teacher approve your plan.

Using a Laboratory Balance

The laboratory balance is an important tool in scientific investigations. Different kinds of balances are used in the laboratory to determine the masses and weights of objects. You can use a triple-beam balance to determine the masses of materials that you study or experiment with in the laboratory. An electronic balance, unlike a triple-beam balance, is used to measure the weights of materials.

The triple-beam balance that you may use in your science class is probably similar to the balance depicted in this Appendix. To use the balance properly, you should learn the name, location, and function of each part of the balance.

Triple-Beam Balance

The triple-beam balance is a single-pan balance with three beams calibrated in grams. The back, or 100-gram, beam is divided into ten units of 10 grams each. The middle, or 500-gram, beam is divided into five units of 100 grams each. The front, or 10-gram, beam is divided into ten units of 1 gram each. Each gram on the front beam is further divided into units of 0.1 gram.

Apply Concepts What is the greatest mass you could find with the triple-beam balance in the picture?

....

Calculate What is the mass of the apple in the picture?

....

The following procedure can be used to find the mass of an object with a triple-beam balance:

1. Place the object on the pan.

2. Move the rider on the middle beam notch by notch until the horizontal pointer on the right drops below zero. Move the rider back one notch.

3. Move the rider on the back beam notch by notch until the pointer again drops below zero. Move the rider back one notch.

4. Slowly slide the rider along the front beam until the pointer stops at the zero point.

5. The mass of the object is equal to the sum of the readings on the three beams.

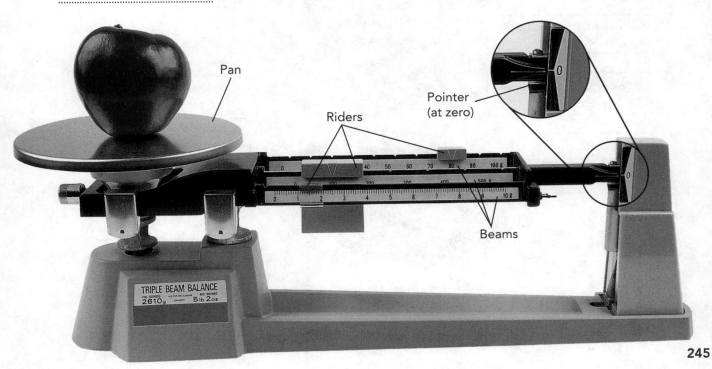

Using a Microscope

The microscope is an essential tool in the study of life science. It allows you to see things that are too small to be seen with the unaided eye.

You will probably use a compound microscope like the one you see here. The compound microscope has more than one lens that magnifies the object you view.

Typically, a compound microscope has one lens in the eyepiece (the part you look through). The eyepiece lens usually magnifies 10×. Any object you view through this lens will appear 10 times larger than it is.

A compound microscope may contain two or three other lenses called objective lenses. They are called the low-power and high-power

objective lenses. The low-power objective lens usually magnifies 10×. The high-power objective lenses usually magnify 40× and 100×.

To calculate the total magnification with which you are viewing an object, multiply the magnification of the eyepiece lens by the magnification of the objective lens you are using. For example, the eyepiece's magnification of 10× multiplied by the low-power objective's magnification of 10× equals a total magnification of 100×.

Use the photo of the compound microscope to become familiar with the parts of the microscope and their functions.

The Parts of a Microscope

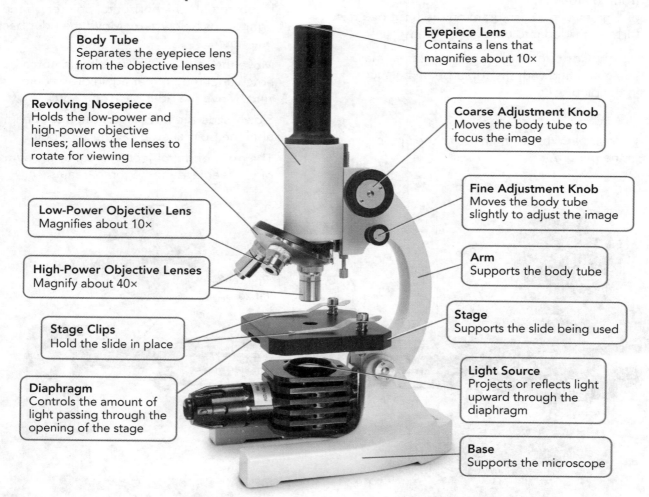

Body Tube
Separates the eyepiece lens from the objective lenses

Revolving Nosepiece
Holds the low-power and high-power objective lenses; allows the lenses to rotate for viewing

Low-Power Objective Lens
Magnifies about 10×

High-Power Objective Lenses
Magnify about 40×

Stage Clips
Hold the slide in place

Diaphragm
Controls the amount of light passing through the opening of the stage

Eyepiece Lens
Contains a lens that magnifies about 10×

Coarse Adjustment Knob
Moves the body tube to focus the image

Fine Adjustment Knob
Moves the body tube slightly to adjust the image

Arm
Supports the body tube

Stage
Supports the slide being used

Light Source
Projects or reflects light upward through the diaphragm

Base
Supports the microscope

Using the Microscope

Use the following procedures when you are working with a microscope.

1. To carry the microscope, grasp the microscope's arm with one hand. Place your other hand under the base.

2. Place the microscope on a table with the arm toward you.

3. Turn the coarse adjustment knob to raise the body tube.

4. Revolve the nosepiece until the low-power objective lens clicks into place.

5. Adjust the diaphragm. While looking through the eyepiece, adjust the mirror until you see a bright white circle of light. **CAUTION:** Never use direct sunlight as a light source.

6. Place a slide on the stage. Center the specimen over the opening on the stage. Use the stage clips to hold the slide in place. **CAUTION:** Glass slides are fragile.

7. Look at the stage from the side. Carefully turn the coarse adjustment knob to lower the body tube until the low-power objective almost touches the slide.

8. Looking through the eyepiece, very slowly turn the coarse adjustment knob until the specimen comes into focus.

9. To switch to the high-power objective lens, look at the microscope from the side. Carefully revolve the nosepiece until the high-power objective lens clicks into place. Make sure the lens does not hit the slide.

10. Looking through the eyepiece, turn the fine adjustment knob until the specimen comes into focus.

Making a Wet-Mount Slide

Use the following procedures to make a wet-mount slide of a specimen.

1. Obtain a clean microscope slide and a coverslip. **CAUTION:** Glass slides and coverslips are fragile.

2. Place the specimen on the center of the slide. The specimen must be thin enough for light to pass through it.

3. Using a plastic dropper, place a drop of water on the specimen.

4. Gently place one edge of the coverslip against the slide so that it touches the edge of the water drop at a 45° angle. Slowly lower the coverslip over the specimen. If you see air bubbles trapped beneath the coverslip, tap the coverslip gently with the eraser end of a pencil.

5. Remove any excess water at the edge of the coverslip with a paper towel.

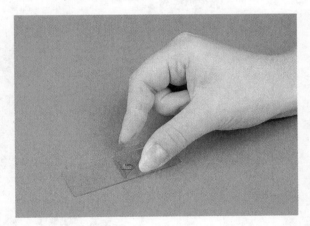

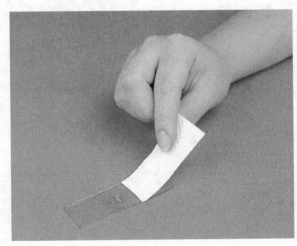

Periodic Table of Elements

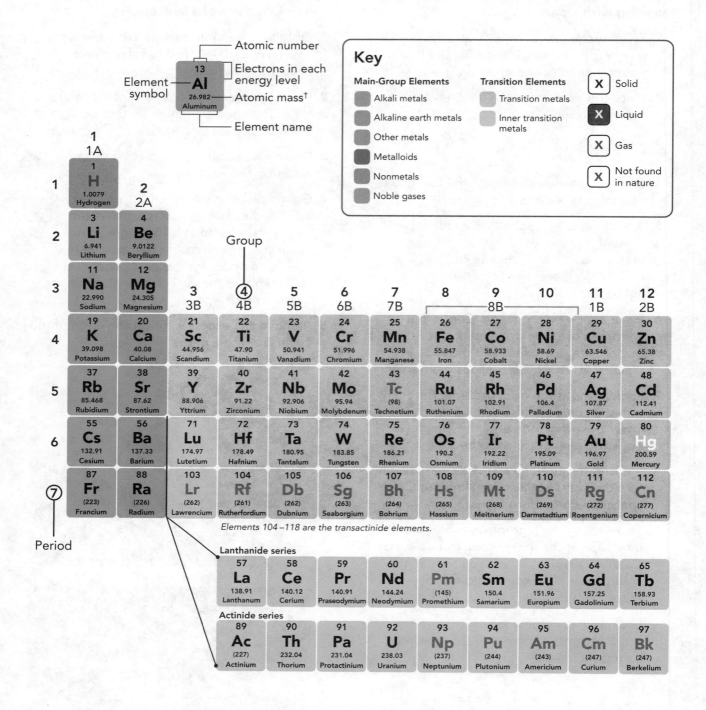

Elements 104–118 are the transactinide elements.

Key

Main-Group Elements
- Alkali metals
- Alkaline earth metals
- Other metals
- Metalloids
- Nonmetals
- Noble gases

Transition Elements
- Transition metals
- Inner transition metals

- X — Solid
- X — Liquid
- X — Gas
- X — Not found in nature

Element symbol — **Al**
- 13 — Atomic number
- Electrons in each energy level
- 26.982 — Atomic mass[†]
- Aluminum — Element name

Group — ④

Period — ⑦

Lanthanide series

| 57 La 138.91 Lanthanum | 58 Ce 140.12 Cerium | 59 Pr 140.91 Praseodymium | 60 Nd 144.24 Neodymium | 61 Pm (145) Promethium | 62 Sm 150.4 Samarium | 63 Eu 151.96 Europium | 64 Gd 157.25 Gadolinium | 65 Tb 158.93 Terbium |

Actinide series

| 89 Ac (227) Actinium | 90 Th 232.04 Thorium | 91 Pa 231.04 Protactinium | 92 U 238.03 Uranium | 93 Np (237) Neptunium | 94 Pu (244) Plutonium | 95 Am (243) Americium | 96 Cm (247) Curium | 97 Bk (247) Berkelium |

†The atomic masses in parentheses are the mass numbers of the longest-lived isotope of elements for which a standard atomic mass cannot be defined.

18
8A
2
He
4.0026
Helium

13	14	15	16	17
3A	4A	5A	6A	7A
5	6	7	8	9	10
B	**C**	**N**	**O**	**F**	**Ne**
10.81	12.011	14.007	15.999	18.998	20.179
Boron	Carbon	Nitrogen	Oxygen	Fluorine	Neon
13	14	15	16	17	18
Al	**Si**	**P**	**S**	**Cl**	**Ar**
26.982	28.086	30.974	32.06	35.453	39.948
Aluminum	Silicon	Phosphorus	Sulfur	Chlorine	Argon
31	32	33	34	35	36
Ga	**Ge**	**As**	**Se**	**Br**	**Kr**
69.72	72.59	74.922	78.96	79.904	83.80
Gallium	Germanium	Arsenic	Selenium	Bromine	Krypton
49	50	51	52	53	54
In	**Sn**	**Sb**	**Te**	**I**	**Xe**
114.82	118.69	121.75	127.60	126.90	131.30
Indium	Tin	Antimony	Tellurium	Iodine	Xenon
81	82	83	84	85	86
Tl	**Pb**	**Bi**	**Po**	**At**	**Rn**
204.37	207.2	208.98	(209)	(210)	(222)
Thallium	Lead	Bismuth	Polonium	Astatine	Radon
113	114	115	116	117	118
Nh	**Fl**	**Mc**	**Lv**	**Ts**	**Og**
(284)	(289)	(288)	(292)	(294)	(294)
Nihonium	Flerovium	Moscovium	Livermorium	Tennessine	Oganesson

66	67	68	69	70
Dy	**Ho**	**Er**	**Tm**	**Yb**
162.50	164.93	167.26	168.93	173.04
Dysprosium	Holmium	Erbium	Thulium	Ytterbium

98	99	100	101	102
Cf	**Es**	**Fm**	**Md**	**No**
(251)	(252)	(257)	(258)	(259)
Californium	Einsteinium	Fermium	Mendelevium	Nobelium

GLOSSARY

A

aggression A threatening behavior that one animal uses to gain control over another animal. (205)

allele A different form of a gene. (186)

alveoli Tiny sacs of lung tissue specialized for the movement of gases between air and blood. (154)

artery A blood vessel that carries blood away from the heart. (151)

asexual reproduction A reproductive process that involves only one parent and produces offspring that are genetically identical to the parent. (183)

auxin A hormone that controls a plant's growth and response to light. (214)

B

bacteria Single-celled organisms that lack a nucleus; prokaryotes. (30)

behavior The way an organism reacts to changes in its internal conditions or external environment. (203)

binomial nomenclature The classification system in which each organism is given a unique, two-part scientific name indicating its genus and species. (17)

brain The part of the central nervous system that is located in the skull and controls most functions in the body. (163)

bronchi The two passages that direct air into the lungs. (154)

C

capillary A tiny blood vessel where substances are exchanged between the blood and the body cells. (151)

carbohydrates An energy-rich organic compound, such as a sugar or a starch, that is made of the elements of carbon, hydrogen, and oxygen. (138)

cell The basic unit of structure and function in living things. (6, 63)

cell cycle The series of events in which a cell grows, prepares for division, and divides to form two daughter cells. (96)

cell membrane A thin, flexible barrier that surrounds a cell and controls which substances pass into and out of a cell. (75)

cell theory A widely accepted explanation of the relationship between cells and living things. (66)

cell wall A rigid supporting layer that surrounds the cells of plants and some other organisms. (74)

chloroplast An organelle in the cells of plants and some other organisms that captures energy from sunlight and changes it to an energy form that cells can use in making food. (77)

circulatory system An organ system that taransports needed materials to cells and removes wastes. (149)

classification The process of grouping things based on their similarities. (17)

cones The reproductive structures of gymnosperms. (197)

convergent evolution The process by which unrelated organisms evolve similar characteristics. (23)

courtship behavior Activty that prepares males and females of the same species for mating. (205)

cytokinesis The final stage of the cell cycle, in which the cell's cytoplasm divides, distributing the organelles into each of the two new daughter cells. (100)

cytoplasm The thick fluid region of a cell located inside the cell membrane (in prokaryotes) or between the cell membrane and nucleus (in eukaryotes). (76)

D

diffusion The process by which molecules move from an area of higher concentration to an area of lower concentration. (85)

digestion The process that breaks complex molecules of food into smaller nutrient molecules. (137)

domain The most basic level of organization in the classification of organisms. (18)

dormancy A period of time when an organism's growth or activity stops. (215)

E

endocytosis The process by which the cell membrane takes particles into the cell by changing shape and engulfing the particles. (88)

enzyme A type of protein that speeds up chemical reactions in the body. (141)

evolution Change over time; the process by which modern organisms have descended from ancient organisms. (22)

excretion The process by which wastes are removed from the body. (156)

exocytosis The process by which the vacuole surrounding particles fuses with the cell membrane, forcing the contents out of the cell. (88)

external fertilization When eggs are fertilized outside a female's body. (207)

F

fertilization The process in sexual reproduction in which an egg cell and a sperm cell join to form a new cell. (184, 194)

fruit The ripened ovary and other structures of an angiosperm that enclose one or more seeds. (198)

G

gene A sequence of DNA that determines a trait and is passed from parent to offspring. (184)

genus A taxonomic category that names a group of similar, closely-related organisms. (17)

germination The sprouting of the embryo out of a seed; occurs when the embryo resumes its growth following dormancy. (199)

gland An organ that produces and releases chemicals either through ducts or into the bloodstream. (128, 166)

H

homeostasis The condition in which an organism's internal environment is kept stable in spite of changes in the external environment. (12)

hormone The chemical produced by an endocrine gland. (128); A chemical that affects growth and development. (214)

host An organism that provides a source of energy or a suitable environment for a parasite to live with, in, or on. (28)

I

inheritance The process by which an offspring receives genes from its parents. (186)

instinct A response to a stimulus that is inborn. (203)

internal fertilization When eggs are fertilized inside a female's body. (207)

interphase The first stage of the cell cycle that takes place before cell division occurs, during which a cell grows and makes a copy of its DNA. (98)

invertebrate An animal without a backbone. (44)

L

lymph Fluid that travels through the lymphatic system consisting of water, white blood cells, and dissolved materials. (153)

M

mammal A vertebrate whose body temperature is regulated by its internal heat, and that has skin covered with hair or fur and glands that produce milk to feed its young. (46)

mating system Behavior patterns related to how animals mate. (204)

metamorphosis A process in which an animal's body undergoes major changes in shape and form during its life cycle. (219)

microscope An instrument that makes small objects look larger. (64)

migration The regular, seasonal journey of an animal from one place to another and back again. (209)

mitochondria Rod-shaped organelles that convert energy in food molecules to energy the cell can use to carry out its functions. (77)

mitosis The second stage of the cell cycle during which the cell's nucleus divides into two new nuclei and one set of DNA is distributed into each daughter cell. (99)

multicellular Consisting of many cells. (6)

GLOSSARY

N

negative feedback A process in which a system is turned off by the condition it produces. (168)

nephron Small filtering structure found in the kidneys that removes wastes from blood and produces urine. (157)

neuron A cell that carries information through the nervous system. (161)

nonvascular plants A low-growing plant that lacks true vascular tissue for transporting materials. (43)

nucleus In cells, a large oval organelle that contains the cell's genetic material in the form of DNA and controls many of the cell's activities. (76)

nutrients Substances in food that provide the raw materials and energy needed for an organism to carry out its essential processes. (137)

O

organ A body structure that is composed of different kinds of tissues that work together. (44, 117)

organ system A group of organs that work together to perform a major function. (117)

organelle A tiny cell structure that carries out a specific function within the cell. (73)

organism A living thing. (5)

osmosis The diffusion of water molecules across a selectively permeable membrane. (86)

ovule A plant structure in seed plants that produces the female gametophyte; contains an egg cell. (197)

P

parasite An organism that benefits by living with, on, or in a host in a parasitism interaction. (33)

peristalsis Waves of smooth muscle contractions that move food through the esophagus toward the stomach. (140)

pheromone A chemical released by one animal that affects the behavior of another animal of the same species. (205)

photoperiodism A plant's response to seasonal changes in the length of night and day. (215)

pollination The transfer of pollen from male reproductive structures to female reproductive structures in plants. (195)

protist A eukaryotic organism that cannot be classified as an animal, plant, or fungus. (33)

R

reflex An automatic response that occurs rapidly and without conscious control. (165)

replication The process by which a cell makes a copy of the DNA in its nucleus before cell division. (98)

response An action or change in behavior that occurs as a result of a stimulus. (7, 127)

S

saliva A fluid produced in the mouth that aids in mechanical and chemical digestion. (141)

selectively permeable A property of cell membranes that allows some substances to pass across it, while others cannot. (84)

sexual reproduction A reproductive process that involves two parents that combine their genetic material to produce a new organism which differs from both parents. (184)

species A group of similar organisms that can mate with each other and produce offspring that can also mate and reproduce. (17)

spinal cord A thick column of nervous tissue that links the brain to nerves in the body. (163)

spontaneous generation The mistaken idea that living things arise from nonliving sources. (8)

stimulus Any change or signal in the environment that can make an organism react in some way. (7, 127)

stress The reaction of a person's body to potentially threatening, challenging, or disturbing events. (132)

synapse The junction where one neuron can transfer an impulse to the next structure. (162)

T

taxonomy The scientific study of how living things are classified. (18)

territory An area occupied and defended by an animal or group of animals. (205)

tissue A group of similar cells that perform a specific function. (42, 116)

trait A specific characteristic that an organism can pass to its offspring through its genes. (184)

tropism A plant's growth response toward or away from a stimulus. (214)

U

unicellular Made of a single cell. (6)

V

vaccine A substance used in a vaccination that consists of pathogens that have been weakened or killed but can still trigger the body to produce chemicals that destroy the pathogens. (28)

vacuole A sac-like organelle that stores water, food, and other materials. (78)

vascular plants A plant that has true vascular tissue for transporting materials. (42)

vein A blood vessel that carries blood back to the heart. (151)

vertebrate An animal with a backbone. (44)

virus A tiny, nonliving particle that enters and then reproduces inside a living cell. (28)

Z

zygote A fertilized egg, produced by the joining of a sperm and an egg. (194)

CREDITS

Take Notes

Use this space for recording notes and sketching out ideas.

Use this space for recording notes and sketching out ideas.

Take Notes

Use this space for recording notes and sketching out ideas.

Take Notes

Use this space for recording notes and sketching out ideas.

Take Notes

Use this space for recording notes and sketching out ideas.